DIXIE

DISCOVER
HISTORIC
AMERICA
SERIES

Dixie

A TRAVELER'S GUIDE

BY

Sara Pitzer

A VOYAGER BOOK

The
Globe
Pequot
Press

OLD SAYBROOK, CONNECTICUT

*Photo credits: p. 3, 167: courtesy Mississippi Tourism Development; p.23: courtesy
Mobile Convention and Visitors Corporation; p.29: courtesy Alabama Constitution
Village; p.37: photo by Tim Schick, courtesy Arkansas Department of Parks and
Tourism; p.41: photo by A.C. Haralson, courtesy Arkansas Department of Parks and
Tourism; p. 59: courtesy The Zimmerman Agency, Tallahassee, Fla.; p. 66: courtesy
Road to Tara Museum; p. 69: courtesy Atlanta History Center; p.76: courtesy Hay
House; p. 107: courtesy Danville-Boyle County Tourist Commission; p. 113: cour-
tesy Shaker Village of Pleasant Hill; p. 131: courtesy Nottoway; p.134: courtesy
Tezcuco Plantation; p. 138: courtesy Laura Plantation; p. 191: courtesy North Car-
olina Travel and Tourism Division, photo by Clay Nolen; p. 207: courtesy of Old
Salem Inc.; pp. 217, 233: courtesy Charleston Area Convention and Visitors Bureau;
p. 232: courtesy South Carolina Department of Parks, Recreation and Tourism; p. 273:
courtesy Historic Rugby; p. 276: courtesy National Park Service, Andrew Johnson
National Historic Site; p. 288: courtesy Valentine Museum; p. 289: courtesy The
Museum of the Life and History of Richmond.*

Cover and text design by Nancy Freeborn

Library of Congress Cataloging-in-Publication Data

Pitzer, Sara.
     Dixie : a traveler's guide / by Sara Pitzer. — 1st ed.
        p. cm. — (Discover historic America series)
     "A Voyager Book."
     Includes index.
     ISBN 1-56440-648-2
     1. Southern States—Guidebooks. 2. Historic sites—Southern States—
Guidebooks. I. Title. II. Series.
F207.3.P58   1996
917.504'43—DC20   96-11670
                                            CIP

Manufactured in the United States of America
First Edition/First Printing

This is dedicated to Jon Crane and Michael Smilowitz.
They helped me in ways I don't think they even realize.
It's also for John Andrews. He realizes.

ACKNOWLEDGMENTS

No one writes a book like this alone. I had help from a tremendous number of individuals, publicity departments, and tourism agencies, and I read dozens of books, magazine features, and newspaper articles. Where possible I have tried to mention in the text of this book the individual people who helped me and the books I read. In addition, I am grateful to the following: Arkansas Department of Parks and Tourism; Alabama Bureau of Tourism and Travel; Florida Division of Tourism; Georgia Department of Industry, Trade, and Tourism; Kentucky Department of Travel Development; Louisiana Bureau of Tourism and Travel; Mississippi Division of Tourism; North Carolina Travel and Tourism Division; South Carolina Department of Parks, Recreation, and Tourism; Tennessee Department of Tourist Development; Virginia Division of Tourism; and the National Park Service. Also, people in chambers of commerce and tourist departments of many of the towns I've written about offered valuable suggestions, as did employees of many of the attractions I've included. There are too many to name, but I appreciate their help. Finally, I can hardly overstate the skill of the people in visitor centers associated with all the regions and many of the attractions in this book. Day after day they give directions, answer questions, mark maps, and answer telephones with astonishing patience. They are the true experts on Southern hospitality.

Contents

The Dixie States

Introduction

I am still surprised by the things I learned writing this book. I was born in the South, and I've lived here for a long time. I travel in the region almost continuously, writing about it. At the same time, having lived in other parts of the country, I believed I saw the South more clearly than either a native who'd never known anything else or someone who'd never lived here at all. So writing a guide to the antebellum South sounded like a pleasant, simple task. Well, it was pleasant, but its complexities still have me bemused. I learned that looking at a region, such as the South, with a particular slant in mind brings into focus issues and realities that you simply never thought about before.

Here's what I learned: Hoop skirts, magnolias, and mint juleps tell only a minuscule part of the story. There never was just one Dixie. At the same time that women on lavish plantations were tightening their stays and practicing their piano pieces, other women on much simpler plantations were up to their elbows in lard and flour, women in cities were running businesses or working in various trades, and women in the southern Appalachians were hacking weeds with hoes. Black women were laboring everywhere from the kitchen to the garden. And women of the American Indian tribes were staggering and often dying as they walked the long road of the relocation project that eventually became known as "The Trail of Tears."

1

The differences among men were equally great. Some were, indeed, merchant princes who looked for increasingly extravagant ways to flaunt their wealth. But others owned plantations that used little or no slave labor. In the Tennessee and North Carolina mountains, a man might have a slave with whom he worked side-by-side in the fields. At the same time, utopian experiments such as the Moravian settlement at Old Salem, North Carolina, and several Shaker communities in Kentucky rose in the South, looking for ways to live a celibate, God-centered life. It's hard to realize that all these different people were living in the South at the same time and certainly must have considered themselves Southern.

For all their differences, virtually all Southerners were touched by one event—the Civil War—in ways not good for any of them. Until you study the details, it's hard to realize how little of the reality of the Civil War actually fits the romanticized ideas about it that persist to this day. This was America's bloodiest war. In it 620,000 people died—almost as many as died in all other American conflicts combined.

You also can't realize, until you've been here, how strong feelings run about the Civil War. In the South it used to be called "the recent unpleasantness between the states" or in stronger language "the war for independence." Many Southerners make a compelling argument that the war was not about abolition but about power and property. They say there was no legitimate justification for using military force to keep states who had joined the Union voluntarily from also leaving it if they so chose.

This war also destroyed an astonishing amount of property, especially in Sherman's long March to the Sea, during which Union troops pretty much burned everything they encountered, including precious architecture. As a result, antebellum buildings are rare in many southern cities.

As devastating as the loss of property was to the South, the loss of life was much worse. The South essentially lost a generation of young men. In many towns almost none of the men who marched off to fight came back, which meant no one was left to keep the community going but the women, the very young boys, and the very old men. This further destroyed an economy that was already ruined in many places, because railroads and shipping ports had been occupied and then burned by Union troops.

Manufacturing plants were burned. Plantations that had been earning huge amounts of money fell to ruin because their crops were gone, their markets were gone, and the slave labor that had made such huge planta-

Grand mansions like Dunleith, in Natchez, Mississippi, come to mind first when we think about the antebellum South.

tions possible in the first place was gone, too. The South has only recently risen from the resultant poverty and regained a healthy economy.

It's hard to find much romance in any of this. Yet, amazingly, romance persists, preserved by Southerners who love the old ways and work without ceasing to restore plantations, re-create mansions, set up museums, and tell stories of the antebellum years. And, astonishingly, a lot of that romance is related to the Civil War itself. Of course the antebellum life on the wealthy plantations still comes across as romantic, with memories of gracious socializing and fine furnishings carefully nurtured by the people who staff the homes and grounds that are open for tours.

In some places a generous chunk of fiction reinforces the real history. In Atlanta, for instance, you find a number of attractions related to the novel *Gone With the Wind,* the home and haunts of its author, Margaret Mitchell, and the countryside homesites of her friends and neighbors. In some ways, Rhett and Scarlett are more real than the people who actually lived in Atlanta at the time of the Civil War. The Cyclorama, part of the Atlanta Museum, had to add the figures of Rhett and Scarlett to their diorama because patrons kept asking for them.

At the other end of the spectrum, the Valentine Museum, in Lexington, Virginia, has dedicated itself to studying and depicting life as it really was in that part of Virginia. They've gone so far as to write scripts of conversations among slaves, conversations among the society folk who lived in the mansion, and interaction between the two groups. The scripts are fiction, of course, but they are based on a wealth of material found in old diaries, letters, and papers. This approach gives you yet another view of Dixie, emphasizing not the architecture or antiques but the sociological aspects of daily life.

What this all adds up to is that when you travel the South in search of the Dixie experience you will inevitably find everything you expected as well as things you never even imagined before. You'll discover that the diversity that people find so appealing in the "New South" today seems almost homogeneous compared to the diversity of the antebellum years. And I promise, no matter where you go, you will see something you haven't seen before and learn something you didn't know before.

The prices and rates listed in this guidebook were confirmed at press time. We recommend, however, that you call establishments before traveling to obtain current information.

Alabama

 ALABAMA TYPIFIES THE OLD SOUTH, with plantations, live oaks swathed in Spanish moss, magnolia trees, an early economy based on cotton, and a history as controversial as that of any state in the South. Because the plantations here operated with many slaves, abolishing slavery would have threatened the owners with economic disaster. After Abraham Lincoln's election as president, Alabama left the Union and joined the Confederate States of America. Although Jefferson Davis was sworn in as president of the Confederacy in Montgomery, there were no major Civil War land battles in this state. Alabama's greatest involvement in the war was producing iron for ordnance. Nearly a century later in Montgomery, a black woman descended from slaves, Rosa Parks, refused to give up her bus seat to a white man, thus setting into motion the bus boycotts and other events that began the Civil Rights movement.

In spite of these periods of discord, the languid speech and gracious manners of the Old South endured in Alabama through the Civil War, the rigors of Reconstruction, and the long climb back to economic stability. Parts of the state have become too modern to compare their culture to a Southern time warp, but even in the bustling new areas the gentility of Alabama folk continues.

Alabama's most popular antebellum attractions cluster around Mobile, on the Gulf of Mexico; Montgomery, the capital, near the center of the

Alabama

Huntsville

North Alabama

N

Birmingham

Greensboro   Montgomery

South and Central
Alabama

Mobile

The Gulf Coast

state; and Huntsville, in northern Alabama. North of Montgomery, in the center of the state, is Birmingham, a larger but younger city, having been mostly farmland until its founding in 1871. Traveling to these areas in each part of the state will give visitors a variety of Southern experiences.

SOUTH AND CENTRAL ALABAMA

It makes sense to begin your explorations in **Montgomery** because so much happened here. Promoters call the city the first capital of the Confederacy and the birthplace of the Civil Rights movement. The "first capital" appellation owes to the fact that Jefferson Davis was sworn in as president of the Confederate States of America in Montgomery. From here he sent the telegram—"Fire on Fort Sumter"—that began the Civil War. The second nickname grew from the groundswell of Civil Rights activity that began in December 1955, when Rosa Parks's act of quiet defiance triggered the Montgomery bus boycott.

To orient yourself in Montgomery and get an overview of all that the city has to offer, stop first at **Thompson Manor Montgomery Visitor Center,** 401 Madison Avenue (corner of Madison and Hull Streets) in **Old Alabama Town.** Here you can pick up brochures about attractions and events in Montgomery and spend a few minutes viewing a video about the city. The restored 1850s mansion housing the center was originally built in Tuskegee by a judge. After the Civil War it became City Hotel. Then, like so many fine old mansions whose original families were no longer in control of a property, the building deteriorated, unoccupied. Finally, it was saved, dismantled, relocated, and restored through the combined efforts of the Montgomery Landmarks Foundation, the city of Montgomery, and the local Kiwanis Club. While you are picking up brochures, take time to tour the mansion. It's especially known for its examples of faux graining and marbleizing.

The other buildings in Old Alabama Town also have been projects of the Montgomery Landmarks Foundation. In an area of three blocks, there are thirty-five restored buildings, including some brought from other places. Walking through this area, you'll see the diversity that made up Alabama life—from slave quarters to townhouses, from pioneer cabins to town gentry. More than a dozen of the buildings are open to the public, furnished to show how different people lived in successive periods of the nineteenth century. Those buildings that are not open to the public can still be enjoyed from the outside.

Costumed craftspeople in the **Ross–Morris Craft House** demonstrate such crafts of the period as weaving, spinning, and dulcimer making. Some of their work is sold in the gift shop in **Lucas Tavern,** where you will begin your tour with an audiovisual orientation and, if you wish, listen to a story read by Kathryn Tucker Windham, a Selma fiction writer. She tells it not exactly as it was, but certainly as it might have been. The tavern was built about 1818, on Old Federal Road at Waugh, where pioneers would have stopped on their way into Alabama Territory.

Among the other buildings you'll see and may enter are **Grange Hall,** once used by farmers around Pintala for town meetings, and a doctor's office, filled with the somewhat grotesque paraphernalia that were part of medicine before modern pharmacies and surgical suites developed. You'll also see shotgun houses, including one that was the home of the Fitzpatricks, a black family, and a modest Presbyterian church in which such families as the Fitzpatricks worshiped.

Some of the buildings—the Adams Chapel School, for instance—were built later than the early Dixie years, but having all the buildings in a relatively small area allows you to see that history doesn't stay holed up in tidy categories; one period runs into the next, one trend affects the next. Old Alabama Town is open Monday through Saturday 9:30 A.M. to 3:30 P.M.; Sunday 1:30 P.M. to 3:30 P.M. Closed major holidays. Admission is about $5.00 for adults, $2.00 for children, and $12.00 for families with children. Phone (334) 240–4500.

About four blocks away, the **First White House of the Confederacy,** 644 Washington Street at Union, was the home of Jefferson Davis when Montgomery was the capital of the Confederacy. President Davis lived here with his wife and three children. He also entertained and held cabinet meetings in the home. This Italianate frame house, across from the current Capitol Building, was built in 1835. The parlors downstairs are furnished with period antiques. Queen Anne furniture in formal arrangements, balanced with crystal chandeliers and impressive mirrors, reflects the elegant lifestyle to which Mrs. Davis, formerly a belle of Natchez, was accustomed. Upstairs, the bedrooms are still furnished as they were when the Davis family slept in them. A Confederate museum in the house displays war relics and some personal items of the Davis family. The house is

Free at Last

Just a few blocks from the state capitol and the First White House of the Confederacy, the **Civil Rights Memorial** tells the story of the forty people who died between 1955 and 1968 in the Civil Rights struggle. Maya Lin, who designed the Vietnam Veterans Memorial, created the Civil Rights Memorial with a similarly solemn simplicity: The name of each person killed, the date it occurred, and what happened are etched in lines running from the center to the perimeter of a circle of black polished granitelike spokes in a wheel. A shallow flow of water runs over the surface. Inscribed on a 9-foot-high black wall behind the circle is the quote from the book of Amos used by Martin Luther King, Jr., at the beginning of the Montgomery bus boycott: "Until Justice rolls down like water, and Righteousness like a mighty stream . . ."

open Monday through Friday 8:00 A.M. to 4:30 P.M.; Saturday and Sunday 9:00 A.M. to 4:30 P.M. Closed major holidays. Admission is free, but donations are accepted. Phone (334) 242–1861.

An interesting site that reflects changes in taste over time is the restored **State Capitol,** built in 1851. With its great white dome, this building, once the capitol of the Confederacy, looks a lot like the U.S. Capitol. Over the years the building was remodeled and changed as people's ideas of what was desirable changed, but it has been restored to the way it looked before the Civil War, as have the original governor's office, the senate chamber, and some other government chambers. The building is open Monday through Friday 8:00 A.M. to 5:00 P.M. Admission is free. Phone (334) 242–3184.

Even if you are traveling with children, don't let the name fool you into skipping another state building, the **Archives and History Museum.** You'll find much more here than documents. This place has something like 500,000 different items, ranging from domestic displays to the Bible on which Jefferson Davis swore his oath of office as president of the Confederacy. Not surprisingly, a military room has weapons and uniforms from both the Revolutionary and Civil Wars as well as subsequent wars. In another section crafts of Indian tribes who lived in the area are displayed. The kids will enjoy **Grandma's Attic,** a section of the museum in which children can play with old clothes, toys, and household items. If they get involved enough, you might be able to spend some time in the reference library on the first floor. Here you might try to trace a runaway ancestor in the museum's military service records, which date back to the American Revolution and, of course, include the Civil War.

If you are interested in architecture, a worthwhile stop is **St. John's Episcopal Church,** at 113 Madison Avenue. The church is a Gothic structure with an inspiringly high spire. Built in 1855, this is Montgomery's oldest Episcopal church. Many Confederate leaders worshiped here; Jefferson Davis rented a pew in the church, even though he was not an Episcopalian. The pew still stands in its assigned place, eleventh from the rear, marked by an old plaque. The church has a blue-stenciled wooden ceiling, preserved from when it was painted in 1869. Needlepoint prayer stools throughout the church provide rest for kneelers.

Here's an interesting historical note: This church is the second edifice built for St. John's. After this second one was complete, the original St. John's, built in 1837, was donated to black Episcopalians. Since they then had their own church, the new church did not include the usual slave gallery but used the space instead to accommodate an organ and choir. The church is open Monday through Friday 9:00 A.M. to 4:00 P.M.; Saturday and Sunday 9:00 A.M. to noon. Admission is free. Phone (334) 262–1937.

When you work up an appetite, you'll find a wealth of possibilities for true Southern cooking. It's what most people eat in Montgomery—no special program for tourists! **Martha's Place,** 458 Sayre Street, serves the real soul food for which black Southern cooks are famous: fried chicken, black-eyed peas, rice, greens, and corn bread. The restaurant is in a black neighborhood near the downtown area, but devotees of this kind of cooking have long since stopped thinking in terms of color. As one regular puts it, "You don't have to be black to know good eatin'." The restaurant is open Monday through Friday 11:00 A.M. to 3:00 P.M. Phone (334) 263–9135.

Three **Farmer's Market Cafes** serve country cooking for breakfast and lunch. The cafes are known for their modest prices, fresh vegetables, fried fish, and a good variety of meats. Lunch is served cafeteria style. One restaurant is at 315 North McDonough Street, one is in the new farmer's market complex, and one is at 1250 Air Base Boulevard. They are open for breakfast and lunch, Monday through Friday. Phone (334) 262–9163.

Right in downtown Montgomery, **Young House Restaurant** serves true Southern cooking in an 1820s Greek Revival mansion furnished with antiques. The place serves outstanding gumbo, chicken pot pie, and desserts. The bread pudding in whiskey-honey sauce is famous. Not only are the furnishings, architecture, and food Southern, but so is the hospitality. People really do say, "Yes, ma'am" and "Yes, sir," as a matter of routine. The restaurant is open Monday through Friday 11:00 A.M. to 2:00 P.M. Phone (334) 262–0409.

Assuming that you choose one of these places for lunch, then you might prefer to have a lighter meal for dinner. For very fresh seafood in a casual environment, go to **Jubilee Seafood.** Located at 1057 Woodley Road, it serves everything from shrimp to snapper, broiled, fried, blackened, and, sometimes, sauced. The restaurant is open Monday through Saturday 5:00 P.M. to 10:00 P.M. Phone (334) 262–6224.

Finally, if you're trying to taste all the kinds of barbecue available throughout the South, try **Country's Barbecue** on the Southern Bypass. Pork is served sliced or chopped, with mild, medium, or hot sauce. Country's has all the standard barbecue accoutrements—slaw, butter beans, okra, and so on. This is a family-style restaurant decorated with old advertising signs and geared up for fast, lively business. Phone (334) 284–1411.

When the day is done, Anne and Mark Waldo at **Red Bluff Cottage,** 551 Clay Street, invite you to spend the night in their inn. It sits on a hill from which you can see the State Capitol, much of Montgomery, and the Alabama River. The building is new—it was built specifically to be an inn—but what goes on inside is the epitome of Southern hospitality at its best. The four guest rooms are furnished with antiques that have been passed down in the family. There are the bed that was Anne's as a child, an antique sleigh bed that belonged to her great-great-grandmother, an old leather trunk that belonged to Mark's grandmother and had in it party invitations dated 1850, and a spread crocheted by her. The public areas are furnished with oriental antiques. In the formal dining room, Mark and Anne serve a full breakfast on fine china with sterling. The inn is surrounded by Anne's flower gardens, which thrive, looking as colorful as Monet's gardens, in the moist, temperate Alabama climate. Rates begin at about $60 per room. Phone (334) 264–0056.

If Anne's gardens whet your appetite for learning more about Southern gardens, you'll enjoy two stops north of Montgomery on Highway 231. **Jasmine Hill** uses gardens as a setting for imported reproductions of such famous Greek statuary as Venus de Milo and the Lions of Delos. A full-scale copy of the ruins of the Temple of Hera, where the first Olympic torch was lighted, dominates the scene. A lily pond with fish fills the center, and a large reservoir feeds water to interlinked ponds and pools. A 6-foot marble Winged Victory soars over a reflecting pool. And all these reproductions are set off with blooming plants, including azaleas, water lilies, bougainvillea, daylilies, roses, and many others, depending on the season. You can phone (334) 567–6463 for a recorded message telling what plants are currently at peak.

The admission fee to Jasmine Hill includes a tour map that delineates the best way to walk the gardens so that you won't miss anything. The text tells you about the original works that are reproduced here. The gardens, statues, and fountains took nearly twenty-five years to assemble—an elaborate display in the best tradition of old Southern grandeur. Jasmine Hill is open Tuesday through Sunday 9:00 A.M. to 5:00 P.M. Admission is about $3.50 for adults, $2.50 children. Phone (334) 263–1440. To get to Jasmine Hill, drive about 4 miles north from downtown Montgomery on U.S. Highway 231, turn right onto Jasmine Hill Road, and follow the signs about 2 miles to the gardens.

Thus inspired, maybe you'll contemplate getting into gardening yourself, which will certainly take you to **Southern Homes and Gardens,** a retail operation that seems the size of a small city. Here you can buy everything from home furnishings, shrubbery, and garden plants to the tools and supplies you will need to create your gardens. Part of the genius of the place is that everything is so effectively displayed that you want it all—even (or especially) the Japanese garden with a pool. If you garden even minimally, treat yourself to a stop here. Open Monday through Saturday 9:00 A.M. to 5:00 P.M. Phone (334) 277–6746. To get to Southern Homes and Gardens, take the Northern Bypass from I–65 and go north on 231. You can't miss the complex.

Driving west on U.S. Highway 80 about 50 miles brings you to **Selma.** Lee Sentell, the Southern writer, historian, and traveler, calls Selma a romantic city that has "maintained the character, style, and even accent of the Old South." In antebellum years this was a fabulously wealthy area in the Black Belt. (The Black Belt is a stretch of fertile, dark soil that runs 300 miles through the center of Alabama from Georgia into Mississippi.) As Sentell explains it, plantation owners in this region profited hugely from the fertile soil and owned more slaves than were in any other area in

Alabama. The area also specialized in producing munitions for the Confederate troops.

When the slave population was freed after the Civil War, many blacks remained in the area but did not prosper because they had so few economic opportunities. Things never got much better for them. Their numbers and desperation were one reason why the early Civil Rights marches took place here.

As a visitor, you should walk the **Old Town Historic District,** where some of the finest mansions of the South once stood, and tour **Sturdivant Hall,** a plantation-style mansion erected in town. Then drive out to the **Old Depot Museum** to see the exhibits relating to local history, black history, and Civil War history.

The Old Town Historic District, one of the largest historic districts in Alabama, has about 1,200 buildings dating from the 1820s. Many private dwellings have been restored and are in good condition.

Sturdivant Hall is a Greek Revival mansion begun in 1853. Designed by a cousin of General Robert E. Lee, the house is so elaborate that it took until 1855 to complete. This building has everything you would expect in an antebellum mansion. The exterior is stucco, with six Corinthian columns rising 30 feet to the portico roof. Iron grillwork trims the second-story balcony, and a cupola tops the slate roof. Inside, the period furnishings, many of which belonged to the Sturdivant family, include oriental rugs set off with huge gold-leafed mirrors and marble mantels. The house is noteworthy for its fine handcrafted woodwork and plaster ceiling medallions. In the detached kitchen and cook's living quarters, you'll find a museum gift shop. The ten-room house is surrounded by splendid formal gardens that are at their peak in early spring. Although this is a museum house, it retains a sense of life because it is supported by local people who use it for special occasions and parties. Open Tuesday through Saturday 9:00 A.M. to 4:00 P.M.; Sunday 2:00 P.M. to 4:00 P.M. Admission is about $5.00 for adults, $2.00 for children. Phone (334) 872–5626.

The Old Depot Museum, at the intersection of Water Avenue and Martin Luther King Street, displays its historical materials in a restored brick railroad-depot building. The Civil War displays include cannon balls produced at Selma's munitions works. There are also displays of old farming equipment, Confederate money printed in Selma, and such homely items as spinning wheels, quilts, silver, and china. The museum is open Monday through Saturday 10:00 A.M. to 4:00 P.M.; Sunday 2:00 P.M. to

5:00 P.M. Admission is about $4.00 for adults, $3.00 for senior citizens, $2.00 for students, and $1.00 for children. Phone (334) 874–2197.

The Chamber of Commerce, 513 Lauderdale Street (phone 334–875–7241), and the Visitor Information Center, 2207 Broad Street (phone 334–875–7485), both offer driving tour maps and brochures for touring the Old Town Historic District and for a "Black Heritage Tour." Cassettes are available for a driving tour.

You can spend the night in Selma in **Grace Hall,** 506 Lauderdale, a two-story house built in 1857, now restored and run as a bed-and-breakfast and tour home. Later additions to the house included a New Orleans–style gallery and a walled-in Williamsburg English garden. When the Civil War began, the mayor of Selma lived in the house, and it was here that he received Union officers when the Confederacy surrendered. In 1865 the house was occupied by Union troops. Later the house was purchased by the Jones family to run as a boardinghouse. The family stayed in it for the next 110 years; sixty pieces of their furniture can still be found in the house. A serpentine marble-top table sits in the bay window, exactly where it was photographed in the 1890s. The six guest rooms are also furnished with elegant period antiques, elaborate draperies, and oriental rugs. Your stay in Grace Hall includes a full breakfast that can be Southern—grits, country ham, biscuits, and gravy—or something lighter. Rates begin at about $67. Phone (334) 875–5744.

For a fine Southern dinner in Selma, try **Tally Ho Restaurant,** 507 Magnum Avenue. The restaurant, in an old log cabin, serves oysters, chicken, shrimp, rice, all staples in the Southern diet, as well as steaks. The Tally Ho is open for dinner Monday through Saturday. Phone (334) 872–1390. To get to the restaurant, from U.S. Highway 80 turn north onto Summerfield Road. Drive a half mile and turn right at the Tally Ho sign onto Magnum Avenue.

After Selma, drive west on State Highway 14 to **Marion** and then on to **Greensboro** to check out two small Black Belt towns where the traditions of the romantic Old South still flourish. Marion is a pretty place, with many antebellum houses in good shape to enjoy by driving or walking, especially in the area south of the town square on Monroe, Washington, and Lafayette Streets. Turning east from Washington onto Early Street brings you to the main campus of **Judson College,** a woman's college started by local Baptists in 1838. In the business district, an unusual 1856 courthouse, shaped like a temple, dominates the scene.

In Greensboro, **Magnolia Grove**, 1002 Hobson Street, features land-scaped gardens, outbuildings, and an 1840 Greek Revival antebellum mansion that is now a museum. This could be a movie set, with its formal gardens, double parlors, and antique furnishings. Colonel Isaac and Mrs. Sarah Groom, a wealthy planting family, built the house about 1840. Its grounds include a detached kitchen, a slave cottage, and a separate office. In the home are furnishings and memorabilia of Richard Pearson Hobson, a hero of the Spanish–American War in Cuba, who was born here in 1870. Magnolia Grove is open Tuesday through Saturday 10:00 A.M. to 4:00 P.M.; Sunday 1:00 P.M. to 4:00 P.M. Admission is about $3.00 for adults, $2.00 for students, and 50 cents for children. Phone (334) 624–8618. To get to Magnolia Grove, go to the western end of Main Street and Hobson, in the historic district.

At this point you might opt to drive the 20 or so miles west to I–20 and head up past Tuscaloosa toward Birmingham. Birmingham is not really an antebellum city, but south of the city, just off the interstate, **Tannehill Historic State Park** preserves the Tannehill Ironworks. Ordnance for Confederate soldiers was produced here from 1829 until Union troops destroyed the works in 1865. After being shut down for more than one hundred years, a blast furnace was restored. You probably would not drive so far just to see a blast furnace, but many other important old buildings have been brought to the site, forming a complex that instructs you in many aspects of antebellum life in Alabama. Thirty pioneer homes and log cabins have been transported to the park from elsewhere in the state, along with a blacksmith shop, an 1822 dairy barn, and a cotton gin house with the original gin in place. (A cotton gin is the machine that separates the seeds from the fibers of cotton.) In some of the cabins, craftspeople demonstrate and sell their pots, quilts, candles, and other wares. The visitor information center is in a restored 1879 house on the property. With admission you'll receive a map describing all the attractions in the complex and discussing their significance. From March through October a miniature train takes visitors to some of the more distant spots.

This is one of the most popular tourist attractions in Alabama, and one of the most interesting. In addition to the historical sites, the park has a restaurant that serves down-home cooking—plate lunches with meat or seafood and vegetables. There are also public campgrounds. To get to the park, exit I–59/I–20 onto Tannehill Parkway, following the signs, and continue east for 2 miles. The park is open daily from 7:00 A.M. to dusk. The restaurant is closed Monday. Admission is about $2.00 for adults, half that for children and senior citizens. Phone (205) 477–5711.

From the park you're close enough to warrant at least a short stop in **Bessemer,** an industrial city where you realize how much more there is to Dixie than just plantations. At 321 North 18th Street, three **Bessemer Pioneer Homes** date back as far as 1817. The Sadler Home was built in 1818 and expanded into a two-story home with a dogtrot in 1830. The Owens Home was built in 1833 and was added onto later. And the McAdory House, 1840, is built of handhewn logs and wooden pegs. All three houses are on the National Register of Historic Places. The grounds are open daily, but you will need an appointment for interior tours. Phone (205) 425–3253 for details. To get to the pioneer homes, take exit 10 off I–459, drive 3 miles, and turn left onto Eastern Valley Road.

Downtown in Bessemer, in the Old Southern Railway Depot, the **Bessemer Hall of History Museum,** 1905 Alabama Avenue, displays artifacts relating to local history. Pieces range from ancient fossils and Indian-mound excavations to pioneer tools and Civil War items. The museum is open Tuesday through Saturday 10:00 A.M. to 4:00 P.M. Closed holidays. Admission is free. Phone (205) 426–1633. To get to the depot, take exit 112 off I–59/I–20.

Traveling east instead of west from Montgomery takes you to **Tuskegee.** If Bessemer and Tannehill illustrate Alabama's old iron industry and Magnolia Grove in Montgomery epitomizes the wealthy planter's life, Tuskegee, about 30 miles east of Montgomery via I–85, represents the accomplishments and indomitable spirit of black Southerners. The town has some interesting early history, having been a fort from which Andrew Jackson and his troops mounted a campaign against the Creek Indians. But today Tuskegee is better known as the home of **Tuskegee Institute** (now Tuskegee University), founded in 1881 by Booker T. Washington, a former slave. The school began in buildings on an abandoned farm with thirty students, who helped build the campus.

Tuskegee Institute National Historic Site, at 1212 Old Montgomery Road, has twenty-seven landmarks related to Booker T. Washington and to George Washington Carver, who pioneered at the institute in finding uses for peanuts and sweet potatoes, both of which grow read-ily in the South. In the **Carver Museum,** exhibits show the range of Carver's experiments, not just with peanuts and sweet potatoes but also with other local plants and materials. There are examples of house paint made from clay, for instance, and inks and dyes made from plants. The museum also has an exhibit of photographs of the institute during its early days. The museum is open daily 9:00 A.M. to 5:00 P.M. Admission is free. Phone (334) 727–3200.

Also on the campus is **The Chapel.** This contemporary building, which replaces the original one built by students, which burned in 1957, marks the burial spot of both Washington and Carver. **The Oaks,** on old Montgomery Road, is the restored home of Booker T. Washington. The Queen Anne structure was built by students with locally manufactured materials in 1899, from plans designed by the architect Robert R. Taylor, the first black graduate of Massachusetts Institute of Technology. Tours of the Oaks begin on the hour from the Carver Museum. The last tour begins an hour before closing. Admission is free. Maps for a walking tour of the campus are available at National Park Service Headquarters, 1212 Old Montgomery Road. Phone (334) 727–6390.

Traveling north of Montgomery for about 90 miles via I–65, you will come to **Birmingham,** a city more notable for its recent development than for its antebellum attractions. If you are in the area, the house museum **Arlington Antebellum Home and Gardens,** 331 Cotton Avenue Southwest, is open for tours and easy to reach from I–65. The Greek Revival mansion, dating from about 1840, first belonged to Judge William Mudd. Like so many important mansions, this one played a brief role in the Civil War. A Union officer dispatched troops from here to Tannehill, Selma, and Tuscaloosa. The house is worth seeing for its fine collection of period antiques, including a Louis XV bed in one of the upstairs rooms. In formal gardens edged with boxwood, azaleas, magnolias, and roses bloom in season. The house and gardens are open Tuesday through Saturday 10:00 A.M. to 4:00 P.M.; Sunday 1:00 P.M. to 4:00 P.M. The last tour begins thirty minutes before closing. Closed major holidays. Admission is about $3.00 for adults, $2.00 for children. Phone (334) 780–5656. To get to Arlington from I–65 South, take the Sixth Avenue North exit. From I–65 North, take the Third Avenue North exit. Follow the signs.

THE GULF COAST

She wasn't wearing petticoats and handing around mint juleps, but she seemed like she would be at home in that role. Miss May stood amid the huge floral displays at Bellingrath Gardens as if she owned them and said to her guests, "You see, dears, Mobile is the *real* south." **Mobile** truly does have a population of Southern belles of all ages who, apparently effortlessly, practice the coquetries and courtesies of the grand early days. They don't wear hoop skirts and bonnets, but you will see full skirts and feminine fashions, hear Southern drawls better than Vivian Leigh ever managed for Scarlett, and find yourself admiring the determination with which the citizens of Mobile continue in the old ways.

It is not what you expect when you first come upon the city from one of the interstates. The perimeter of the city is an active manufacturing and shipping area. But you get an entirely different picture after you take the Government Street exit to get to the **City of Mobile Museum,** located at 355 Government Street, in a restored 1872 Italianate townhouse. Government Street is famous for its live oaks, which were replanted after being cut down during the Civil War to provide fortification against Yankee incursions. Later, you'll probably want to drive the length of the street, but in the beginning, a stop at the museum can orient you to the city's history. Exhibits cover Mobile's development from the first French contacts in 1702 through the attempts at rule of the British, Spanish, and then British again, as the European nations struggled to control this area. The Diamond Horseshoe in the museum displays costumes worn by Mardi Gras queens from the 1860s to the 1960s. These bejeweled gowns, complete with trains, are astonishing in their grandeur—and, incidentally, their weight. It seems like a Mardi Gras queen would have to go into weight training just to walk while wearing one of these hefty gowns. Mobile claims to have held the first Mardi Gras celebration in 1703. New Orleans copied it later, they say. Seeing this exhibit, you realize that in its mentality, Mobile is more like New Orleans than like Montgomery.

Other displays include local silver, old photographs and documents, and, of course, Civil War artifacts. An 1850s carriage is displayed at the Rutherford Carriage House inside the museum. The museum is open Tuesday through Saturday 10:00 A.M. to 5:00 P.M.; Sunday 1:00 P.M. to 5:00 P.M. Admission is free. Phone (334) 434–7569.

An Oak with a Hundred Roots

The Church Street Cemetery, behind the public library on Government Street, is a graveyard dating back to 1819. One of the people buried there is Charles R. S. Boyington, who, as a young man, was convicted of murder and hanged. He protested his innocence to the end and, from the scaffold, claimed that an oak tree with one hundred roots would grow from his grave to prove he was wrongfully hanged. Boyington was buried in a part of the cemetery that is now on the outside of the wall. An oak tree did, indeed, start to grow there. Today the huge tree, growing near where the murder was supposed to have happened, has more than one hundred roots. Although the tree is not marked, it is the first large oak against the cemetery wall as you walk toward it down Bayou Street. Locals refer to it as the Boyington Oak.

This story is told in the book The Best of Alabama, *by Lee Sentell.*

The city's welcome center is in **Fort Conde,** 150 South Royal Street. The fort was built between 1734 and 1735 and headquartered the French colony in Mobile. In 1829 it was torn down, but Mobile reconstructed it for the 1976 American Bicentennial. Costumed guides fire replicas of old French firearms and give tours of the fort. In addition to a variety of displays on the city's history, including an exhibit about early Mardi Gras celebrations, the center has brochures for most of the attractions, lodgings, and eating places in the area. The fort is open daily 8:00 A.M. to 5:00 P.M., except Christmas and Mardi Gras days. Admission is free. Phone (334) 434–7304. To get to the fort, take I-10, exit 26B, and turn left onto Church Street. The fort is at the corner of Church and Royal.

From Fort Conde it's a quick walk to **City Hall,** on Royal Street, where murals in the lobby depict the history of Mobile. There are scenes of early forts, Indian fights, steamboats and rail shipping, slave transport, and the building of the Confederate submarine *Hunley* (a replica of which stands outside the museum in Charleston, South Carolina). The building itself is Renaissance Italianate style, built in 1857 to serve as a market and city hall. The building is open Monday through Friday during normal business hours.

Also close to Fort Conde is **Conde-Charlotte House,** 102 Theatre Street. Built in 1822, it was the city's first jail; now it's the city's oldest house museum. You can actually see the marks on the brick floor where four jail cells stood. When the building became a private residence in 1845, the jail doors were shifted to the kitchen wing. The house is furnished with eighteenth- and nineteenth-century antiques to represent various periods in the city's history. A walled Spanish garden is designed in the style of the eighteenth century. The house is open Tuesday through Saturday 10:00 A.M. to 4:00 P.M. Admission is about $4.00 for adults and about half that for children. Phone (334) 432–4722.

Mobile has four downtown historic districts. Another historical district is near downtown, and one is farther away from the waterfront, which was originally built as an escape from summers in the city. Each preserves a different aspect of Mobile's early years. **Church Street East** has most of the important sites between the public library and Fort Conde. **Old Dauphin Way,** just on the edge of the downtown area, north of Government Street and south of Spring Hill Avenue, has the nineteenth-century homes of middle-class merchants and steamboat captains and the modest cottages of some of the people who worked as servants in the mansions on Government. It was one of the first preservation neighborhoods in Alabama. The **Lower Dauphin Street Commercial District** comprises many smaller brick business buildings from the 1800s, set close together.

Between Dauphin and Conti Streets, on the west side of Claiborne, is the **Cathedral of the Immaculate Conception.** Built in the years from 1835 to 1890, it is the only church in the South to be named a minor basilica. The cathedral has twin towers supported by ten fluted Doric columns. Inside, the windows are of German art glass. Fourteen handcarved scenes mark the stations of the cross. The church is open daily 8:00 A.M. to 3:00 P.M. Admission is free. Phone (334) 434–1576.

De Tonti Square has the in-the-city look of mid- to late-1800s townhouses, with their balconies and ironwork fences.

Spring Hill was essentially a summer suburb in the woods. Houses here date from the 1820s.

Bragg-Mitchell Mansion, in this district, is considered one of the most imposing antebellum mansions on the Gulf Coast. Judge John Bragg, originally from North Carolina, built it in 1855. The mansion has twenty rooms, with 15-foot-high ceilings downstairs. Double parlors flank a wide center hall. Both the high ceilings and the center hall were intended to improve air circulation in the muggy Mobile summers in the days before air conditioning. Everything in the mansion is just a tad more ornate than the norm for the time. The heart pine floors and wainscoting in the lavish dining room, for instance, are painted to look like mahogany. The marble mantels over the fireplaces have silver fenders. Gold-leaf glitters on the cornices from which damask draperies hang. Outside, sixteen fluted columns reflect Italianate and Greek Revival influences.

The mansion sits romantically amid fine old live oaks. Even this has a story. The original oaks were cut down during the Civil War to clear space for firing at the Yankees. Judge Bragg saved acorns from those trees and planted them when the war was over. Most of the trees that are here now grew from the judge's acorns. The mansion is open Monday through Friday 10:00 A.M. to 4:00 P.M.; Sunday 1:00 P.M. to 4:00 P.M. Admission is about $4.00 for adults, $2.00 for children.

Oakleigh Garden District, which incorporates the oak canopy of Government Street, centers around **Oakleigh Mansion,** originally the elaborate raised-cottage–style home of a merchant from South Carolina. Detailed brochures for walking tours are available at the welcome center in Fort Conde.

Oakleigh Mansion, 350 Oakleigh Place, is worth some attention as an antebellum house museum. It was built with slave labor of bricks made on the grounds. The hollows from which the clay was dug have been turned into sunken gardens. The house is furnished in true antebellum elegance, with fine antiques, silver, and china. Costumed guides take you through the house, pointing out such notable collections as the portraits of important society people of Mobile in the 1800s. In spring, though, the displays of blooming azaleas outside steal the show. The price of admission includes a tour of the 1850 **Cox-Deasy House,** a more modest raised Creole cottage on the grounds. The cottage was built with French doors and a hall down the center. When you consider the climate of Mobile, in the days before air conditioning, raising cottages and keeping them as open as possible made a lot of sense. The Oakleigh complex is open Monday through Saturday, 10:00 A.M. to 4:00 P.M.; Sunday 2:00 P.M. to 4:00 P.M. Admission is about $5.00 for adults, and there are discounts for senior citizens and children. Phone (334) 432–1281.

An interesting variation on the Creole-style cottage is **Carlen House Museum,** 54 Carlen Street, on the campus of Murphy High School. Here you see another aspect of the need to catch the breeze. The 1842 cottage had wide galleries (porches) running the length of the house. The place is furnished to demonstrate day-to-day life in the mid-1800s in Mobile. Clothing of the period is also displayed. The house is surrounded with brilliant flowering plants—crape myrtle, azaleas, and magnolias. Carlen House is open Tuesday through Saturday, 10:00 A.M. to 5:00 P.M.; Sunday 1:00 P.M. to 5:00 P.M. Admission is free. Phone (334) 470–7768.

With its splendid interior, Bragg-Mitchell Mansion is said to be the most photographed house in Mobile. For outdoor pictures **Bellingrath Gardens and Home** would surely be photographers' choice. These sixty-five acres of landscaped gardens attract at least 20,000 visitors a year. The gardens weren't ready for public showing until 1932, well past the antebellum era, but their scope and elaborate design, patterned on the formal gardens of Europe, would make them perfectly at home in those prewar years when wealth was fabulous and labor plentiful. The admission fee includes a printed guide to the gardens.

A tour guide first leads you toward a rose garden, beside the Oriental Garden, past lakes with water plants and birds. Paths take you to fountains and reflecting pools and through great displays of blooming plants. Something is always blooming at Bellingrath: azaleas, dogwoods, daffodils, and other spring blooms, then roses and annuals, on to chrysanthemums, followed by camellias. It's hard to convey the sheer masses of bloom—250,000 azaleas, millions of chrysanthemums, a one-acre rose garden shaped like a Rotary Club emblem, and so on. If you're a gardener accustomed to acquiring special plants a few at a time, these gardens will boggle your mind.

The Bellingraths also assembled the largest collection of Boehm porcelain on public display. The home was built in 1937, but it is trimmed with antebellum wrought iron and furnished with priceless antiques, exquisitely arranged—well worth the time if you enjoy these things. Also on the grounds are a conservatory of exotic plants, a gift shop, a patio filled with plants that you can buy, a visitors' lounge housing the Boehm porcelain collection, and a cafeteria.

Both the Bellingrath gardens and home are open for tours. The gardens are open daily from 7:00 A.M. to dusk, the house from 8:00 A.M. to dusk. Admission for house and garden is about $14 for adults, $11 for children. Admission for the gardens alone is about $6.50 for adults, half that for children. Phone (334) 973–2217 or (334) 973–2365. The gardens are about 20 miles south of Mobile. To get there take I–10 west from Mobile. Exit at 15–A to the Theodore/Bellingrath Highway, then follow the signs.

Alabama's warm temperatures and high humidity are part of what keeps Bellingrath Gardens blooming from one glorious season to the next.

Bellingrath Home and Gardens

Walter D. Bellingrath was a Coca-Cola bottler. He bought the land that is the heart of Bellingrath Gardens as a rustic fishing camp to entertain his friends. Before long his wife began moving some of her azalea plants from their overplanted city garden. Then the Bellingraths began touring the great gardens of Europe and decided to create their own garden estate. The fact that they had the wealth to work with a landscape architect, acquire the huge volume of plants, and pay for the gardens' maintenance are all factors in the success of the project. So are the Bellingraths' innate good taste and their abiding interest in gardens. Over the years their gardens were expanded and improved. Mrs. Bellingrath died in 1943. Her husband continued to live there, in the center of the gardens until he died in 1955. The home is as they left it, with nothing added or removed. In 1892 Mr. Bellingrath wrote to his mother, ". . . by God's help I am going to try to make the world better and brighter by my being here." The thousands of visitors that the gardens attract each year attest to his success in that goal.

For romantic lodging, spend a night back in Mobile at the **Malaga Inn,** at 355 Church Street, in the downtown historic district. The inn started out as two townhouses, built in 1862 by two brothers-in-law so that their families could live privately but close. After the Civil War the homes fell into decline and were not restored until 1968. Since then the restoration and renovation have been ongoing. Now the two old homes have a patio, garden, swimming pool, and a new building connecting them.

About half of the forty guest rooms are in the restored homes. Some still have their original wallpaper and hardwood floors. The furnishings are fairly standard—mostly traditional with some good antiques—though the newer rooms are more elaborate. Those rooms overlooking the courtyard, with its plants and fountain, call earlier days to mind. The inn has a nice restaurant that serves Cajun and Creole dishes, emphasizing fresh seafood. Rates begin at about $60 per room. Phone (334) 438–4701 or (800) 235–1586.

bama

If you'd like to dine in a restored mansion, try **The Pillars,** amid the
live oaks at 1757 Government Street. The house has eleven dining rooms
and serves continental dinners with seafood, pasta, beef, and veal specialties. The restaurant has a good wine cellar. Phone (334) 478–6341.

Or try seafood in a more casual setting at **Rousso's,** 166 South Royal
Street. The restaurant is an old warehouse next to Fort Conde, decorated
in a nautical motif, with nets, buoys, and so on. It is open Monday through
Saturday 11:00 A.M. to 10:00 P.M.; Sunday 11:30 A.M. to 9:00 P.M.

Across Mobile Bay, the little resort town of **Fairhope** has several attractions based on its colorful past. Fairhope was started as a utopian community based on the ideas of Henry George, who wrote in 1879 that people
would prosper if they were taxed only for the land on which they lived and
not for their capital and labor. Thus when a community increased in value,
the benefits would go to those who did the work and not benefit land
owners unfairly. About that time, Ernest B. Gaston, a newspaper man from
Iowa, led a group of disgruntled people from Iowa to build a community

Fairhope

Fairhope was unusual not only for its economic philosophy but also
for its liberal attitude toward women and social experiments. In
Women of Fairhope (Black Belt Press, 1993; originally published by
University of Georgia Press, 1984) Paul M. Gaston, grandson of the
town's founder, writes about three women who significantly shaped
the character of the town. Nancy Lewis was a black woman who
insisted that she had the same right to lease colony land as white people. She persisted until she found a way to become a land holder just
about a mile from the spot where she was first denied it. Marie How-
land spent time in other utopian communities, brought her ideas to
Fairhope, and worked all her life for social reform. There she campaigned for cooperative living, homes without kitchens, and scientific
childrearing to liberate women from "household drudgery and male
exploitation." Marietta Johnson, an education innovator, determined
that education should not be allowed to become a mill to "crush the
childish mind." All three women were born in the mid-1800s.

that would be such a single-tax corporation. Instead of owning their land, the families lease it for 99 years. Leases are renewed automatically; the corporation pays all the taxes. The town got its name because the first colonists in 1894 speculated that they had a "fair hope" of success.

It worked. Fairhope is the oldest, most successful single-tax corporation in the country. This means that you, as a visitor, pay no local sales tax as you enjoy the beautifully kept downtown and bay-front public areas of a thriving historic community. This is not an antebellum community in time, but in spirit it represents the best of Southern cooperation and hospitality. Walking about the downtown is a treat, as is wandering through the rose gardens in the waterfront park. The **Fairhope Municipal Pier** on Fairhope Avenue is open daily.

Fairhope has two charming bed-and-breakfast inns, both run in old family homes by Becky and Bill Jones. The houses were built sometime after the Civil War, the furnishings go back for generations, and the Southern hospitality is timeless. **Bay Breeze Guest House,** 742 South Mobile Street, sits on a three-acre site right on the shores of Mobile Bay. The stucco building was built as a small home and has been variously remodeled and enlarged over the years, so there are nooks and crannies and surprising little rooms to discover. The entire downstairs—even the kitchen, which is considered off limits in many inns—is devoted to guests.

The mix of wicker, stained glass, hooked rugs, and antique furniture is homey. Most of the furnishings are family heirlooms going back as far as five generations. Becky says that every piece has a story. She has a good Southern hostess's ability to know when to tell the story and when to leave guests alone. She also has the knack of finding out what you like and providing it, such as a favorite jelly or coffee or bread. Once she knows, you can count on having it again anytime you stay there. Rates begin at about $85 a room. Phone (334) 928–8976.

Staying at **Church Street Inn** is staying in a Southern home—literally. Becky's mother lived in the stucco house until she had to move to where she could receive extra care. She left almost everything behind—furniture, photographs, knickknacks, even dishes. Guests use all these things just as she did. The guest rooms are named after great-grandchildren and are furnished with such family antiques as spool furniture and a Jenny Lind bedroom suite. The front porch has romantic rockers, and the house is next door to an old-time tearoom. Rates begin at about $85 a room. Phone (334) 928–5144.

Two forts that guarded Mobile Bay during the Civil War are now historic sites. **Fort Gaines,** on Dauphin Island, guarded the western side of the bay. Directly across from it—about 8 miles as the fish swims—**Fort Morgan,** at Gulf Shores, guarded the eastern approach. This fort is a National Historic Landmark. Both forts fell to the Union in 1864, in what has been described as the most important sea battle of the war. Fort Morgan was used as late as World War II, but Fort Gaines stood abandoned for a long time and even now has been only partly restored. Each fort has a museum of Civil War and naval artifacts, awesomely thick walls, and cannons.

Fort Gaines is open daily April through August 9:00 A.M. to 6:00 P.M. It closes an hour earlier the rest of the year. Admission is about $2.00 for adults, $1.00 for children. Phone (334) 861–6992. To get to Fort Gaines, take I–10 west from Mobile. Exit at Theodore Dawes and take Highway 59 south, turn east on Highway 188, and go south on Highway 163 to Dauphin Island. The fort is 2 miles east of the LeMoyne Drive intersection.

Fort Morgan is open Monday through Friday 8:00 A.M. to 5:00 P.M.; Saturday and Sunday 9:00 A.M. to 5:00 P.M. Closed major holidays. Admission is about $2.00 for adults, $1.00 for senior citizens and children. Phone (334) 540–7125. To get to Fort Morgan, follow the signs on Highway 180 west from Gulf Shores to Mobile Bay for 21 miles. The Mobile Bay Ferry runs back and forth between Fort Gaines and Fort Morgan regularly. Rates are $1.00 per person walking on, $13.00 for car and passengers one way, $20.00 round trip. Phone (334) 973–2251 or (800) 634–4027 for details.

NORTH ALABAMA

People tend to think of **Huntsville** as the space center where the rockets that took the astronauts to the moon were developed. It's true that when you come into Huntsville from the west, the 363-foot *Saturn V* rocket is the first thing you see. But one of the most impressive attractions in the state commemorates what happened in Huntsville well before Jules Verne had even thought about space shots.

The first British settlement in Alabama began here. Later some wealthy Georgians decided that they wanted to make this the county seat for Madison County. It first was to be named Twickenham, after the hometown of an English poet, but people didn't like that choice. By 1811 the name had become Huntsville, for John Hunt, a pioneer squatter from Tennessee. A convention was held here in 1819 to write Alabama's first constitution.

In 1982 **Alabama Constitution Village,** 301 Madison Street, was opened, in observance of the 150th anniversary of Alabama's becoming a state. Its creators excavated the original site and did research for years to learn exactly what the old village and its buildings had been like. Their efforts paid off: Some old-timers who had known the original buildings inside and out could not tell that the re-creations were new structures.

The spirit and pride that went into re-creating the village continues. Talking with the volunteers who work in the project, watching them duplicate the times, and sharing their enthusiasm for it is as much a pleasure as exploring the buildings and learning their history.

Costumed guides take you through a cabinetmaker's shop, print shop, theater, library, and post office. This is a living-history village, so guides and "interpreters" are engaged in appropriate activities. In the Stephen Neal House, for instance, a domestic-skills interpreter cooks over an open fire, bakes from old recipes, and demonstrates the culinary arts as practiced in the 1800s. Other interpreters spin, garden, pick cotton, dye textiles, and put up food for winter. In another complex, an interpreter shows you how the weekly newspaper, *The Alabama Republican,* was printed on a handpress.

Constitution Village is open Monday through Saturday 9:00 A.M. to 5:00 P.M.; closed major holidays. Admission is about $6.00 for adults, with discounts for children and senior citizens. Phone (205) 535–6565 or (800) 678–1819. To get to the village, take exit 19C from I–565 and turn right. Drive 4 blocks on Jefferson/Madison. The village is 1 block south of the courthouse square.

Take some time to walk through the **Twickenham Historic District,** within which Constitution Village is set. Given that Twickenham was a name inspired by British literary connections, you may find it appropriate that some of the homes in this district were built by physicians and merchants with British connections. Some of the homes were part of plantations before the land was sold off. This is one of the most dense neighborhoods of antebellum homes in the South. One reason so many of the original buildings remain is that even though Yankee soldiers occupied Huntsville for a while, no major battles were fought in the town, so it sustained relatively little damage. Also, in the years after the Civil War, money was so tight that the people who owned these homes could not afford to modernize the exteriors.

Alabama Constitution Village is a faithful recreation on the original site. It was so carefully researched and executed that some old-timers who had known the original buildings didn't know they were looking at newly created structures.

Of the homes, only the **Weeden House Museum,** a block east of Constitution Village, 300 Gates Avenue Southeast, is open to the public, but you can still appreciate the others from the outside. Weeden House is an 1819 Federal Style High House, furnished with antiques of the Federal period. It has handcarved woodwork, leaded–glass fanlight windows with the original glass, and a spiral staircase. Weeden House was the home of the artist and poet Maria Howard Weeden, who supported her family after the Civil War by teaching art and writing poems, which she also illustrated, about ex-slaves. Her watercolor portraits of the slaves who were her friends are displayed in the museum, and a guide reads the poetry during the tour. Weeden House is open Tuesday through Sunday 1:00 to 4:00

P.M.; closed January and February. Admission is about $2.00 for adults, with discounts for senior citizens and children. Phone (205) 536–7718.

Another fine building that survived undamaged is the **Episcopal Church of the Nativity,** at the corner of Eustis and Green Streets, a block from the courthouse square. This is an outstanding example of ecclesiological Gothic architecture and is a National Historic Landmark. The church, with its 151-foot metal spire, was built in 1859. During the Civil War Union soldiers were supposed to stable their horses in the church, but for some reason they did not, so it remains in fine condition.

The only bed-and-breakfast inn in the Twickenham Historic District is **Stockton House,** 310 Green Street Southeast. This Queen Anne brick structure with white columns overlooks both the Weeden House and the Episcopal church. It is only 2 blocks from the courthouse square. The interior of the inn is furnished with oriental rugs and family antiques, set off with Tiffany stained-glass windows and intricately carved paneling. The three guest rooms are also furnished with antiques. The bathrooms, however, are thoroughly modern, as are the refrigerator and ice machine provided on the second floor for guests. Rates, which include a continental breakfast served on a tray in your room or on the porch, begin at about $70 per room. Phone (205) 539–3195.

Stockton House is walking distance to the **Huntsville Depot Transportation Museum,** 320 Church Street, which shows how early Southerners got from place to place. Built in 1860, it's one of America's oldest railroad buildings, complete with grafitti from the Civil War that was probably inscribed when Union forces took the depot in 1862 and used it as a prison for Confederate soldiers. Model-railroad enthusiasts will enjoy the HO-gauge re-creation of the depot and surrounding Huntsville as they were in the 1860s.

The guided tour of the museum includes an audiovisual presentation in which animated cartoon characters explain what the telegraphers, engineers, and mechanics did in the old depot. The museum is open March through December, Tuesday through Saturday 10:00 A.M. to 4:00 P.M. Admission is about $3.50 for adults, with discounts for senior citizens and children. Phone (205) 539–1860 or (800) 239–8955. The depot is at the ramp of exit 19 off I–565.

A walk in the historic district might help justify a genuine old-fashioned Southern breakfast at **Eunice's Country Kitchen,** 1004 Andrew Jackson Way off I–565. It has already been discovered by the late Southern humor writer Lewis Grizzard and NBC weatherman Willard Scott. Biscuits and country ham are the classic breakfast. The place is known as a level playing field or mixing pot for people of all classes and colors and occupations. There's as much coffee as you want, but tradition has it that you first help yourself and then walk around filling the cups of everyone else in the house. This creates a fair amount of commotion and a lot of good humor.

Between Huntsville and Decatur on Alabama Highway 20, the town of **Mooresville,** the oldest incorporated town in Alabama, delights those in search of Dixie. The entire town is listed on the National Register of Historic Places. Most people just drive through the tiny town, because the old homes, which date back to the 1820s, are not open to the public. But you can certainly park your car and stroll among the magnolias to admire the homes from the outside. Be sure to look at the brick 1839 Cumberland Presbyterian Church, with its slave gallery, and the 1854 frame church nearby. You can go into the post office, a small wooden building, to see the old call boxes that have been there since 1840. The town also has an old tavern and a stagecoach shop dating to pre-Civil War days. To get to Mooresville, take the Mooresville exit from I–565 East.

If you continue northwest on Highway 20, you will come to **Florence,** notable for **Pope's Tavern Museum,** 203 Hermitage Drive. Built of handmade brick, the museum began its existence in the early 1800s as a stage stop and inn. Later it was used as a Confederate hospital. The city of Florence operates the museum. It displays frontier relics, many antiques of the period, decorative glass, Civil War artifacts, and framed engravings. The museum is open Tuesday through Saturday 10:00 A.M. to 4:00 P.M.; closed major holidays. Admission is about $2.00 for adults, with a discount for children. Phone (205) 760–6439.

One more stop in Florence reminds you of the role that music has played in Southern life. The **W. C. Handy Home & Museum,** 620 West College Street, is the birthplace of the composer William Christopher Handy, who wrote "St. Louis Blues," "Memphis Blues," and "Beale Street Blues." Handy was born in this log cabin in 1873 into a family of Methodist ministers who disapproved of his musical inclinations. In 1950 the cabin was dismantled to make way for a housing project and was moved to College Street. Among the displays are Handy's trumpet and the piano where he wrote "St. Louis Blues." The museum is open Tuesday through Saturday 10:00 A.M. to 4:00 P.M. Admission is about $2.00 for adults, with a discount for children. Phone (205) 760–6434.

Arkansas

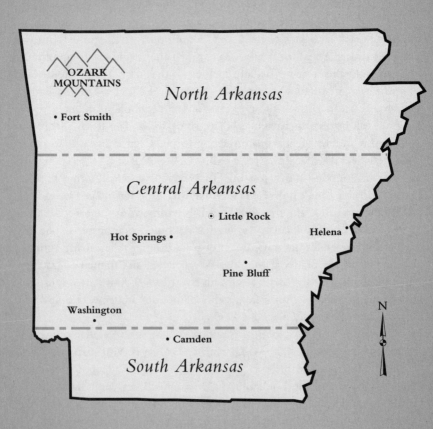

OZARK
MOUNTAINS

North Arkansas

• Fort Smith

Central Arkansas

⊙ Little Rock

Hot Springs •

Helena •

Pine Bluff

Washington •

N

• Camden

South Arkansas

Arkansas

 ARKANSAS GOT ITS NAME FROM THE QUAPAW INDIANS, which doesn't make sense at first, since this isn't the state of Quapaw. But the Quapaw Indians were known as the Arkansas, or "South Wind People," by other tribes. Although Europeans came into this area as early as 1541, settlements other than those of the existing Native American tribes did not develop for a long time; in fact, you can still drive many miles in the northern part of the state without seeing much in the way of habitation. Major population areas seem far apart. What is more, even the older towns in the state date their historic buildings from about the turn of the century. There just wasn't a lot there earlier.

When you visit Arkansas, you will discover remnants of several distinctly different kinds of antebellum life. Arkansas was still a territory until 1836, belonging first to Louisiana and then Missouri. It became Arkansas Territory in 1819. Arkansas was admitted to the Union as the twenty-fifth state in 1836.

In the southern region bordering Louisiana and the southeastern stretch along the Mississippi River, where the relatively flat land and good soil encouraged crops, a planting society evolved, as it did in Louisiana and part of Tennessee. (Because of its plantations, Arkansas was admitted to the Union as a slave-holding state, so the state seceded in 1861 to join the Southern Confederacy.) The people of the mountains, however, were not part of this culture; instead, they lived in small, clannish pockets widely separated from one another, often at near-subsistence levels. They had come mainly from the Appalachian Mountains, choosing to settle in the Ozarks because of the similarity in climate and topography. Along the western border of the state there are also signs of the early Arkansas frontier, where law and order weren't exactly the rule because the rules had not even been made yet.

No Southern state has greater social contrasts. The most logical place to begin exploring the state today is at its center, where much of its population is concentrated.

CENTRAL ARKANSAS

Little Rock, the capital of Arkansas, was founded in 1814 with fewer than two dozen people and did not grow significantly until after the Civil War. In 1865 the population was about 4,000 people; by 1900 it had risen to nearly 40,000. This means that much of the city is comparatively new. These days Little Rock is an up-and-coming city, with lots of new businesses and other growth. Perhaps the energy is contagious, because the attractions that preserve the city's history are being promoted as enthusiastically as is its modern development.

A major preservation effort is in process in **Quapaw Quarter,** an area of 9 square miles, including the central business district and some residential neighborhoods. This is the oldest part of Little Rock. The Quapaw Indians lived in this part of Arkansas in the early 1800s. Within the quarter, the **MacArthur Park Historic District** and the **Governor's Mansion Area** each have some fine old homes. A few date back as far as 1842, more were built in the late 1800s, and some in the early 1900s. Except for the commercial buildings, most of these are private residences. The **Little Rock Convention and Visitors Bureau** will provide you with excellent walking-tour guides, complete with maps, photographs, and commentary. They are free. Write the bureau at P.O. Box 3232, Little Rock, AR 72203, or phone (800) 844–4781.

Most of the city's oldest buildings are in the MacArthur Park Historic District. Three of them are open for public tours. The **Arkansas Museum of Science and History,** in the old Little Rock Arsenal Building, has more than 15,000 scientific and anthropological objects. The structure, built in 1842, is listed on the National Register of Historic Places. Adults will be interested in the building; children should enjoy the hands-on exhibits about early Arkansas explorers and Indians. The museum is open Monday through Saturday 9:00 A.M. to 4:30 P.M.; Sunday 1:00 to 4:30 P.M. Closed Thanksgiving, Christmas, and New Year's Day. Admission is about $1.00 for adults, half that for children and senior citizens; free to all on Monday. Phone (501) 324–9231.

Villa Marre, 1321 Scott Street, is a restored nineteenth-century Italianate Victorian home furnished as it would have been in the period. The house is known for its elaborately carved woodwork and overall elegance. Villa Marre is open Monday through Friday 9:00 A.M. to 1:00 P.M.; Sunday 1:00 to 5:00 P.M. Closed Saturday. Admission is about $3.00 for adults, with discounts for senior citizens and children. Phone (501) 374–9979.

The **Decorative Arts Museum,** at the corner of Seventh and Rock Streets, is housed in the 1839 Pike-Fletcher-Terry House. It is interesting both for its architecture and for the collections it contains. Some of the exhibits are of contemporary crafts. Others include nineteenth-century European and American glass and toys designed by contemporary artists. Changing exhibits include collections of historical interest as well as contemporary items. The museum is open Monday through Saturday 10:00 A.M. to 5:00 P.M.; Sunday noon to 5:00 P.M. Closed Thanksgiving and Christmas. Admission is free, but donations are accepted. Phone (501) 372–4000, extension 357.

Continuing on Scott or Cumberland Street, moving from the 700 block toward the Arkansas River, you will come to the **Arkansas Territorial Restoration,** 200 East Third Street, in what is known as the oldest neighborhood in the state. The museum's staff research, collect, and interpret materials related to the frontier period of Arkansas. Five early nineteenth-century houses are open for guided tours. One of them, the **Hinederliter Grog Shop,** built with hand-hewn logs and covered in hand-beaded cypress siding, is the oldest building in Little Rock, dating from 1820.

Another, the **Woodruff Exhibit,** includes the 1824 print shop of *The Arkansas Gazette,* the oldest newspaper west of the Mississippi River. In other buildings are old offices, displays of needlework, including antique quilts, kitchens, and handcarved woodwork. All the buildings are furnished with pieces collected by the Restoration project to show how the interiors would have looked in their day. Costumed actors play scenes to convey how the early residents of these homes thought and behaved. Tours begin hourly except at noon; the last tour begins one hour before closing. Although the exhibits are historical, you won't find history isolated here. In the museum store Arkansas artists and crafters sell their work, some of it contemporary in design, creating a pleasing link between the past and the present. The Restoration is open Monday through Saturday 9:00 A.M. to 5:00 P.M.; Sunday 1:00 to 5:00 P.M. Closed major holidays. Admission $2.00 for adults, with discounts for children and senior citizens. The first Sunday of every month is free to all. Phone (501) 324–9351. To get to the Restoration from I–30, take exit 141–A. It leads right to the museum.

To visit the **Old State House,** 300 West Markham Street, walk even closer to the river. Construction on the building was begun in 1833, and it became the state's capitol in 1836. Construction was finished in 1842. Its oval office replicates the Oval Office of the White House. This is the oldest surviving capitol building west of the Mississippi River and is considered an outstanding example of Greek Revival architecture. It no longer serves as a capitol building but is exclusively a museum. Exhibits include the gowns worn by Arkansas first ladies and an assortment of Victorian costumes, along with items relating to the history of the state, including a wilderness gallery showing what the state was like in its earlier years. Two legislative chambers have been restored. The museum is open Monday through Saturday 9:00 A.M. to 5:00 P.M.; Sunday 1:00 to 5:00 P.M. Closed major holidays. Admission is free. Phone (501) 324–9685.

From Little Rock, it's about 42 miles heading south on I–65 to **Pine Bluff,** the second-oldest city in Arkansas. It was occupied by Union troops in 1863. Located in Jefferson County, the city has a population of less than 60,000 and the county population is about 90,000. The amount of energy and enthusiasm for preserving historic sites and for making Pine Bluff an appealing place to visit or live would be impressive coming from twice that many people. When you're visiting, don't be surprised if you start thinking about living here.

Your search for antebellum Dixie should begin at the **Dexter Harding House,** 110 North Pine Street, at the Pine Street exit off Highway 65 Expressway. The visitors' center, where you can pick up a detailed map for a tour of the city's historic buildings, is in this house, but the house is an important site in itself. The Dexter Harding restoration re-creates the original three rooms of the home of, no surprise, Dexter Harding. It stood on the banks of Harding Lake, near Texas Street and East Twelfth Avenue. The

The Old State House in Little Rock is where President Clinton was sworn into office.

materials and style of construction (hand-hewn logs for sills, doweled studs, no nails) suggest that the original three-room house was probably built about 1850. The Harding family had a sawmill that was converted to a grist mill at the beginning of the Civil War to help feed the Confederate Army. Generations of the family occupied the house over many years, adding rooms all around until the three original rooms were totally encompassed. When the land on which the house stood was purchased to become part of the Civic Center complex, an architect and some preservationists worked to save the old structure. They dismantled the house, marking each piece of the original three rooms, and stored the materials. They preserved the grist mill stones similarly. Then they received grants to rebuild the house on its current site. The house was put back together as closely as possible to the original plans, using many of the original materials. The Dexter Harding House is open daily 8:30 A.M. to 4:30 P.M. Phone (501) 536–7606.

For an overview of Pine Bluff's history from 1830 to the present, stop at the **Pine Bluff/Jefferson County Historical Museum,** 201 East Fourth Street (corner of Fourth and State Streets), in the restored Union Station train depot. The building itself is on the National Register of Historic Places. This three-room museum displays antique farm equipment, old clothes and furniture, quilts, and so on. A cotton exhibit includes a cotton gin, built in 1840, that could be operated by one man. The Farm Bureau provided a three-dimensional model of a farm growing cotton and corn that is a big favorite with children. The museum is open Monday through Friday 9:00 A.M. to 5:00 P.M. Admission is free, but donations are welcome. Phone (501) 541–5402.

Another unique exhibit, **Keepers of the Spirit,** on the campus of the University of Arkansas at Pine Bluff, traces the 120-year history of the school, using photographs, texts, and memorabilia. The university, formerly known as A & M College, has been important in the lives of black people in Arkansas. The exhibit is a follow-up to an earlier exhibit, "Persistence of the Spirit," which provided a chronological survey of the black experience in Arkansas. "Keepers of the Spirit" is divided into four periods in the history of the school. The displays, in the west wing of the Leedell Moorehead-Graham Fine Arts Gallery, consist of twenty-five 4- by 8-foot panels. The gallery is part of the Fine Arts Center, 1200 North

"The Judge Is a Very Involved Kind of Man!"

The story behind the Pine Bluff/Jefferson County Historical Museum is as interesting as its displays. Funded through the County Court, the museum used to be crowded into two rooms in the old courthouse. Judge Jack Jones, who grew up in the area and loves its farming history, searched for a better location, finally managing to situate the museum in the restored train station owned by the city. The judge, described by a staff member as "a very involved kind of man," is active in supporting the museum and personally helps pay for its advertising. A staff member at the museum says that the museum does not rely on court funding alone. An annual fish fry raises several thousand dollars.

University Drive. The gallery is open Monday through Friday 8:30 A.M. to 4:30 P.M. Admission is free. Phone (501) 543–8236.

Pine Bluff also has an "outdoor gallery." As you travel around the city, pay special attention to the murals on the outside walls of some of the downtown buildings. The long-range plan calls for twenty-two murals depicting nostalgic scenes from local history. As this is being written, six are complete, including a scene showing an Indian chief. Another shows an old-time view of Main Street lined with businesses along both sides and the courthouse at its end, all under a blue sky dotted with a few fluffy white clouds. For more information about the murals project, phone Pine Bluff Downtown Development, Inc., (501) 536–8742 or (800) 638–7698.

When you're ready to eat, for old Arkansas country cooking that practically everyone recommends, try **Jones Cafe,** a quick drive to 3910 Highway 65 south. The cafe, owned and operated by three generations of the same family, has been serving home-cooked meals for more than half a century. The offerings include plate lunches, especially catfish and chicken, with all the fresh vegetables for which Southern cooking is famous, as well as homemade pies and other award-winning desserts. The restaurant is open Monday through Saturday 9:00 A.M. to 6:00 P.M.; Sunday 11:00 A.M. to 2:00 P.M. Phone (501) 534–6678.

Similar food is served at **Southern Cook's Kitchen,** at 3007 Olive Street, out where the street becomes State Highway 15, on the south side of town. Southern Cook's Kitchen promises catfish and shrimp every night. The restaurant is open daily 6:00 A.M. to 8:30 P.M. Phone (501) 534–0625.

Margland Bed and Breakfast Inns, 703 West Second Street, provide lodging in seventeen guest rooms in a hospitable atmosphere. The inns comprise three restored turn-of-the century homes, with gardens and decidedly un-antebellum creature comforts such as Jacuzzis and cable TV. Rates begin at about $65 per room and include a country breakfast. Phone (501) 536–6000.

Approximately 20 miles south of Pine Bluff on State Highway 35, **Rison Pioneer Village,** shows what life was like in a typical south Arkansas community during the late 1800s. Mount Olivet Methodist Episcopal Church, in the village, is listed on the National Historic Register. Other buildings include a couple of log cabins, a barn, a tenant cottage, a post office, a store, and a doctor's modest Victorian-style home, all dating from about the turn of the century. Everything is furnished in the style of the era. A stop here gives you an interesting glimpse of how areas in

Arkansas not developed before the Civil War emerged after the war ended. Crafts are sold in the store. The village is open most weekday mornings, except holidays. For more information or to arrange a tour, call Rison City Hall, (501) 325–7444.

Continuing approximately 20 miles more to the south, you will come to the little town of **New Edinburg,** at the junction of Highways 97 and 8. A historical marker identifies **Marks' Mills Battle Site,** where Confederate soldiers captured a federal supply train in 1864. A park at the site has outdoor exhibits.

West of Pine Bluff, at the junction of U.S. Highways 167 and 270, in the little town of **Sheridan,** the **Grant County Museum** displays many artifacts related to the Red River Campaign in Arkansas, a Civil War campaign in which the Confederates thwarted the Yankees' attempt to take over Texas (see page 44). The displays give details of the Battle of Jenkins' Ferry. Other exhibits cover pioneer life and American Indians, demonstrating the continuity of development in the area. The museum includes several log cabins dating from the mid-1800s and a library. Open Tuesday through Saturday 9:00 A.M. to noon and 1:00 to 5:00 P.M. Closed holidays. Admission is free. Phone (501) 942–4496. The museum is on Shackleford Road, off State Highway 46.

Jenkins' Ferry State Park is also on this road. The park is the site of an important battle in the Red River Campaign (see page 44).

From here you can get back to U.S. Highway 270 and go on to **Hot Springs National Park,** once an important resort for planters driven from their plantations by summer's heat. It's a little confusing to describe this area because the national park is partly inside the city of Hot Springs, and in normal travel you can't tell which is which. The park, which advertises itself as "America's only national park located in a city," covers nearly 6,000 acres. The American Indians considered the thermal water of the hot springs curative. Its heat still seems magical, and the water is still pure. It wells up from deep inside the Earth and comes out hot enough to have been sterilized, through fissures in the rock.

In the antebellum years the area was set aside as a park because so many people went to Hot Springs to "take the waters." You can still do it. **Bathhouse Row,** on Central Avenue in downtown Hot Springs National Park, has eight turn-of-the-century bathhouses. One of them, **The Fordyce,** has been restored and now contains the **National Park Visitor Center.** Another, **The Buckstaff,** is still in use. The water runs through two separate pipes—one for hot water and one for water that has cooled—to the bathhouse, where the two are mixed to a comfortable temperature. You bathe in individual tubs, women on one floor, men on the other. For a bath only, the charge is $12.25. A full treatment, including bath, hot pack, steam, and massage is $26.40. The Buckstaff is open Monday through Friday 7:00 A.M. to 11:45 A.M. and 1:30 to 3:00 P.M.; Saturday 7:00 to 11:45 A.M. Phone (501) 623–2308.

At **Hot Springs Health Spa,** 501 Spring Street, a new facility that is not on Bathhouse Row, you have a variety of choices. You might choose a simple tub bath or time in a spa pool that, in design, resembles a Japanese bathhouse. Everyone wears bathing suits. The spa is open seven days a week 9:00 A.M. to 9:00 P.M. Prices depend on the services you choose. Phone (501) 321–9664.

To get the idea without actually taking a bath, visit the two thermal

People used to go to Hot Springs to soak in the mineral waters that bubbled hot and pure from the ground. They would "take the waters" for their health. You can still try this at Bathhouse Row in Hot Springs National Park.

springs at the **Display Hot Springs,** behind the Maurice Bathhouse on Central Avenue. For a thorough orientation to the park, the springs, and the baths, spend a little time in the visitors' center in Fordyce Bathhouse. Guided tours are offered, and a film about the area is shown every twenty minutes. The center is open daily 9:00 A.M. to 8:00 P.M. from Memorial Day to Labor Day. It closes at 5:00 P.M. during the rest of the year.

While you're in Hot Springs, you might spend a night at the **Williams House,** 420 Quapaw Road. This restored Victorian house has a turret, a tower with notched battlements, and wonderful interior woodwork. Mary and Gary Riley practice a personal, accommodating brand of Southern hospitality here, doing whatever it takes to make sure you have what you need. In the guest rooms you find some material describing how a thermal bath is taken in Hot Springs National Park. Jugs of mineral-spring water are always available in a refrigerator just outside the kitchen, so that guests may take the waters even without taking the baths. Rates, which include full breakfast, begin at about $60 per room. Phone (501) 624–4275.

If you drive east from Pine Bluff, taking U.S. Highways 79 and then 49 (a total drive of about 100 miles) until you come to the Mississippi River, you will reach **Helena,** a Delta town that advertises itself as the place "where the ridge and the river meet." (The ridge is Crowley's Ridge, which rises as high as 200 feet above the Mississippi alluvial plain.)

Because the land is fertile, as river deltas tend to be, a variety of successive populations have left evidence of their lives here. Artifacts indicate that Native Americans had flourishing communities here as early as 1000 B.C. In 1541 the Spanish explorer Hernando de Soto encountered large villages in the area. Over the ensuing years European diseases destroyed much of the native population; the rest of the Indians were forced to move away. The next wave of settlement came in the antebellum years with the pioneers, who created a lively city incorporating trade, farming, plantations, and the professions. In the Civil War, when Helena was occupied by Union troops, thousands of freed slaves came through the depot in town looking for work. What remains for visitors is a well-preserved downtown historic district replete with the fine mansions that seem to go hand-in-hand with successful planting regions. Some of the homes are turn-of-the-century, past the antebellum years, but they were built on that earlier grand scale, in keeping with the spirit of the good years. They are well worth seeing. Be sure to pick up a copy of the driving tour with a map, a splendid seventeen-page booklet that gives a short history of the town, identifies important sites, and provides full-color photographic illustrations of the major structures. The booklet is available from the Helena Tourism Commission, 226 Perry Street, Helena, AR 72342. Phone (501) 338–9831.

Among the important buildings is **Estevan Hall,** 623 Biscoe Street, built in 1826. It was occupied during the Civil War by Union troops. Another, **Allin House,** 513 Columbia Street, built in 1858, cooperates with the **Edwardian Inn,** 317 Biscoe Street, in offering bed-and-breakfast accommodations. Edwardian Inn, built by a wealthy cotton merchant, was an astonishingly expensive project, but the house deteriorated over the years. Now that it has been restored, you can't help but marvel over its details: barleytwist balusters on the banister of the oak stairway, ornately carved wainscoting, wood carpeting parqueted in 1-inch-wide strips, and all eight original fireplaces. The twelve guest rooms are furnished with excellent period antiques. Cathy Cunningham, owner of the Edwardian Inn, also owns Allin House, which she calls "a more modest kind of building." Built in 1858, the two-story brick home is notable for its New Orleans–style balcony overlooking the street. The house contains five two-room suites, furnished with antiques. Sometimes the suites are rented for long terms, so rooms are not always available for short stays. Guests who spend the night at the Allin House eat breakfast at the Edwardian Inn. Rates, which include continental breakfast, begin at about $50 per room at either inn. Phone (800) 598–4749 or (501) 338–6868.

Magnolia Hill Bed and Breakfast, 608 Perry Street, also built by a wealthy cotton merchant, provides another luxurious lodging alternative. This restored Queen Anne Victorian landmark is large enough to have once been a Presbyterian church and elegant enough to make you feel like royalty. The house has a wraparound veranda, the antique furnishings include museum-quality Japanese porcelains, and the guest-room beds are made up with satin sheets. The innkeepers serve a three-course Southern breakfast with homemade biscuits and imaginative egg and sausage entrees. Rates begin at about $65 per person, $10 more for each additional person in room. Phone (501) 338–6874.

SOUTH ARKANSAS

The southern part of Arkansas has several small towns that are developing their historic sites. Widely spaced as they are, however, they probably do not have enough attractions to warrant a special trip to any one of them. You might make a pleasant day of driving to see them all.

South of Pine Bluff, 71 miles on U.S. Highway 79, the city of **Camden,** on the banks of the Ouachita River, has antebellum homes, historic landmarks, and Civil War history. Coming up the river, de Soto found the place in 1541. In subsequent centuries the area was a pioneer town, a cotton center, and then a casualty of the Civil War. The city has more than thirty structures on the National Register of Historic Homes, including the **1847 McCollum-Chidester House,** 926 Washington Street, an example of classic plantation home architecture. Both Confederate and Union commanders used this house at different times. Touring here you see the original furnishings, including a bed slept in by Union general Frederick Steele. There are bullet holes in the upstairs walls. The house is open April through October, Wednesday through Saturday 9:00 A.M. to 4:00 P.M. Admission is about $3.00 for adults, with a discount for children. Phone (501) 836–9243. The house is ½ mile west of Camden on State Road 4.

Poison Spring State Park, just 10 miles west of Camden on State Highway 76, is one of several Civil War battle sites from the Red River Campaign. The Union goal was to capture Texas, a large cotton-producing state, because the Union was suffering a serious cotton shortage. Because the resistance while passing through Arkansas on their way to Texas was stronger than Union troops had expected, their attempt failed. The Union troops had captured Little Rock in September 1863. Six months later troops began marching to Texas, but at Poison Spring Confederates captured the troops' cannons, wagons, and teams, took more than one hundred prisoners and buried nearly 200 more Union soldiers. After similar serious losses, in the Battle of Marks' Mills and the Battle of Jenkins' Ferry, General Frederick Steele and his Union troops abandoned the campaign. They straggled back to Little Rock. Like Poison Spring, Marks' Mills (at the junction of Highways 96 and 8 just southeast of Fordyce) and Jenkins' Ferry (about 30 miles west of Pine Bluff on State Highway 46) are state parks with interpretive markers (see page 40).

The site with the most to see is **Old Washington Historic State Park,** about 100 miles southwest of Little Rock via I–30, some 9 miles northwest of Hope, on State Highway 4. This is an important stop because it reflects the territorial, antebellum, Civil War, and Reconstruction periods in the state. The unpaved streets are lined with catalpa and other trees as they have been for more than 150 years, but fire destroyed some of the old buildings in the 1800s. Washington was the state's Confederate capital during the Civil War, after Little Rock fell to the Union.

The park was a major stop on General Steele's route. A guide will lead you on a walking tour of the reconstructed museum village, narrating the history of Washington. The tour, called **Pioneers, Planters, Printers and Merchants Bring Life to Old Washington,** takes you through the years 1824 to 1840. You can inspect a reconstructed blacksmith shop, the 1836 courthouse, a log home built in about 1835, the Tavern Inn reconstruction, and the print museum. The tour **Living in Town: The Washington Community—1840–1875** focuses on the community's politics and professions and includes several houses and the Methodist church. Another building holds a gun museum, with more than 600 weapons. Important for researchers, the old courthouse contains the Southwest Arkansas Regional Archives (SARA). Holdings range across many categories: obituary-notice clippings files, library books, court records, Civil War records, and personal manuscripts and letters. You are allowed to use these resources without the presence of a guide. In addition to scheduled tours, a number of shorter visiting arrangements are offered.

Some buildings in the complex have not been restored yet, and others are used for administration, but you can count on getting into more than enough buildings to give you a sense of the old community. The park is open daily 9:00 A.M. to 5:00 P.M. Closed Thanksgiving, Christmas, and New Year's Day. Admission is about $6.00 for adults, half that for children. Purchase tour tickets at the visitors' center in the courthouse. Phone (501) 983–2684, weekends (501) 983–2733.

To enjoy a bite to eat in the midst of all this history, try **Williams Tavern Restaurant,** in the park. The building was the home of John W. Williams from 1832 to 1869, but at the time it was located 7 miles northeast of Washington at Marlbrook. In that location, Williams provided food and camping space for as many as sixty men and horses a night. In 1985 the building was moved to the park and restored as a restaurant. The cooking is good Southern staples—plate lunches and soups, homemade yeast rolls and cornbread, and homemade desserts, especially cobblers. The restaurant is open daily 11:00 A.M. to 3:00 P.M. Phone (501) 983–2890.

You can spend the night in **The Old Washington Jail Bed and Breakfast** in the park. The building was constructed in 1872 and served as the Hempstead County Jail until 1939. It has been renovated to operate as a seven-room bed-and-breakfast inn. The renovations left some of the graffiti, presumably written by prisoners, in the dining room. They also kept the 2-foot-thick concrete walls. Otherwise, however, the ambience is not at all "jailish." The rooms are furnished in appropriate antiques, with rockers and swings on the two porches inviting you to take your ease. Rates begin at about $55 per room. Phone (800) 747–JAIL or (501) 983–2461.

"It Was Almost Too Horrible for Human Endurance"

A CONFEDERATE PRIVATE

The Red River Campaign in Arkansas, led by Union general Frederick Steele, commanding 20,000 men, followed a route roughly paralleling present-day I–30. In his unsuccessful attempt to move into Texas, Steele lost 635 wagons, 2,500 horses and mules, and 2,750 men before he was able to get back to Little Rock and safety. The Arkansas State Parks offer a four-page brochure, complete with map, describing the campaign, its significance, and where to go to trace Steele's trail. Quotes from the writings of Confederate soldiers lend the text drama that goes beyond that of straight narrative. To order a copy of the brochure, write Arkansas State Parks, One Capitol Mall, Little Rock, AR 72201; or phone (501) 682–1191.

NORTH ARKANSAS

In the Ozark Mountains of Arkansas, antebellum life never included vast plantations or grand mansions, or slaves. People lived in small communities in the valleys, growing most of what they ate and producing most of the items they needed for daily life: brooms, baskets, pots, horseshoes. That way of life has been both preserved and re-created at the **Ozark Folk Center State Park,** near Mountain View. The park covers 637 acres and includes a sixty-room lodge, a full-service restaurant, a swimming pool, and various facilities for groups and conferences. The attraction for those in search of early Dixie is the lively pursuit of the old mountain folkways. The place pulses with energy and enthusiasm. In centers so widespread that a tram service operates, appropriately costumed staff people play music, dance, and practice all the mountain crafts, demonstrating such homely activities as gardening and making dyes. They offer classes and special programs related to all these homestead skills. In the crafts area you find what the staff call the "cabin craft demonstrations." Crafters in twenty-four buildings duplicate the activities of the years 1820 to 1920 in the Ozarks. For instance, the Heritage Herb Garden is designed to grow and show not just the culinary herbs but also those that homesteaders once used for medical treatment. Herbalists explain how each plant was used. The skills that the staff demonstrate and teach are researched and passed on to new practitioners through apprenticeship programs. Outdoor musical programs are held here, too. You can buy the crafts and tapes of mountain music in the Homespun Gift Shop and also in the General Store, where the welcome center is located. I treasure a small, carved wooden bowl, filled with miniature handmade wooden apples, that I found in the gift shop.

Musically, expect to hear mountain pickin', strummin', and singing. Musicians play dulcimers, mandolins, banjos, fiddles, and even spoons, played as they have been for generations in these mountains. These instruments do not plug in! Performers square dance, clog, and dance old-time jigs. The music ranges from ballads to gospel songs. Special concerts are held evenings in the Ozark Folk Center Theatre. Sing along, dance along, take a turn. It's bound to make you hungry.

The **Iron Skillet Restaurant** serves homestyle Southern cooking, including traditional favorites such as hickory-cured ham and fried chicken with fresh vegetables, corn bread, and homemade desserts. Costumed wait-

resses serve you in unfailing good humor. And if you like what you ate in
the restaurant, you can buy the jellies and relishes in the shop to take home.

You can easily spend a couple of days here; anything less than at least
one full day simply does not do the place justice. The rooms in the lodge
are comfortable, motel-like rooms arranged in groups like the cluster-
classroom arrangements of the past decade. Large sliding-glass doors look
out onto the Ozark forests. The park is open every day April through
October. Crafts demonstrations are featured 10:00 A.M. to 5:00 P.M. Musical programs in the auditorium begin at 7:30 P.M., Monday through Saturday. Special events are scheduled throughout the year. Admission to the
crafts area is about $6.50 for adults, with a discount for children; the fam-
ily rate is $17.25. Musical programs cost about $7.00 for adults, with discounts for children; the family rate is $17.25. Combination crafts and
musical program rates are about $12.25 for adults, with discount for chil-
dren; the family rate is $31.25. For details about specific events, phone
(501) 269–3851; for information about lodging, phone (800) 264–FOLK
or (501) 269–3871. The restaurant is open daily 7:00 A.M. to 8:00 P.M.
Phone (501) 269–3139. To get to the folk center, go 1½ miles north of
Mountain View on State Highways 9/5/14, then drive 1 mile west on the
State Highway 382 spur. When you come into the complex, stop first at
the General Store near the parking lot. Here you can work out details of
tickets and lodging. If you wish, a tram will take you to the top of the hill
to the theater and crafts area. You'll receive a map showing the location of
everything from the restrooms to the old lye soap shed and the vintage-
clothing displays.

Florida

IN FLORIDA, THE MOUSE GETS ALL THE ATTENTION. Retirement in Miami, races in Daytona, and spring parties at Fort Lauderdale come in a close second. History just isn't what comes to mind first when you mention Florida. In fact, Orlando is so young a city that the S.S. Kressge building, originally a five-and-dime store built in 1938, has been marked as a historical landmark. But other parts of the state go back to some of the most important early events in the country.

As in much of the South, it seems in Florida as though someone was always fighting. In the 1600 and 1700s, both Spain and Great Britain tried to make the land their own. Florida did not become part of the United States until 1819, about the time the Seminole Indians were attacking settlers in the area. Andrew Jackson's attempt to control the Indians led to the Seminole Wars, which were followed shortly by the Civil War. The activities of the early settlers and the subsequent wars left sites that have every bit as much drama as the fantasy theme parks for which Florida is more famous these days. Several cities in "old Florida" had significant Native American populations and figured heavily in the Civil War. Visiting these places, you will discover "the other Florida," where the ambience is that of the Deep South rather than of a transplanted New York. Historic sites, preserved and reconstructed districts, and museums tell the story of Florida before the Mouse.

Florida

Pensacola

Inland North

⊙ Tallahassee

Amelia Island

St. Augustine

The Atlantic Coast

The Gulf Coast

St. Petersburg

N

Miami

THE ATLANTIC COAST

Amelia Island, near the Georgia border on the Atlantic Coast, is the last in the string of southern barrier islands. The island claims to be the only place in the United States to have been ruled under eight different flags: French, Spanish, British, and U.S., as well as the Patriots of Amelia Island, Green Cross of Florida, Mexican Rebels, and Confederate.

The major site from the Civil War years is **Fort Clinch.** This was a 1,086-acre Civil War outpost (never completely finished) with massive brick fortress walls. Fort Clinch is in what is now a state park at the north end of the island. From State Road A1A you will drive to the fort down a long road canopied by live oaks draped with Spanish moss. It was occupied by Confederates until Yankees took it in 1863. You can still see the thick brick walls and some of the black cannons that defended the fort. The guides, dressed as Union soldiers, give you highly specific details about what it was like in the fort during the Civil War. They talk as if they were the soldiers, observing that it's a lot of work to build a fort and hoping the war will end soon so they don't have to finish it.

The story behind having the guides dressed as Yankees in a fort originally built to defend a Southern site reminds you that while war always separates people, it also sometimes brings them back together. It seems that some of the Northern troops enjoyed the Florida climate so much during their occupation that after the war they abandoned the cold climate of their original New England homes, coming back to live in the Florida sun. The park is open daily 8:00 A.M. to dusk. The fort is open daily from 9:00 A.M. to 5:00 P.M. Admission to the fort is $1.00; admission to the park is $3.25 for each private automobile. Phone (904) 277–7274.

The only city on Amelia Island is **Fernandina Beach,** a town with a 50-block Victorian district. Many of the old homes in downtown Fernandina have been restored and opened as bed-and-breakfast inns. The oldest is the antebellum **Williams House,** 103 South Ninth Street. Built in 1856 for a banker from Boston, it was purchased shortly before the beginning of the Civil War by Marcellus Williams, who surveyed much of Florida. The Civil War figured significantly in the history of the house: Confederate president Jefferson Davis visited often and stored some of his personal items here. The Marcellus family left when the war began, and the house became an infirmary for Northern soldiers. Later, when the family returned, it was among the first to free its slaves. The house still has a secret chamber in which slaves were hidden back when the house was a safehouse in the underground railroad for runaway slaves.

Staying here, you can enjoy the kind of opulence for which wealthy Southerners were once famous. The first thing you see as you come into the front center hall is a mahogany and cherry staircase lined with the original stained-glass windows, which rise 24 feet. The house is furnished with fine museum-quality antiques and is decorated with oriental carpets and art. There is a ceremonial robe that belonged to the last emperor of China, and a prayer rug displayed here was a gift from Napoleon Bonaparte.

Three of the four guest rooms have handcarved fireplaces. The rooms are elaborate, with fine antiques plus the contemporary creature comforts, such as private baths and television, that we have come to associate with good lodging. The Chinese Blue Room has a bay-windowed sitting area larger than some B & B guest rooms. Rates begin at about $100 per night. Phone (904) 277–2328.

The Fairbanks House, 227 South Seventh Street, offers bed-and-breakfast accommodations in a restored Italianate villa, with piazzas, a swimming pool, and gardens. A tower rises from the center of the building, dominating the view from the street. The interior moldings are handcarved; the fireplace tiles in the living room and dining room illustrate scenes from *Aesop's Fables* and the works of Shakespeare. The ten-room inn is furnished with comfortable antiques throughout. Continental breakfast is provided in the dining room, at an antique table beneath a crystal chandelier. Rates begin at about $85 per room. Phone (904) 277–0500 or (800) 261–4838.

In the downtown area of the historic district, at 22 South Third Street, the **Florida House Inn,** built in 1857, is said to be the oldest hotel in Florida. It has been in business continuously since it first opened and is listed on the National Register of Historic Places. Outside, this long, two-story facility is dark green, trimmed with white. Inside, ivory walls are decorated with antique quilts. The feel of this place is similar to that of the old-time Southern inns in the mountains, with long verandas upon which to sit and catch a breeze. The furnishings are simple but comfortable. All eleven guest rooms have private baths. Rates begin at about $70 per room. The hotel has a small pub and a restaurant in which you can eat old-fashioned Southern cooking—fried chicken, biscuits, barbecue, green beans, and so on—served family style at long tables, three meals a day. Phone (904) 261–3300.

Another place to season your Southern cooking with historical nostalgia is the **Palace Saloon,** 113 Center Street. This is the oldest bar in

Florida. The place has a beautiful handcarved bar setting off wall murals with characters such as Falstaff and Mr. Pickwick, in scenes drawn from English literature. Along with spirits, the saloon serves good, quick food for lunch and supper, including a shrimp burger that reminds you of how good shrimp can be when you eat it close to the source and how creative Southern cooks can be when ingredients like shrimp are available to them in generous quantities. Phone (904) 261–6320.

Your next stop along the coast is **St. Augustine,** about 60 miles south of Amelia Island via A1A, where Ponce de León came looking for the Fountain of Youth in 1513. This is the oldest city in the United States.

St. Augustine has its share of souvenir shops and hokey attractions mingled with its history. Ripley's Believe it or Not! Museum is here, as is Potters Wax Museum, featuring wax-figure celebrities of earlier times. But the Old City is rich in historic and architectural detail. Perhaps most impressive are the restored **Spanish Quarter Museum** and **Castillo de San Marcos National Monument.** A visitors' information center at the **Triay House,** at Castillo Drive and Avenida Mendez, has maps and printed information for a walking tour as well as exhibits of regional artifacts. You'll find a parking lot here, too. Use it—parking is extremely difficult in St. Augustine, and because of the narrow streets and one-way routing, trying to see anything from an automobile is almost impossible. You can amble through the area in a couple of hours with less frustration than trying to drive.

The Spanish Quarter Museum represents the homes and lives of a variety of Spanish colonists. Among the restored and reconstructed buildings you'll find the **Lorenzo Gomez House,** a one-room house typical of the housing for a Spanish soldier in the 1760s. The **Martin Martinez Gallegos House,** a two-room reconstruction, is made of tabby—a building material of lime, ground oyster shells, and salt water. The **Bernardo Gonzales House,** made of coquina, a soft rock composed of shells and other marine remains, represents the lifestyle of a Spanish cavalryman. Children enjoy the **Geronimo de Hita y Salazar House,** the house of a soldier with a large family, where kids have an opportunity for hands-on experience with old-time children's chores such as sweeping and helping with crafts. In the manner that has become typical of living museums, costumed craftspeople demonstrate the spinning, weaving, and smithy of the 1740s.

Everywhere you walk, you feel and hear the grit of centuries of sand and shells.

The **Castillo de San Marcos National Monument** is a coquina fort with walls (some of them reconstructed) 33 feet high and 12 feet thick at the base. It has a moat; Native Americans and slaves built the fort from a medieval design. The fort was begun in 1672; its last official use was during the Spanish American War. Men in the garb of eighteenth-century Spanish soldiers parade and demonstrate cannon firings as part of the exhibits about Spanish-era military history.

St. Augustine also has what is believed to be the oldest school building in the United States and a Spanish military hospital, fitted out as it would have been in the late 1700s and early 1800s. It also has a cathedral on the site of the oldest Catholic parish in the country. These old Spanish buildings and a number more in the historic district stand in marked contrast to the eating places and tourist shops that line the beaches outside the city.

You can, however, spend the night at **Casa de la Paz,** 22 Avenida Menendez, which is the only remaining example in St. Augustine of pure Mediterranean Revival architecture from the turn of the century, complete with barrel-tile roofing. The house overlooks Mantanzas Bay. Turn-of-the-century construction takes the building itself out of the antebellum era, but the feel is right nonetheless. A sunporch with white walls and white wicker furniture feels spacious and airy, almost as though you were in an outdoor courtyard. The rest of the inn is furnished with English antiques and oriental rugs, reminiscent of older, more elegant times. Beds in the guest rooms are made up with luxurious all-cotton sheets and feather pillows. Breakfast is served at a mahogany table set with sterling. Rates begin at about $75 per room. Phone (904) 829–2915.

Another bed-and-breakfast accommodation, at 146 Avenida Menendez, **Westcott House,** also has the feel of luxury from earlier times. This little inn, which also overlooks Mantanzas Bay, was originally built by Dr. John Westcott in about 1890. It's the kind of place that Cinderella must have dreamed about when she was sweeping the hearth and scrubbing floors. The exterior is pink, with elaborate blue trim. Three verandas call to mind formal parties with women in billowing gowns and gentlemen in formal dress. In the absence of a ball, you can sit in a rocker and watch the bay. The elegant antiques, oriental rugs, brass, china, crystal, white paddle fans, and high ceilings practically scream "romance." Rates begin at about $100 per room. Phone (904) 824–4301.

St. Augustine has numerous pleasant restaurants featuring local cuisines. **Shrivers Barbecue,** at 152 San Marco Avenue, offers some classic Southern choices, including mustard-based barbecue with fried okra, slaw, and beans. Phone (904) 829–2344. For more upscale dining, **Champ's of Aviles,** 8 Avile Street, offers especially well-prepared seafood and vegetable dishes for dinner, in a relatively plain building. Phone (904) 824–6410. And **Raintree Restaurant,** at 102 San Marco Avenue, is a favorite spot for special-occasion dinners. The restaurant prepares mainly continental cuisine, but the Southern touch creeps in to produce the kinds of dishes that well-to-do early Southerners with roots in Europe might have favored. Phone (904) 829–5953.

THE GULF COAST

On Florida's Gulf Coast, almost into Alabama, **Pensacola** attracted Spanish settlers, followed later by the French and British. The Civil War accounts for a major attraction in Pensacola, too. **Fort Pickens** is the largest of four forts built, with slave labor, to defend Pensacola Bay. It was finished in 1834 and used for more than a hundred years after that. During the Civil War Pensacola was divided between Union and Confederate soldiers. Union troops held Fort Pickens, while the Confederates held Fort McRee. After the war Geronimo and some fifty Apache warriors were imprisoned in Fort Pickens, turning the place into a tourist attraction as early as 1886. Fort Pickens is part of the Gulf Islands National Seashore, administered by the National Park Service, which provides an elaborate brochure about the fort, sketching the positions of Union and Confederate forces and their armaments and giving details of the fort's construction. The fort is 9 miles west of Pensacola on Fort Pickens Road. It is open April through October, daily 9:00 A.M. to 5:00 P.M., 8:00 A.M. to 4:00 P.M. the rest of the year. Admission is $4.00 for each automobile. Phone (904) 934–2635.

Historic Pensacola Village, beginning at Palafox and Zaragoza streets, is a complex of restored and preserved buildings of the 1800s representing a variety of architectural styles and inhabitants. **Charles Lavalle House,** 203 East Church Street, is a Gulf Coast Creole cottage from the 1800s. **Clara Barkley Door House,** 311 South Adams Street, built in the late 1800s and furnished in Victorian style, is a Classical Revival building. 1804 **Julee Cottage,** at Zaragoza and Barracks streets, belonged to a free black woman. Three museums in the complex depict the history of industry, commerce, and natural history in the area. The complex is open Easter to Labor Day, daily 10:00 A.M. to 4:00 P.M.; the rest of the year, Monday through Saturday 10:00 A.M. to 4:00 P.M. Admission is $5.50 for adults, $4.50 for senior citizens, and $2.25 for children. Phone (904) 444–8905.

One important stop in pursuit of the Dixie experience is a relatively new, privately owned museum at 108 South Palafox, **The Civil War Soldiers' Museum.** This project is the personal passion of Dr. Norman W. Haines, Jr. Dr. Haines grew up next to the battlefield at Antietam, which inspired an interest in the Civil War. He used to wander the fields looking for artifacts. So great was his fascination with the subject that for his fourteenth birthday, his parents gave him an authentic Springfield rifle. He's been collecting ever since.

His museum houses all kinds of objects related to the war, including documents, flags, photographs, covers (stamps), and currency. A sign in the front window announces a display of the largest collection of Civil War medical materials in the country. Nothing deglamorizes the Civil War faster. Browsing through here, you will find a wheelchair, artificial limbs, boxes of glass eyes, an amputation table, and many surgical tools. A diorama shows an amputation in process in the field. Just inside the entrance of the museum, a gift shop offers souvenirs such as model soldiers handpainted by a craftsperson in Georgia. The shop sells a lot of books—more than 600 Civil War titles. You can buy a Confederate flag here, too, though, interestingly, there are no Union flags with the proper number of stars for those times. Apparently, Yankee flags are not manufactured; where's Betsy Ross when you need her? The museum is open Monday through Saturday 10:00 A.M. to 4:30 P.M. Admission is about $4 for adults, $2 for children, under six free. Phone (904) 469–1900.

To sleep and eat surrounded by Pensacola's history, try **New World Inn,** at 600 South Palafox Street. This is a first-class, European-style inn in a restored section of the waterfront. Originally, the building was a box factory, situated on the waterfront for easy shipping. The restoration of old warehouses in Charleston, South Carolina, influenced the restoration here. The hotel reflects Pensacola's international history, with rooms decorated and furnished to reflect the nationalities of the five flags that have flown over Pensacola: French, British, Spanish, U.S., and Confederate. Each room in the inn is named for a famous person in the history of Pensacola and decorated to fit the nationality of that person. The inn's three dining rooms also reflect Pensacola's past. The Barcelona Room has a Spanish decor; large photographs of the city fill the Pensacola Room; and French influence permeates the Marseilles Room. The food in the dining rooms is elegantly continental, reflecting the availability of varied and fresh seafood. Rates begin at about $75 per room. Phone (904) 432–4111.

Pensacola, Amelia Island, and St. Augustine are not the only places in Florida where you find life before the Mouse, but because of their concentrations of important sites, they are good places to start. Moving inland, you will come to a part of Florida that has much the same character as the states near the border, Georgia and Alabama, where you retreat easily into history.

INLAND NORTH

Tallahassee is sometimes called "Florida with a Southern accent." Tallahassee became the capital of Florida after an attorney boated east from Pensacola and a physician rode horseback west from St. Augustine. The two met on a hill that they decided would make a good central meeting place for the state legislature. In earlier times Native Americans used the same space as a tribal center. In this area are the Spanish moss–draped trees and old mansions that seem to typify the antebellum South. Scenic roads running almost like tunnels under old live oak trees covered with moss are known in the area as "canopy roads." On roads designated as official canopy roads, the live oaks are protected. While driving is a bad idea in St. Augustine, in the Tallahassee area you can see a lot by taking one of several scenic auto tours mapped out by the Historic Tallahassee Preservation Board. The printed tour guides are available at the Tallahassee Area Convention and Visitors Bureau, 200 West College Avenue, P.O. Box 1369, Tallahassee, FL 32302; phone (800) 628–2866 or (904) 413–9200.

The first tour, which covers 23 miles and takes about four hours, is called "The Native Trail." This archaeologically based tour begins at the **Museum of Florida History** (open Monday through Friday 9:00 A.M. to 4:30 P.M.; Saturday 10:00 A.M. to 4:30 P.M.; Sunday noon to 4:30 P.M. Admission is free. Phone 904–562–0042). For sheer drama, the 12,000-year-old mastodon skeleton that was discovered at Wakulla Springs steals the show. But the Indian artifacts, including beautifully executed pottery, probably do more to develop a sense of life in Florida before European settlement. The exhibits in the museum preview the archaeological sites you will visit later in the tour. These include the **Lake Jackson Mounds State**

Archaeological Site and the **San Luis Archaeological and Historic Site: 1656–1740.**

At the Lake Jackson site, mounds that were a ceremonial center for Apalachee Indians testify to their complex civilization before the 1500s. Three mounds remain, along with parts of a nineteenth-century cotton plantation, mute affirmation of the continuity of human history.

The San Luis remains further develop this sense. The printed tour guide explains that the Apalachees were agrarian and that as many as 30,000 of them lived in towns in the countryside, growing maize, beans, and squash. Spanish missionaries were headquartered in San Luis from 1656 to 1704, working to convert the Apalachees to Christianity. The remains of Mission San Luis de Apalachee has been designated a National Historic Landmark.

The tour continues to the **De Soto State Archaeological Site,** where archaeologists found artifacts, including pieces of an olive jar, that came from the winter encampment of Hernando de Soto and his soldiers during the winter of 1539. Don't expect to see buildings or even foundations here. What you find is contemporary buildings, but knowing that de Soto was here first in what was then the Apalachee capital of Anhaica puts a special spin on it. Eventually, interpretive displays will tell the story on this hilltop. From here the tour turns onto Old St. Augustine Road, another canopy road, that dates back to at least the 1600s. This road, looking like a scene from *Gone With the Wind,* leads back to the city.

A second tour, "The Cotton Trail," covers about 50 miles in about three and a half hours. It takes you past an assortment of antebellum mansions, plantations, farms, churches, and stores from the days of Leon County's slave-based cotton years. The tour begins at the **Brokaw-McDougall House,** 329 North Meridian Street. This property, built in 1856, is notable for its formal gardens, which were designed at the time the house was built, its huge live oaks, and its cupola. The house is open Monday through Friday 8:00 A.M. to 5:00 P.M. Admission is free. Phone (904) 488–3901.

The tour continues along Miccosukee Road, taking in **Goodwood Plantation,** with more fine old gardens and lots of fragrant roses. The plantation was created in the 1830s; the main house and three outbuildings survive from the 1840s. Fifteen more buildings were added early in this century. Don't expect to see a completed restoration when you visit Goodwood. The place had deteriorated seriously, and its restoration is an ongoing process. The first phase involves restoring the old kitchen and several other buildings.

Grief at Goodwood

Hardy Croom, from North Carolina, created Goodwood as a special home for his family in Florida, but he, his wife, and their three children never got to live in it. They all died when their steamship sank on the way to Florida. Hardy's brother, Bryan, finished the house. But the family of Hardy's dead wife sued Bryan and succeeded in wresting Goodwood away from him. Arvah Hopkins later bought the place and entertained lavishly there from the 1850s through the 1880s. After the Civil War and Arvah's death, Mrs. Hopkins had to sell the property. In subsequent years it was bought and sold three more times. The plantation's restoration began with the death of the last owner, Thomas Hood, who had established a fund for turning Goodwood into a public museum.

Goodwood Plantation is a restoration in process. Its fully restored main building is shown here.

Restoration is beginning on the exterior of the main house, too. The grounds are open Tuesday through Sunday 9:00 A.M. to 5:00 P.M.

Along this route you will drive along more canopy roads, pass by red hills of clay, great stretches of undeveloped scenic countryside, and huge groves of live oaks that slaves may have planted to provide shelter in sweltering summer weather. This route includes a couple of optional detours. The one to Reeves Landing offers a chance to see the kinds of wildlife that have always appealed to Southern men—ring-necked ducks, bass, and bream in an isolated lake setting—but it's a fairly hair-raising ride on unpaved roads with steep embankments.

A third tour, "The Quail Trail," traces the development of hunting after the Civil War. It takes you along more canopy roads, past plantations especially created for hunting, and into an area where the live oaks are still young, giving a suggestion of how the venerable old oaks began. On this route stop at the **Alfred B. Maclay State Gardens,** 3540 Thomasville Road, U.S. Highway 319. This property was originally bought for hunting, but the owner turned out to like gardening better. The garden display includes nearly one hundred varieties of camellias and about half that many varieties of azaleas, along with other seasonal flowering plants. Nobody does gardens better than Southerners. The place takes your breath away, especially in March. In addition to flowers, the state park has nature trails, boating, swimming, and fishing. The restored house is a center for camellia information. It is open daily 9:00 A.M. to 5:00 P.M. The park, one of four ornamental gardens in Florida, is open daily 8:00 A.M. to sunset. Admission May through December is $3.00 for adults, $1.50 for children. Phone (904) 487–4556.

The Tallahassee Area Convention and Visitors Bureau offers walking tours of the downtown. These focus on downtown architecture, by district. The **Park Avenue Historic District** and the **Calhoun Street Historic District** each have 1800s houses and appealing landscaping. Civil War dead, black leaders, and state politicians are buried in the **Old City Cemetery,** an eleven-acre site in the Park Avenue district. The cemetery is the oldest public burying ground in Tallahassee. It was laid out by the Territorial Legislature in 1829. At the kiosk at the entrance, you can read the history of the cemetery and pick up a brochure for a self-guided walking tour.

Three attractions in Tallahassee have special significance for people interested in African-American history. **First Presbyterian Church,** 110

North Adams Street, built in 1838, is the oldest church in Tallahassee. It was unusual in that slaves were always welcome to worship as independent church members, without the consent of their owners. Phone (904) 222–4504. And on the campus of Florida A & M University, at Martin Luther King, Jr. Boulevard and Gamble Street, the **Black Archives Research Center and Museum** has one of the country's most extensive collections of African-American artifacts and one of the largest collections in the world of African-American history. You can listen to taped recollections of life as it was for blacks in earlier times and to tapes of gospel music. The archives and museum are open Monday through Friday 9:00 A.M. to 4:00 P.M. You need to request a visitor's parking permit at the security office. Phone (904) 599–3020.

In two side-by-side graveyards, **Old City Cemetery** and **Episcopal Cemetery,** at Park Avenue and Bronough Street, some slaves and early graduates of Florida A & M University are buried, along with Confederate and Union soldiers who died in the Battle of Natural Bridge and the Battle of Olustee, near Lake City. In 1841 an epidemic of yellow fever killed several hundred local people, which led the city of Tallahassee to lay out grids and lots in the cemetery. Whites were buried in the eastern half, blacks in the western half. Request a map of the cemetery from the visitors' information center in the New Capitol building. Open sunrise to sunset. Admission is free. Phone (904) 488–3901 (Historic Tallahassee Preservation Board).

Sometime during the day you might seek Southern home-style cooking at **The Wharf,** 4141 Apalachee Parkway, about 2 miles east of Capitol Circle. In some states this kind of restaurant is known as a "fish camp." Folks say the Wharf has the best seafood in the area. It includes everything from fried mullett, to grouper stuffed with crab, to seafood gumbo. Hush puppies, cheese grits, Key lime pie, and peanut-butter pie are other Southern favorites to try. The place is big (seats 400), loud, rustic, and friendly. It's the kind of restaurant where everyone eats too much and laughs a lot in the process. The food is relatively inexpensive. The restaurant does not serve spirits, but you are welcome to bring your own. The restaurant is open Monday through Thursday 11:00 A.M. to 9:00 P.M.; until 10:00 P.M. Friday; Saturday 4:00 P.M. to 10:00 P.M.; Sunday 4:00 P.M. to 9:00 P.M. Phone (904) 656–2395.

Sometime during your visit to this part of Florida, plan on eating at **Nicholson Farmhouse,** generally acknowledged as the ultimate "dining in Dixie" experience. The restaurant is north of Tallahassee, near Havana. To get there, drive on Highway 27 north for about 15 miles, then turn left onto State Highway 12 and proceed 3.5 miles to the restaurant. Nicholson Farmhouse Restaurant is actually a complex of three old farmhouses—the Nicholson House, the Littman House, and the McCall House—plus some outbuildings, set in forty acres of woods and pasture. The Nicholson House, built by Malcolm Nicholson in 1828, housed the restaurant when it first opened in 1987. In the antebellum years the house was part of a 4,000-acre cotton plantation and was built with slave labor from wood cut on the plantation; its bricks were fired in a kiln there. Apart from adding restrooms and making repairs, the Nicholsons did not change the house much for its incarnation as a restaurant. The spot quickly became so popular that the Nicholsons brought in another farmhouse, the Littman House, built in 1890, from about 2 miles west. Then the McCall House, built in 1905, was moved in from its former nearby location and opened as part of the restaurant in 1991.

The food is simple but carefully prepared country cooking, including steaks cut from western beef and aged on the premises, for which the restaurant first became famous. It also serves grilled pork chops, shrimp, and grilled chicken, with potatoes, salad, and bread baked on the premises. The atmosphere is down-home country, appropriate for children and for casual dress. The restaurant does not sell spirits, but you are welcome to bring your own. Open Tuesday through Saturday 4:00 to 10:00 P.M. Phone (904) 539–5931.

If you drive farther west of Tallahassee, about 50 miles on I–10, you will find another plantation tour house in **Torreya State Park,** beside the Apalachicola River. Wooded bluffs reach to 150 feet above the river. The park has camping, hiking facilities, and nice spots for a picnic. The **Gregory House,** built in 1849 as part of Ocheesee cotton plantation on the other side of the river, was dismantled, moved, and restored in the park. It is furnished in 1850s antiques. Rangers give guided tours of the house and can tell you about the park's history as well. General Andrew Jackson and the army crossed the river at this bend in 1818 during the Seminole Wars.

From this part of Florida, it's an easy jaunt up into Georgia, which seems to be part of this area anyhow. It's also an easy trek into Alabama.

Georgia

 GEORGIA, ONE OF THE ORIGINAL THIRTEEN COLONIES, was established by the British at Savannah in 1733. In those early years Creek and Cherokee Indians lived throughout the area, but their numbers diminished as European settlers took over. Otherwise the state prospered until the Civil War. Georgia left the Union in 1861, after Abraham Lincoln was elected president. During the Civil War, General Sherman's troops marched across the state, burning cities, homes, plantations, and businesses as they went. The cost to the people of Georgia in death, destruction of property, and money was devastating. But with agriculture, commerce, and a temperate climate on their side, the state recovered more rapidly than some of the states in the deeper South.

Georgia, more than any other Southern state, is a place where fact and fiction, fantasies and reality have intermingled for so long that it is hard to tell what's real and what isn't. The plantations were grand, the gardens were glorious, the women were gracious, the gentlemen were gallant. But life was really hard—hardest, obviously, for slaves, but demanding also for the people who ran the plantations. Men often died young, but even so, plantation masters frequently outlasted two or three wives. A couple might have six or more children and count itself lucky if half survived. Still, the notion of the romantic South persists, nurtured faithfully by Georgians themselves.

Georgia

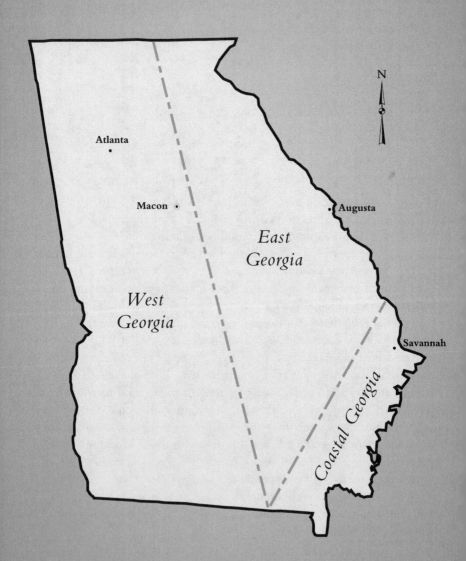

Today Georgia offers some attractions that remind you about the hard times and others that reinforce your belief in the romance. And then there are those areas you can't sort out—Scarlett and Rhett, "born" in Georgia, are quoted more often than any real figures of the era. What words are more entrenched in American history than "Frankly, my dear, I don't give a damn!" except, possibly "Fiddle-de-dee, I'll worry about it tomorrow"?

WEST GEORGIA

There's a good chance that most of what you know, or think you know, about **Atlanta** started with *Gone With the Wind*. The phenomenon of Margaret Mitchell's novel and the film it generated defies rational explanation. The book was basically a lively, historical romance told with a remarkable sense of place. The film embellished as only film can. "I'll go back to Tara," Scarlett said. She could have gone to Mitchell's Tara, perhaps, but there's no

Gone With the Wind

Gone With the Wind was published in 1936, seventy-five years after the Civil War began. It was the only novel Margaret Mitchell wrote. The original hardcover edition had 1,037 pages. Within three weeks of the book's release, 176,000 copies had been sold. Within six months a million copies had been sold. The book has been translated into twenty-eight languages, and sales have gone into the tens of millions.

Mitchell received $50,000 for the film rights. The book and film have spawned a continuing stream of interest, from scholarly study to collecting pop culture memorabilia. In fact, *Gone With the Wind* is written about so much, it has become customary to use the abbreviation *GWTW* in referring to it.

Some of this information comes from a book entitled *Looking for Tara* (Longstreet Press, 1994), by Don O'Briant, a features writer for *The Atlanta Journal-Constitution*. He describes Mitchell's life and the places she lived and then suggests places to go to have the fictional "Scarlett Experience."

way Scarlett could have found the film version of Tara, with its fine columns and verandas, anywhere near Atlanta. *That* Tara was filmed at Linden, in Natchez, Mississippi (see page 168). Mitchell's version of Tara was a plain farmhouse set in the middle of a working plantation, and she was always unhappy with the film producers insistence on glamorizing it.

At the **Road to Tara Museum,** 659 Peachtree Street, Suite 600, you'll find a huge collection of *Gone With the Wind* memorabilia, including costumes, and dolls dressed like Scarlett. A special collection consists of fifteen intimate letters exchanged between Margaret Mitchell and Henry Love Angel, a childhood friend who eventually asked her to marry him. Even though she declined, they remained friends. There are also fifty photographs and a 107-page unpublished manuscript entitled "Lost Laysen." Ten costume replicas and costume prints are displayed from the film, along

The Road to Tara Museum features a huge collection of Gone With the Wind *memorabilia, including dolls dressed like Scarlett and Rhett.*

with more than one hundred pictures of the making of the film. Also on display is a piece of mirror from Mitchell's apartment at Seventeenth and West Peachtree Streets in Atlanta. She called the apartment "The Dump." It's where she lived when she wrote *GWTW*. Admission includes a documentary film about Margaret Mitchell's life. The museum is open Monday through Saturday 10:00 A.M. to 6:00 P.M.; Sunday 1:00 P.M. to 6:00 P.M. Closed Thanksgiving, Christmas, and New Year's Days. Admission is about $5.00 for adults; there are discounts for children and senior citizens. Phone (404) 897–1939.

Perhaps in response to Mitchell mania, the **Atlanta History Center** has adopted the slogan "There's more to Atlanta's past than Tara and some guy named Sherman." You could easily spend several days enjoying all that the Atlanta History Center, 130 West Paces Ferry Road, has to offer. The complex is bordered on the north by West Paces Ferry Road, on the west by Andrews Drive, and on the east by Slaton Drive. The scope of the center's holdings makes it a fine place to get an overview of Atlanta's *real* past.

Atlanta was created by railroads. In 1837 the Western and Atlantic Railroad route was laid out from Chattanooga, Tennessee, to a point marked with a stake in the rural red clay. At that point several other railroads connected. This spot was the center of what was to become Atlanta. By 1845 the town had about 2,000 people and was surrounded by farms and more small railroad towns. By the time of the Civil War, the population had grown to about 9,000 people. Although Atlanta had slave markets and used slave labor in industry, African Americans were a small percentage of the total population. The real issue in Atlanta at the beginning of the war was not slavery but the railroads in the center of the city; these were the threat that Sherman had to destroy. Ironically, by 1865—when the war finally ended—all the city's railroads were in service again.

All this is explained in exhibits at the Atlanta History Center. The center includes the **Atlanta History Museum and Museum Shop, Tullie Smith Farm, Swan House** (1928), **The Victorian Playhouse, Horticultural Gardens,** and **McElreath Hall.** In your search for Dixie, the museum, Tullie Smith Farm, the gardens, and McElreath Hall will be especially pertinent.

Begin your visit with the museum. It is the largest museum in Georgia devoted exclusively to interpretations of history. Although some of the exhibits change, you can count on always finding ample information about antebellum Atlanta and the Civil War. A permanent exhibit entitled "Metropolitan Frontiers: Atlanta 1835–2000," for instance, contains displays in the transportation center related to those early railroads that essentially started the city. Other displays tell you about the Civil War, cotton growing, business growth in the black and white communities, Civil Rights, and so on, right up to the 1996 Olympic Games. Particularly interesting items include a slave bill of sale from 1861 and a reconstructed shotgun house.

Among the changing exhibits, one about the black upper class in Atlanta and another about the Jews of Atlanta may be gone by the time you visit, but they will be replaced with comparable new exhibits. Many items from another exhibit, looking at the Civil War through the eyes of a common soldier, will be moved into permanent display.

As if to demonstrate that fantasy and reality simply will *not* stay separated in Atlanta, you will always find items related to *Gone With the Wind* on display. And the museum gift shop sells copies of *GWTW,* books about Margaret Mitchell, and such souvenirs as T-shirts and mugs with the *GWTW* theme.

Outside the museum but still in the History Center complex, Tullie Smith Farm represents a typical, mid–1800s Piedmont Georgia farm. The buildings include the farmhouse, a detached kitchen, and, among the outbuildings, a corncrib and a reproduction blacksmith shop. The buildings were moved here from about 5 miles away. The farmhouse survived Sherman's fires because it was beyond the city limits. The home is simple and plain, as if to remind visitors that not all antebellum houses had columns.

Spread throughout the complex, thirty-two acres of gardens have thousands of plants labeled with historical and botanical information. The Tullie Smith Farm gardens show you a typical period-house garden, with a vegetable garden, cotton patch, and roadside bed.

A wealth of garden information is covered in the holdings of McElreath Hall, which houses a library and archives collection of 3.5 million items, ranging from maps, photographs, and manuscripts to the **Cherokee Garden Library,** which has more than 3,000 publications with historical and current information about all aspects of gardening. Scarlett, of course, is here, too. McElreath Hall has one of the largest public Margaret Mitchell collections.

The center is open Monday through Saturday 10:00 A.M. to 5:30 P.M. Ticket sales stop at 4:30 P.M. A minimum of three hours is recommended to tour the entire center. Closed Thanksgiving, Christmas Eve, Christmas, and New Year's Day. Opens at noon on holidays. Admission is about $7.00 for

The Tullie Smith House demonstrates the simplicity of most Piedmont Georgia farms of the mid-1800s.

adults, with discounts for children and senior citizens. There is a small additional charge for admission to the historic houses. Phone (404) 814–4000.

To get to the center going north on I–75 from downtown Atlanta, take the West Paces Ferry Road exit. Turn left at the end of the ramp onto Northside Parkway. Turn right at the next intersection onto West Paces Ferry Road. Going south on I–75 from Marietta, take the West Paces Ferry Road exit and turn left at the end of the ramp onto West Paces Ferry Road. Once there, continue east for 2.6 miles. Pass the center and turn right onto Slaton Drive. The entrance for the center is on the right. Free parking is available.

To get to the center using public transportation, take MARTA to Lenox rail station. Transfer to bus #23 to Peachtree and West Paces Ferry Roads. Walk 3 blocks west on West Paces Ferry Road. The pedestrian entrance is in front of the Atlanta History Museum.

The history center has another branch, **The Atlanta History Center Downtown,** at **Atlanta Heritage Row,** 55 Upper Alabama Street in **Underground Atlanta.** A self-guided tour features photographs, videos, and walk-through exhibitions telling Atlanta's story. In the replica of a

Getting around Atlanta

Traffic in Atlanta is awful. The city began as a transportation town, however, and continues to be so. You can get practically anywhere in the city by the Metropolitan Atlanta Rapid Transit Authority (MARTA) and a little walking. The system has 39 miles of track and 1,500 miles of feeder bus routes, and it really does work.

bomb shelter, you watch Civil War action. In another exhibit you can stand at the pulpit from which Martin Luther King, Jr., once spoke and hear a recording of his words. The uptown center is open Tuesday through Saturday 10:00 A.M. to 5:00 P.M.; Sunday 1:00 P.M. to 5:00 P.M. Admission is about $3.00 for adults, with discounts for senior citizens and children. Phone (404) 584–7879.

The entrance to Underground Atlanta is across from the MARTA Five Points Station. Underground Atlanta encompasses twelve acres under the city and is filled with restaurants, nightclubs, and specialty shops. In addition to Heritage Row, you find the **Zero Milepost** down here. That's the spot where Colonel Stephen Long pounded a stake into the wilderness ground to mark the southern end of the Western and Atlantic Railroad (see page 67)—although, of course, he did it above ground.

Your next stop, **The Cyclorama,** 800 Cherokee Avenue Southeast, gives you a near virtual-reality experience of the July 22, 1864, Battle of Atlanta in the Civil War. The battle is painted in the round, 42 feet tall and 358 feet around. To add perspective, mannequins and models stand in front of the painting. You sit on a slowly revolving platform in the center while lights, narration, and sound effects bring the whole diorama to life. The painting was done in 1884; the figures were added later. Fact and fiction are blended here, too: One of the figures in the diorama is *GWTW*'s Rhett Butler, added because tourists kept asking for him. The Cyclorama is next to the zoo, which has no particular historical significance but needs to be mentioned since the two attractions are side by side in Grant Park, southeast of downtown. The Cyclorama is open daily October through May 9:30 A.M. to 4:30 P.M.; daily June through September 9:30 A.M. to 5:30 P.M.

You should probably visit The Cyclorama and be revolved on a platform *before* eating. When you are ready for food, however, Atlanta is full of good restaurants representing every cuisine that you would expect to come across in what has become a pretty sophisticated city. A restaurant in the History Center serves fairly standard fare for lunch Monday through Saturday in the Swan Coach House, once the garage and servants quarters for Swan House.

Probably the Atlanta restaurant best known for southern ambience is **Pittypat's Porch,** 25 International Boulevard Northwest. Pittypat's serves upscale dinners with a regional emphasis in a friendly place decorated to evoke nostalgia for the Old South. This place is popular, so be sure to make reservations if you want to try it. Phone (404) 525–8228. To get to Pittypat's from Interstate 75/85, take the Courtland Street exit if you are going south; take the International Boulevard exit if you are northbound.

You can't find a lot of downtown lodging in old mansions in Atlanta. General William Tecumseh Sherman burned them all. But **Shellmont,** 821 Piedmont Avenue Northeast, in North Atlanta, is one of only thirty-three structures listed as a City of Atlanta Landmark Building. This Victorian home was built in 1891 and has been restored to its original state with the help of family records and photographs. The place has many touches of what must have been the Victorian confusion between fact and fantasy. The house, for example, has a little octagonal nook called the "Turkish Room," which is done in a style that Victorians erroneously imagined to be Turkish. In restoring the house to its original condition, the owners, Ed and Debbie McCord, also restored the Victorian fantasy, down to the last canopy and tassel. The inn has four guest rooms in the main house, plus a two-bedroom carriage house. Rates, which begin at about $85 per room, include continental breakfast.

Moving from the metro area to the suburbs, **Marietta,** about 20 miles northwest of Atlanta in Cobb County, has four National Register Historic Districts. Sherman burned Marietta's downtown, too, but the citizens rebuilt, and the turn-of-the-century structures have been preserved. This has become a popular place to shop for antiques. Many of the homes outside the downtown area were untouched during the war. At the **Marietta Welcome Center,** in the 1898 railroad depot on Marietta Square, you can pick up a map with narrative text for the **Historic Marietta Walking/Driving Tour** (as well as for the **Cannonball Trail Driving Tour**).

Most of the houses on the walking/driving tour are private residences. The map tells you about each one, and you can study their exteriors, but they are not open for tours. The welcome center is open Monday through Saturday 10:00 A.M. to 3:00 P.M.; Sunday 1:00 to 4:00 P.M. Brochures are free; recorder and cassette rental of narrated tours is $4.00. Phone (770) 429–1115. To get to the Marietta Welcome Center, take I–75 north from Atlanta to exit 112. The downtown historic district extends 3.5 miles, between Whitlock Avenue and Green Street.

A short drive from the historic district, **Kennesaw Mountain National Battlefield Park** marks the site of two Civil War battles. Battle details are explained in a short slide show in the visitors' center/museum. Walk the grounds of the park to trace the old earthworks and historic markers.

A different kind of park, **Stone Mountain Park,** about 16 miles from Atlanta on U.S. Highway 78, brings you more antebellum mansions and imposing portraits of three important Confederates—carved onto the face of a mountain! Generals Robert E. Lee and Stonewall Jackson and Confederate president Jefferson Davis, all astride lively horses, with their capes flying and their hats held reverently over their hearts, seem to rise from within the granite outcropping upon which they are carved. The figure of Lee is as tall as a nine-story building; but, even so, the size of the mountain dwarfs the outsized figures. A tape recording tells you the story of the sculpture while you ride to the top of the dome.

A complete plantation is also part of the park. Antebellum buildings were brought from other sites in Georgia to create a typical plantation village, with a big manor house furnished in Baroque style. An overseer's house, slave cabins, and a country store are all furnished as they would have been in the 1840s. There is an old moonshine still here, but it is not officially dated, nor is it functioning.

The park encompasses 3,200 acres, including some distinctly nonantebellum amusements—a waterslide and miniature golf, for instance. It is open daily 6:00 A.M. to midnight. Admission is $5.00 per car. The antebellum plantation is open June through August daily, 10:00 A.M. to 8:30 P.M.; daily 10:00 A.M. to 5:30 P.M. the rest of the year. Closed Christmas. Phone (770) 498–5600.

To see some old mansions still on their original sites, visit **Historic Roswell,** about 20 miles north of Atlanta. Homes and store fronts here date back to 1839. Most of the antebellum structures remained intact during the Civil War, because here Sherman burned only the mill that manufactured gray cloth for Confederate uniforms. That mill and some buildings that used to house mill workers have been restored at the intersection of State

Roads 9 and 120; they now house restaurants and specialty shops. Phone (770) 993–8806. The Roswell **Convention and Visitors Bureau,** 617 Atlanta Street, promotes tourism in the area. You can pick up instructions here for a tour of the historic district. Phone (770) 640–3253.

One building that you can tour is **Bulloch Hall,** 180 Bulloch Avenue, a block west of Roswell Square. This antebellum Greek Revival building, dating from about 1849, was the childhood home of Mittie Bulloch, President Theodore Roosevelt's mother. The home is furnished in period style, with family photographs and documents to add authenticity and interest. The home is open Monday through Friday 10:00 A.M. to 3:00 P.M. Closed holidays. Admission is about $3.00 for adults, with discounts for children and senior citizens. Phone (770) 992–1731.

The **Archibald Smith Plantation House,** 935 Alpharetta Street, was the home of one of Roswell's founders. This is the community's best-preserved landmark; the original outbuildings are still in place. Open Tuesday through Saturday 11:00 A.M. to 2:00 P.M. Phone (770) 992–1665.

Assuming that you use Atlanta as a base, drive south of Atlanta via I–75. You will come to **Jonesboro,** a little town at State Road 138, where **Stately Oaks 1839 Plantation Home and Historic Community,** 100 Carriage Lane, dispenses history and hospitality in equal measures. This 1839 restored Greek Revival plantation includes such authentic outbuildings as the original log kitchen and a schoolhouse. Costumed guides take you through the home. Open Wednesday, Thursday, and Friday 11:00 A.M. to 3:30 P.M.; the second and fourth Sundays of each month 2:00 P.M. to 4:00 P.M. Admission is about $5.00 for adults, with discounts for children and senior citizens. Phone (770) 473–0197.

For dinner, you might try **Greenwood's on Green Street,** 1087 Green Street, where the specialties are the fresh vegetables, for which the South is famous, and catfish. Other entrees include chicken, duck, and beef. The restaurant is in an 1835 house with a brick courtyard. When the weather permits, meals are served in the courtyard as well as inside. The restaurant is open 5:00 P.M. to 10:00 P.M. every day but Monday and major holidays. Phone (770) 992–5383.

In downtown Roswell, next to the Roswell visitor center, **The Public House,** 605 South Atlanta Street, serves lunch, dinner, and Sunday brunch in a historical building. The Southern sweet tooth is honored here with desserts made on the premises. Phone (770) 992–1665.

Continuing south, move toward the center of the state. **Macon** is about

84 miles south of Atlanta on I–75. Just before you get to Macon, the town of **Forsyth,** founded in 1823, has several interesting attractions to illustrate the nature of Georgia's antebellum small towns. Taking exit 61 from I–75 onto Tift College Drive brings you to the **Monroe County Museum and Store,** Tift College Drive. The museum, located in a restored railroad depot, is owned and operated by the Monroe County Historical Society and traces area history. Next door is a restored caboose. The museum is open Tuesday through Saturday 10:00 A.M. to 5:00 P.M.; Sunday 1:00 to 5:00 P.M. Admission is free, but donations are welcome. Phone (912) 994–5070.

A short walk from the museum takes you to Forsyth's *first* train depot, dating from 1846, where wounded Confederate soldiers were unloaded during the Civil War. Railroads were important here, not just for troops, but also for trade. Railroads meant money, as you can tell from the name of this first railroad in Georgia—the Monroe Railroad and Banking Company. This rail line was built in 1838 to run from Macon to Forsyth and back. At one time, as many as thirty-two trains a day passed through Forsyth.

You'll also be close to the **Courthouse Square Historic District,** which was described more than a decade ago by *The Macon News* as looking like "a picture postcard arriving a century late." It still is that way. Most of the buildings are on the National Register of Historic Places. There is the Farmer's Gin Lot, where a cotton gin operated during Forsyth's economic boom in the late 1800s. Visit the statue of a Confederate soldier that stands as a memorial to the 299 unknown Confederate soldiers, plus one identified soldier and one nurse, who are buried in the Confederate Cemetery. Many of the buildings in the district are from the late 1800s, built to carry on businesses and services begun in the antebellum years.

You can pick up an excellent guide for a walking tour at the Monroe County Chamber of Commerce, 267 Tift College Drive. Someone is usually there weekdays 8:00 A.M. to 4:00 P.M. On weekends the museum usually has brochures, but if you want to be sure of getting one, write the Chamber of Commerce at Post Office Box 811, Forsyth, GA 31029; phone (912) 994–9239.

Right on courthouse square, the **Farm House Restaurant** serves country cooking from 7:00 A.M. to 2:00 P.M. every day.

Head east of Forsyth to Juliette, 8 miles on U.S. Highway 41. In Juliette, eat at **The Whistle Stop Cafe.** This is the little restaurant that came to fame when the movie *Fried Green Tomatoes* was filmed on location.

It had been about the only surviving business in the remains of a once-thriving railroad town. In its new life, the town bustles with tourists browsing through the specialty shops that have opened on McCrackin Street. The restaurant is usually so busy that you have to sign in and then wait until someone leaves. The menu includes all the down-home standards—butterbeans, collards, okra, chicken pot pie, and, of course, fried green tomatoes—all cooked from scratch. The restaurant is open 9:00 A.M. to 7:00 P.M. Monday through Saturday and on Sunday from noon to 7:00 P.M.

Outside Juliette, **Jarrell Plantation State Historic Site** has one of the largest and most complete collections of original family artifacts for the years 1847 to 1945. This is an original middle Georgia plantation, with twenty buildings constructed during that period. Jarrell Plantation gives you an excellent opportunity to see the kind of plantation that was self-sustaining but not glamorous—the kind that was most typical, if not most famous, in Georgia. The first building was the 1847 plantation plain-style house. Erected subsequently were a mill complex, barn, carpenter shop, and steam-powered cotton grist mill. Appropriately placed in the buildings you will find cradles, spinning wheels, cooking utensils, and many original furnishings made by members of the Jarrell family. The Georgia Department of Natural Resources operates the plantation. It does it so convincingly that when you call outside regular hours, it seems to make sense to hear a message saying, "We're outside on the back forty right now." The plantation is open Tuesday through Saturday 9:00 A.M. to 5:00 P.M.; Sunday 2:00 to 5:30 P.M. Admission is about $2.00 for adults, $1.00 for children. Phone (912) 986–5172. The plantation is southeast of Juliette, 18 miles from I–75, Forsyth exit 60.

From the plantation, you can drive to Macon, 18 miles south on I–75, but it is more pleasant to travel down U.S. Highway 23 along the Ocmulgee River. Commerce is developing actively in Macon these days, but the city, which dates back to 1823, still has a generous number of antebellum mansions. Macon is also home to two distinguished schools, Wesleyan University (previously Wesleyan College), founded for women in 1831, and Mercer University, founded in 1871.

Macon is probably best known for its Cherry Blossom Festival in March, when the blooming of more than 150,000 cherry trees is celebrated with everything from craft shows and food to fireworks. Whether you should visit for the festival or at a more quiet time depends on your tolerance for crowds and how much you love a party.

Whatever festivities are in process, you have your choice of three different historic walking tours in Macon, or you can gear up and do all three. Stop in the **Macon-Bibb County Convention and Visitors Bureau,** 200 Cherry Street, for advice, maps, and brochures. Guided tours of the historic district are also available. The center is open during normal business hours Monday through Saturday. Phone (912) 743–3401 or (800) 768–3401.

One of the most important tour homes in Georgia is in Macon. **Hay House,** 934 Georgia Avenue, is not only a grand Italianate mansion, but it has features that were not ordinarily part of life when the house was built (beginning in 1855 and continuing until 1860). Start with its size. Hay House has twenty-four rooms in 18,000 square feet. The ballroom alone is 1,296 square feet—larger than many contemporary homes! The indoor bathrooms had an ingenious system for running water: A 20,000-gallon tank in the attic held water to gravity-feed the floors below, where it was piped into tubs. Speaking tubes allowed voice communication from

The ballroom in Macon's Hay House is 1,296 square feet in area; the entire house contains 18,000 square feet.

one floor to the next. The house also has an elevator that operated without electricity, and a ventilating system that provided a pre-freon-and-electrical-power version of air conditioning. The house is furnished with fine antiques and such decorative touches as crystal chandeliers and fine porcelains. The ceiling moldings are considered the best in Georgia. Some other notable features are stained-glass windows, gold leafing, and trompe l'oeil finishes. Hay House is open Monday through Saturday 10:00 A.M. to 4:30 P.M.; Sunday 1:00 to 4:30 P.M. Closed major holidays. Admission is about $6.00 for adults, with discounts for students and children. Phone (912) 742–8155.

Old Cannonball House and Macon Confederate Museum, 856 Mulberry Street, has an interesting history. Built in 1853 by Judge Asa Holt, it got its name by being the only house in Macon to be hit by a cannonball during the Civil War. According to records, the cannonball hit the sidewalk, went through the second column from the left on the gallery, went into the parlor above a window, and landed in the hall without exploding. You can follow the path of the cannonball by studying the repaired column, a patch in the parlor wall, and a dent in the hall floor. For a time Mrs. Holt displayed the cannonball on a table in the parlor.

The house is architecturally important for its perfect proportions, handsome Ionic columns, and drawn-wire railings on the porch and balcony. The Greek Revival home is furnished with antebellum antiques. Two parlors have been furnished to re-create the sorority rooms of Alpha Delta Pi and Phi Mu, two secret sororities organized in 1851 and 1852 at old Wesleyan Female College. The museum, located behind the mansion, is a two-story, four-room house built with hand-molded brick, originally intended for servants' quarters. It contains a variety of Civil War relics. The house and museum are open Monday through Saturday 10:00 A.M. to 1:00 P.M. and 2:00 to 4:00 P.M.; Sunday 1:30 to 4:30 P.M. Admission is about $3.00 for adults, with discounts for children and senior citizens. Phone (912) 745–5982.

In addition to the Civil War Museum, Macon has a museum showing the accomplishments of black Americans in the arts and in cultural development. **Tubman African American Museum,** 340 Walnut Street, offers a video entitled "Black Cultural History in Macon, Georgia." The museum is named for Harriett Tubman, the leader of the Underground Railroad for slaves. In the main gallery, a 40-foot mural by local artist Wilfred Stroud, entitled "From Africa to America," tells the story of black history. Permanent exhibits include artifacts and art from Africa. Upstairs are changing shows of local, regional, and national black artists. The museum is open Monday through Saturday 10:00 A.M. to 5:00 P.M.; Sunday 2:00 to 5:00 P.M. Closed major holidays. Admission is about $1.00. Phone (912) 743–8544. To learn more about the role of black people in Macon, pick up a copy of the tour brochure "An African Experience," which maps out twenty-one important sites in the city.

For dinner in a Southern mansion, go to **Beall's 1860,** 315 College Street. The menu is not particularly Southern—it features some contemporary American low-fat entrees and has a salad bar and buffet. The offerings change, but the restaurant is especially noted for its good seafood (not fried) and prime rib. The ambience, though, is pure Southern graciousness. The restaurant is open from 11:00 A.M. to 2:30 P.M. and 5:00 to 10:00 P.M. Closed Sunday. Phone (912) 745–3663.

It would be worth it to plan your schedule to allow you to spend a night in **1842 Inn,** at 353 College Street, just a few doors from Beall's 1860 and within easy walking distance of the historic district. Experienced travelers agree that this is an outstanding hostelry. The building is a beautifully restored Greek Revival antebellum mansion. The mainhouse connects to a Victorian cottage with a courtyard. The twenty-two guest rooms are luxuriously furnished with a mix of period reproductions and fine antiques. No antiques are in the private baths, though; they are state-of-the art. The innkeeper, Phillip Jenkins, offers what he calls "formal evening hospitality," which means hors d'oeuvres and drinks in the parlors, accompanied by piano music. Rates begin at about $95 per night per room and include continental breakfast.

COASTAL GEORGIA

Savannah has it all—grand mansions, enchanting squares, good food, hospitable people, and rich history. This is where Georgia was founded. The city is on the Atlantic Coast, at the confluence of the Savannah River and the Atlantic Ocean. James Oglethorpe brought the first English settlers to the area and laid out the city according to an unusual plan that has functioned well for more than 250 years. To oversimplify a bit, the plan relied on squares laid out in a pattern that could be repeated as the population grew. Each square was the center of a ward. Along the north and south sides of the squares were lots for personal residences; lots east and west of the squares were for businesses. Streets going east and west were boundaries for the wards. This pattern produced small neighborhoods with a mix of homes and businesses and a feeling of intimacy.

The squares had another function beyond aesthetics. Writing from London in 1744, Francis Moore explained it in *A Voyage to Georgia Begun in the Year 1735:* "The use of this is, in case a War should happen, that the Villages without may have Places in the Town, to bring their Cattle and Families into for Refuge, and to that Purpose there is a Square left in every Ward, big enough for the Out-wards to encamp in."

Originally, the squares were not landscaped, nor did they have sidewalks. These people were, after all, just settling the town. They eventually planted live oaks to line the streets, however, and today the cooling green leaves play an important role in the feeling of tranquillity that you enjoy in the historic district. So do the small, grassy parks in the squares.

The best way to understand the layout of the district is to use the taped walking tour produced by the **Savannah Area Convention and Visitors Bureau.** You can pick it up for $8.00 at the **Visitors Center,** in the restored railroad station at 301 Martin Luther King, Jr. Boulevard, at the end of I–16. Side 1 of the cassette tells you about the north squares, Side 2 the south. Each side runs about thirty minutes. The Visitors Center is open Monday through Friday 8:30 A.M. to 5:00 P.M.; weekends and holidays 9:00 A.M. to 5:00 P.M. Phone (912) 944–0456 or (800) 444–2427.

The railroad depot is also home to the **Savannah History Museum.** The people of Savannah point to this as a good example of "adaptive reuse," which means to restore a historic building and use it in a new way without spoiling the architectural and structural integrity of the original structure. The building was originally the Central of Georgia Railroad Station, Georgia's first railroad and the first chartered railroad in the United States. The station was built in 1860. Highlights of the museum include details about the station; a film about Savannah's history, from its founding in 1733 to the present; and information on the Baldwin locomotive No. 103, which pulled trains along the rails in the late 1800s. The Black Soldiers' Exhibit provides information about the 178,895 black men who fought during the Civil War.

Be sure to visit the **Owen-Thomas House and Museum,** 124 Abercorn Street, on Oglethorpe Square. It was designed by the English architect William Jay in 1816. The architecture of this house, emphasizing simplicity of design, was well ahead of its time. The drawing room has a rounded end wall, against which rare antique furnishings are effectively displayed in a formal setting. The curves are echoed in an unusual, oval-shaped front porch. A formal garden connects the main house with a carriage house. The house is a National Historic Landmark. Guides take you through the house, explaining its history and the significance of its architecture. The house and museum are open Tuesday through Saturday 10:00 A.M. to 5:00 P.M.; Sunday and Monday 2:00 to 5:00 P.M. The last tour begins thirty minutes before closing. Closed January and major holidays. Admission is about $5.00 for adults, with discounts for senior citizens, students, and children. Phone (912) 233–9743.

Farther down on the same street, the **Andrew Low House,** 329 Abercorn Street, on Lafayette Square, was built in 1848 by a successful cotton dealer. It was the adult home of Julia Gordon Low, who founded the Girl Scouts. The house is open for tours Monday through Wednesday and Friday and Saturday 10:30 A.M. to 4:00 P.M.; Sunday noon to 4:00 P.M. Closed holidays. Admission is about $5.00 for adults, with discounts for students and Girl Scouts. Phone (912) 233–6854.

If you have a special interest in the Girl Scouts, you should also plan a stop at the **Juliette Gordon Low Birthplace,** 142 Bull Street, on the corner of Bull and Oglethorpe—the Girl Scout National Center. This house was built between 1818 and 1821. Four generations of Gordons lived here. They were remarkably good record keepers and prolific writers; because of this, restoration and research are continuing projects. It is rare to find so much material to work with in speculating about the past. As a staff member put it, "We just keep learning and changing things to make it even more accurate." Where the emphasis at the Andrew Low House, owned by the Colonial Dames, is on the architecture and furnishings, here it is on family life. The house is furnished in Regency style, much as the Gordon Lows kept it. At Christmas, the staff decorate the house and re-create the celebrations as the Gordon Low family observed the holiday, using information gathered from family writings. Visitors participate in singing and dancing and enjoy refreshments, as guests would have done in earlier times. This site is unusual in the level of involvement that staff people have in the project. That's saying a lot in a city where many important sites are managed with pride and care. The house is open for tours every day but Wednesday 10:00 A.M. to 4:00 P.M. Admission is about $5.00 for adults, with discounts for children. Phone (912) 238–1779.

Historic Savannah Architecture

In his book *The Architecture of Georgia* (University of South Carolina Press, 1993), Tom Spector refers to "the triumph of the preservation movement in Savannah." Specifically, as developers began to chew away at the old downtown to make way for skyscrapers, a group of Savannah women formed the Historic Savannah Foundation, in 1955. They bought endangered properties and resold them to people who agreed, as a condition of sale, to restore them. This activity set the tone for the years since. Only two of the city's original squares were lost. Now the riverfront and market areas are being restored and used in much the same way.

The **Davenport House,** 324 East State Street, a Federal-style home built in 1820–1821, was the first "preservation triumph" of Savannah's Historic Savannah Foundation. The house has been completely restored and furnished with English and American antiques. The house is open for tours daily 10:00 A.M. to 4:00 P.M. Tours leave every thirty minutes. Closed Christmas day. Admission is about $4.00 for adults, $1.00 less for children. Phone (912) 236–8097.

On Telfair Square the **Telfair Mansion and Art Museum,** 121 Barnard Street, is another Savannah house designed by William Jay, this one for Alexander Telfair and his sisters, Margaret and Mary. It was built in 1820. After Mary's death in 1875, ownership of the house passed to the city. Like the Owen-Thomas House (see page 79), Telfair has some curved walls, and one room in the front is octagonal. It is considered a must-see for people seriously interested in period rooms. Many of the antiques in the house belonged to one-time Georgia governor Edward Telfair. The museum in the building features the work of Impressionist artists as well as silver and furniture from America and England in the 1700s and 1800s. Telfair is open Tuesday through Saturday 10:00 A.M. to 5:00 P.M.; Sunday 2:00 to 5:00 P.M. Closed holidays. Admission is about $3.00 for adults, with discounts for senior citizens and children. Phone (912) 232–1177.

The **Hamilton-Turner House and Ghost House,** 330 Abercorn Street, is a privately owned home and a museum that is fun to tour because it is quirky, with more emphasis on what people did in it than on its architecture. It is also fun to visit because it was featured in the book *Midnight in the Garden of Good and Evil,* by John Berendt, which gives the inside story on Savannah's old society. Newcomers and tourists love the book; third-generation Savannah residents hate it.

Your tour will probably be led by Sandra Hinly, a historian and director of tour guides. She or another guide will explain such things as why the house has a few big rooms rather than more, but smaller, ones. (Under English tax law, home owners were taxed for the number of rooms a house had, not for square footage.) The dining table is set as though someone were coming to dinner in a few minutes. The original owner was what the guides call a "financial merchant prince of Savannah," and he enjoyed flaunting his wealth. The rooms of the house were decorated not to display fine taste but to communicate wealth. An overabundance of rich wine tapestry and drapes puddled on the floor, implying that the person who lived in this house could afford to pay for more expensive fabric than was really necessary to cover the windows and furniture. The women living in such wealth seemed to spend a lot of time fainting. You'll see a daybed and learn that the phrase "she has taken to bed" was common, because women struggled with the combined rigors of low-country summer heat and confining corsets.

Savannah's society folk, including corseted ladies, held many a cotillion, debut, and reception in this house. It's still available for such functions, though corsets are only occasionally part of the scene today. A gift shop, located in the old wine cellar, stocks mementos of the city; it donates its profits to a shelter for the homeless.

About the ghost: Nobody's named him, but he's pretty active. At Christmas he seems to sit in a chair at the top of the stairs. He has a long beard, but he's definitely not Santa. At other times you can hear him breaking pool balls on the table upstairs when nobody else is there. Once a pool ball inexplicably came rolling down the steps. On the more gory side, he seems to be associated with an early practice of shooting criminals from the roof of the house; from time to time, very unghostly, noisy buzzards circle as if there were dead prey in the street. The house is open for tours daily 10:00 A.M. to 4:30 P.M. Admission is about $5.00 for adults, with a discount for children. No extra charge for ghostly experiences.

When you've seen enough mansions, walk toward the river to **Factor's Walk** and **Riverfront,** both on the waterfront. Cotton factors (brokers dealing in the sale of cotton) used to thrive here; now tourist spots and small businesses flourish. Factor's Walk is a row of buildings overlooking the river from Bay Street. The buildings are now being renovated and used for offices and small businesses. The area is set off with the original cobblestones and ironwork. Below, on the riverbank, Riverfront Plaza and Riverstreet is packed with pubs and specialty shops in the old cotton warehouses. Nine blocks of parks with benches and footpaths separate the shops from the river and make a nice place to rest while you watch the river.

Given Savannah's fine homes and lovely design, it's not surprising that forts were needed to defend the city. **Old Fort Jackson,** on the banks of the Savannah River at 1 Fort Jackson Road (off President Street, 3.5 miles from historic downtown on the Islands Expressway), is the oldest standing fort in Georgia. It was built beginning in the early 1800s, with slave labor, on Salter's Island, and took more than fifty years to complete. Although the fort was most important during the Civil War, its cannons were manned by soldiers during other times of war and unrest, much as the National Guard is deployed today. Exhibits depict both the uses and construction of the fort. The collection includes an assortment of weapons and equipment that are actually used during special events and living-history presentations. The fort is open daily 9:00 A.M. to 5:00 P.M. Admission is about $2.00 for adults, with discounts for retired military personnel, senior citizens, and students. Phone (912) 232–3945.

Savannah's other fort, **Fort Pulaski National Monument,** completed in 1847, is considered a good example of nineteenth-century seacoast fortifications. It is administered by the National Park Service, which dispenses such information as this: The fort was built with 25 million bricks, and it has walls that are 7½ feet thick.

The original purpose of the fort was to protect the seaport from foreign attack, and people had great faith in it. General Tottethe, U.S. chief of engineers at the time, said, "You might as well bombard the Rocky Mountains." But the fort's strength wasn't actually tested until April 1862, during the Civil War, when a Union cannon fired from more than a mile away on Tybee Island. It took only thirty hours for the Union bombardment to breach the wall. The Confederates surrendered, and military experts of the era concluded that masonry fortifications could not protect against new weaponry and ordnance.

For visitors, the site offers a video and exhibits about the fort. A bookstore sells related material, including publications about the Civil War. The site is manned by park rangers who are well versed in the history of the fort and skilled in communicating it. The monument comprises 5,600 acres, with salt marshes. Audio stations spaced around the fort explain the significance of the area. This site also has nature trails, a boat ramp, and a picnic area. The fort is open daily 8:30 A.M. to 5:00 P.M. Admission for adults is $2.00; children under sixteen and senior citizens are admitted free. Phone (912) 786–5787.

To get to the fort, take either Victory Drive from the south or President Street from downtown to U.S. Highway 80. Fort Pulaski is 14 miles east of Savannah. The entrance is on your left.

Chatham Artillery Punch

1½ gallons catawba wine
½ gallon rum
1 quart gin
1 quart brandy
½ pint Benedictine
2 quarts Maraschino cherries

1½ quarts rye whisky
1½ gallons strong tea
2½ pounds brown sugar
1½ quarts orange juice
1½ quarts lemon juice

Mix from thirty-six to forty-eight hours before serving. Add one case of champagne when ready to serve.

This punch has been famous in Savannah for 200 years. It's named for the Chatham Artillery, the oldest military organization of record in Georgia. Nobody knows for sure where the recipe originated. One theory holds that the "gentle ladies" made up a nice, light punch for a party honoring the artillery and that one by one, the officers sneaked in something extra to give the punch a little punch. The other theory—equally likely or unlikely—you could call "fraternity party desperation": The ladies were giving a party during hard times and scavenged all the spirits they could find in whatever amounts left in the bottles, dumping everything together with enough sugar and fruit juice to make it palatable.

Georgia

In addition to the self-guided tours of the town, the mansion tours, and trips to the forts, you have the option of joining a number of different commercial tours. **Savannah Trolley Tours,** whose tours leave from the Visitors Center on Martin Luther King, Jr. Boulevard, provides narrated trips through the historic district that take about an hour and a quarter. For rates, time schedules, routes, and reservations, phone (912) 234–8687. Or maybe you'd rather try a carriage. **Carriage Tours of Savannah** has tours leaving daily from several different sites in the city. For rates, time schedules, routes, and reservations, phone (912) 236–6756. Then there's **Gray Line Tours,** the official tour operation of the Historic Savannah Foundation. They take you through the coastal low country, in air-conditioned comfort. For rates, time schedules, routes, and reservations, phone (919) 234–8687.

How about a water tour? **Savannah Riverboat Cruises,** aboard the *Savannah River Queen,* offers a variety of narrated sightseeing cruises, brunches, dinners, and moonlight cruises, emphasizing Southern hospitality. The *Savannah River Queen* is a replica of the boats that used to navigate American rivers. The ticket office is behind City Hall on River Street. For rates, schedules, and reservations, phone (912) 232–6404 or (800) 786–6404.

New Forest Studios' tour, **Ghost Talk, Ghost Walk,** takes advantage of the popularity of ghost stories and hauntings in Savannah. It takes about ninety minutes to walk through the old city, while your guide tells stories from Margaret DeBolt's book *Savannah Spectors and Other Strange Tales,* based on research from Duke University and interviews with people in Savannah. The tours leave from John Wesley's Monument in Reynolds Square. Cost is about $10.00 for adults, half that for children. For more details, phone (912) 233–3896, or communicate telepathically.

Want to spend an entire day being shown around? **Tapestry Tours** has a six-hour tour that includes lunch and on-board refreshment. You ride in a comfortable bus that picks you up at your lodging door, and travel in a group no larger than twelve. The same company has a **Wildlife Safari** to take you through abandoned ricefields, which are now rich in wildlife, especially birds. For time schedules, routes, rates, and reservations, phone (912) 233–7770 or (800) 794–7770.

Another interesting option is the **Negro Heritage Trail**—three walking or driving tours that highlight seventeen historic sites significant to black history from slave times to the present. For further details, call the Visitors Center (912–944–0456 or 800–444–2427) or visit the **King-**

Tisdell Cottage, 514 East Huntingdon Street. Tours leave from the Visitors Center, but the exhibits here are worth a separate trip to this museum of black history, set in a restored 1896 Victorian cottage.

These aren't the only tour possibilities in Savannah, but they are some of the more well-established ones. For other possibilities, contact the Visitors Center, where there is always a list of current tour offerings.

Even without a tour guide, you could spend an entire day in Savannah looking at historic churches. They generally don't offer formal tours and some may not be open during the week, but you can still enjoy them from outside, count on getting inside some of them, and attend services on Sunday. **Cathedral of St. John the Baptist,** 222 East Harris Street, is the oldest Roman Catholic church in Georgia. It was organized in the late 1700s, and the current Gothic cathedral was dedicated in 1876. **Christ Episcopal Church,** 28 Bull Street, was built in 1840. The church was the first established in the colony, 1733, though it was Anglican at that time.

First African Baptist Church, 23 Montgomery Street, developed from the oldest Negro congregation in the United States, originating from Brampton Plantation in 1788. The first Negro Sunday school was held in 1826. The existing building was finished in 1861. This church does offer tours emphasizing its history. Phone (912) 233–6597.

Another church was also formed from the Brampton Plantation congregation, **First Bryan Baptist Church,** 575 West Bryan Street, on a worship site that has been owned by African Americans for more than 200 years. The **Second African Baptist Church,** 123 Houston Street, was formed in 1802. From here, General Sherman read the Emancipation Proclamation to the people of Savannah and promised freed slaves "forty acres and a mule." Almost a century later Dr. Martin Luther King, Jr., preached his "I Have a Dream" sermon here before giving it during the March on Washington.

At 25 West Oglethorpe Street, **Independent Presbyterian Church,** founded in 1755, is a replica of an 1815–1819 building that burned in 1889. The new building was put up a year later. **Lutheran Church of the Ascension,** 21 East State Street, was organized by the Germans in 1741. The building was completed in 1844, then added on to about thirty years later. **Temple Mickve Israel,** 20 East Gordon Street, the only Gothic synagogue in America, was built in 1776–1778. The Jewish congregation, established in 1733, was the first in the South. The oldest Torah in America is in the synagogue, and there's a museum next door with nearly 2,000 books about the congregation's activities.

After all the touring, it's time for eating and drinking. Savannah has lots of good restaurants. For a historically steeped experience that is also a lot of fun, try dinner at the **Olde Pink House,** 23 Abercorn Street, on Reynolds Square. It is special in many ways. First, consider the building. The mansion was built for a wealthy planter in 1771. It survived a city fire in 1796, the Civil War, and the general ravages of time, virtually unchanged. The owners say that the Pink House is the only remaining true colonial structure still standing in Savannah. The style is late Georgian. The original house plan remains intact, and the building is notable for the balance and grace of its design. During the Union occupation of the city, General Sherman headquartered in the Olde Pink House, where he was honored at a dinner party. Local people speculate that it was at this party that Sherman decided to give the city to President Lincoln for Christmas instead of burning it (see below).

The Pink House serves contemporary and colonial Georgia cuisine. The chefs do an especially fine job with fresh seafood and made-from-scratch desserts. The praline wafer with ice cream and fruit sauce is spectacular. You have a choice between formal dining upstairs and a more casual environment in the tavern downstairs. Musicians play jazz, blues, and ballads in the tavern. Phone (912) 232–4286.

Music is a big part of the scene at the **Pirates House,** 20 East Broad Street, too. Located in the historic district, this is an authentic 1733 tavern and it's where Bluebeard the pirate is purported to have died. It is a big place, with sixteen dining rooms, serving a variety of standard and low-fat entrees. Open for lunch and dinner. Phone (912) 233–5757.

In a three-story restored brick house that is said to be the oldest brick

Merry Christmas, Mr. President!

Savannah, Georgia, December 22, 1864

To His Excellency President Lincoln, Washington, D.C.:

I beg to present you as a Christmas-gift the city of Savannah, with one hundred and fifty heavy guns and plenty of ammunition, also about twenty-five thousand bales of cotton.

—W. T. Sherman, Major-General

building in Georgia, **The Chart House,** 202 West Bay Street, serves good traditional entrees such as prime rib and fresh grilled seafood. The dining room atmosphere is casual but pleasant, with some interior brick walls and natural wood accents. Open for dinner. Phone (912) 234–6686.

The **Shrimp Factory,** 313 East River Street, is located in what used to be an 1820s cotton warehouse that still has its heart-pine rafters. The restaurant serves lunch and dinner, emphasizing, of course, shrimp and other local seafood. The restaurant specialty is pine bark stew, which doesn't really have anything to do with trees; it is a fish concoction. Phone (912) 236–4229.

And so to bed. Savannah has many bed-and-breakfast accommodations. Three of the best, all in restored mansions, are Magnolia Place, The Gastonian, and the Lion's Head Inn.

Magnolia Place, 503 Whitaker Street, is a thirteen-room inn in a restored Victorian mansion. The inn has exotic antique furnishings, including prints and porcelains from around the world, and a famous butterfly collection in the parlor. It has a ghost, too. The story is that the original owner of Magnolia Place was a cotton magnate who went broke when the boll weevil got into cotton. He committed suicide by falling down the steps and has been hanging around ever since, turning on televisions, opening doors, and moving furniture. High tea is served every afternoon in the parlor. Rates begin at about $90 per room, including continental breakfast. Phone (912) 236–7674.

The Gastonian, 220 East Gaston Street, is elegant, too, located in two side-by-side 1868 buildings and a two-story carriage house, all linked by a garden courtyard and an elevated walkway. The eleven rooms and two suites are filled with English antiques and Persian rugs. Some distinctly nonhistoric plumbing had been added to create exotic baths; each bath complements the theme of its room: French, Oriental, Victorian, and so on. In the public rooms, guests lounge on English antiques, enjoying satin damask drapes and Sheffield silver. Full breakfast is served at large tables. Guests all introduce themselves before breakfast, because, as innkeeper Hugh Lineberger explains, "In the South we don't allow strangers to eat together." By the end of the meal, many lively conversations have inevitably begun, some as fun as the tourist attractions. Rates begin at about $120 per room. Phone (912) 232–0710.

Lion's Head Inn, 120 East Gaston Street, a Federal-style 9,000-square-foot mansion built in 1883, has six guest rooms. The house is built of Savannah gray bricks and is graced with handcarved marble mantels, elaborate wood and plaster moldings, and a Waterford crystal chandelier. The rooms are furnished with nineteenth-century American Federal antiques; each has a fireplace. Rates, including continental breakfast, begin at about $85. Phone (912) 232–4580 or (800) 355–5466.

EAST GEORGIA

Augusta deserves more attention than it has received in recent years. This city on the Savannah River is the second oldest in Georgia. It was an outpost for American Indian trade in 1736; tobacco and cotton later swelled the area's economy. Augusta was the second-largest inland cotton market in the world in the mid-1800s; after that things got tough as the Civil War and Reconstruction took their toll economically. Fortunately, however, the city was not burned, so you can still find good old architecture and historic sites as well as fine gardens and an engaging assortment of dining and lodging possibilities. Since it hasn't been "discovered" in the busload-attracting way of Charleston and Savannah, it is possible to enjoy Augusta's attractions without fighting crowds.

The streets are broad, with lots of trees lending a sense of serenity. Springtime bloom is spectacular in the city, especially when you see it from Riverwalk, a grassy, landscaped park with a splendid view of the Savannah River. Plantings have been planned with attention to succession of bloom, so you will find flowers at every time of year. The park is a nice spot for a picnic-basket lunch.

Riverwalk, which stretches from Oglethorpe Park at Sixth Street to the Riverwalk Amphitheatre at Ninth Street, is the center of downtown development. Restaurants, bars, and art and specialty shops line the walk, with a retail shop and condominium complex at one end. At the other end, the **Morris Museum of Art** has galleries devoted to Civil War art, the African-American presence in Southern painting, and Southern Impressionism and still life. There is also a museum shop. The museum is open Tuesday through Saturday 10:00 A.M. to 5:00 P.M.; Sunday 1:00 to 5:00 P.M. Admission is about $2.00 for adults, half that for senior citizens and children. Phone (706) 724–7501.

The main entrance to Riverwalk is at Eighth and Reynolds Streets. At 32 Eighth Street, the **Cotton Exchange,** a restored building where some

200 brokers used to buy and sell the cotton that was the heart of the economy in Augusta, now contains the **Historic Cotton Exchange Welcome Center** and a museum related to the cotton industry. Here you will find a variety of brochures and maps for self-guided walking and driving tours of the historic district. An Augusta city map shows the locations of twenty-four important sites, annotated with brief descriptions of their significance. The museum shows all the steps of the cotton business beginning with planting and through manufacturing. The building is listed on the National Register of Historic Places. The center is open Monday through Saturday 9:00 A.M. to 5:00 P.M.; Sunday 1:00 to 5:00 P.M. Phone (706) 724–4067 or (800) 726–0243.

Of special interest to preservationists is **Olde Town.** This area, delineated by Fourth Street, the Savannah River, May Park, and East Boundary Street, is one of the oldest residential areas in the city. At its peak it was known as "Pinch Gut," because of the corsets its fashionable ladies wore. In 1916 fire destroyed many of the homes. Renovation and restoration have progressed almost continuously, however, in recent years.

The **Clarion Telfair Inn,** 326 Greene Street, is an entire block of Victorian homes authentically restored and converted into hotel accommodations. They call it a "cluster inn." There are a total of seventy-eight rooms in sixteen restored houses. Each building has special features: hardwood floors, interior brick walls, or exceptionally fine woodwork. Rooms are furnished with antiques and reproductions appropriate to the particular house. Rates begin at about $80 per room; breakfast is extra. Phone (706) 724–3315 or (800) 241–2407.

At 540 Telfair Street is the **Augusta Richmond County Museum,** where you'll find exhibits about the Civil War as well as collections in archaeology, railroading, and natural sciences. The building, which dates to 1802, is a square Tudor style. Originally, it was one of the first boys' high schools in the country; it was later used as a Civil War hospital. The museum is open Tuesday through Saturday 10:00 A.M. to 5:00 P.M.; Sunday 2:00 to 5:00 P.M. Phone (706) 722–8454.

Another aspect of Augusta does not date so far back, but to some people, it matters more: Augusta is the home of the Master's Golf Tournament, partly the result, curiously enough, of the Civil War. Although the city escaped ravaging fires, wealthy families lost enough money in other ways to be willing to take paying Northerners into their homes. By the late 1800s Augusta thrived as a resort area. One hotel owner built a nine-hole course for a new Scottish game called "golf." Any golf widow will tell you: The rest was inevitable.

To see the city from the river, try the antebellum buffet cruise offered by **Augusta River Boat Cruises.** You leave from the Fifth Street dock on a replica of a nineteenth-century sternwheeler. Sightseeing cruises leave in the afternoon. The antebellum buffet cruise is offered Thursday evening. Phone (706) 722–5020 for specific times, details of various cruises offered, and prices.

While you're in the area, take a minute to look at the **Confederate Monument** on Broad Street, between Seventh and Eighth Streets. The marble monument shows the life-size figures of Generals Robert E. Lee and Stonewall Jackson with a Confederate private soldier. Farther down Broad Street, at Fifth Street, **The Haunted Piller** adds a touch of mystery. According to legend, a traveling minister who was not allowed to preach in the Lower Market cursed the place and predicted its destruction. Sure enough, in 1878 a cyclone wiped out everything but this pillar.

Three small towns west of Augusta have interesting antebellum attractions. **Thomson** has a downtown historic district listed on the National Register. **Crawford,** where many movies with Southern themes have been filmed, is the site of the antebellum home of the vice president of the Confederacy, A. H. Stephens. And **Washington** has several historic sites, antebellum homes, and a working plantation open for tours.

You can drive to Thomson on I–20 or drop down onto State Road 223 for a more leisurely drive to soak up the Southern ambience. Robert Inman's *Home Fires Burning* was filmed here. Should you decide to do more than drive through the historic district, stop in the **Thomson Depot,** at the **Thomson/McDuffie Tourism Convention and Visitors Bureau,** for a tour map.

Continue west, which is easier now on I–20. Take the State Road 22 exit, to Crawfordville and the **A. H. Stephens Home and Confederate Museum,** a state historic park, on Park Street. Stephens was vice president of the Confederacy and later was a governor of Georgia. The house, built in 1830, contains many of Stephens's personal items; a museum in the house includes weapons and uniforms. The park has camping, fishing, and boating facilities. The museum is open Tuesday through Saturday 9:00 A.M. to 5:00 P.M.; Sunday 2:00 to 5:30 P.M. Admission is about $1.75 for adults, less for children. Phone (706) 456–2602 for the park or (706) 456–2221 for the museum.

Now take State Road 47 north to Washington, a town established in 1773, where the major attraction is **Callaway Plantation,** about 5 miles west of the city on U.S. Highway 78. This working plantation has five historic houses and the Callaway Country Store. Three of the buildings are restored Early American homes. The oldest is a hand-hewn log cabin, probably built about 1785, where primitive furniture and the cooking and farming tools that would have been used by settlers in about 1780 are displayed. A two-story plantation plain-style house is furnished as it would have been in the 1790s. The main house, an 1869 Greek Revival brick structure, is furnished with period antiques. Everything looks as it did in the early days: The heart-pine floors and original plaster moldings are in excellent condition, and the rooms are lit with candles. The outbuildings include a smokehouse and outdoor toilets. Fields surround the buildings,

What Is a Plantation?

In his introduction to the book *Bases of the Plantation Society* (University of South Carolina Press, 1969), editor Aubrey C. Land writes, "In a sense all the American colonies were plantation colonies." In colonial times the original sense of the word "plantation" was that English settlements were "planted" overseas. But as major crops such as tobacco and rice were cultivated profitably for the empire, "planting" came to relate to growing crops that made a lot of money. Then, the planting colonies were the Southern coastal provinces.

Remarkably few planters' lives fit the image that many people have of plantations—great houses, lavish hospitality, and immeasurable wealth. According to Land, the statistics that historians have found "tell a story of a population composed mainly of smaller producers. . . ." We don't know much about these smaller producers, because, unlike the wealthy, the "small fry" left few records and fewer structures. They were basically farmers. What Land calls the "storybook" plantations developed late in the eighteenth century.

and there is a cemetery, as was usual on plantations. This place gives you a realistic sense of what plantation life would have been like. The plantation is open Tuesday through Saturday 10:00 A.M. to 5:00 P.M.; Sunday 2:00 to 5:00 P.M. Closed Thanksgiving, Christmas, and New Year's Days. Admission is about $2.00, with discounts for children. Phone (706) 678–7060.

Downtown in Washington, the **Washington Historical Museum,** 308 East Robert Toombs Avenue (on U.S. Highway 78), displays furnishings and memorabilia from the antebellum period and the Civil War. The Federal-style structure was built about 1835, but major additions were made about twenty years later. The museum is open Tuesday through Saturday 9:00 A.M. to 5:00 P.M.; Sunday 2:00 to 5:30 P.M. Closed Thanksgiving, Christmas, and New Year's Day. Admission is about $1.50 for adults, half that for children. Phone (706) 678–2105.

About a block away, at 206 East Robert Toombs Avenue, stands the **Robert Toombs Historic Site,** the home of the man for whom the avenue is named. Toombs was a U.S. senator who became a Confederate cabinet member after Georgia left the Union. After the war he vacillated in his feelings about secession, the Confederacy, and the United States. The 1797 home has been restored to its state at the time of Toombs's death, in 1885. The house is furnished with Toombs family antiques and Civil War relics. The house is open Tuesday through Saturday 10:00 A.M. to 5:00 P.M.; Sunday 2:00 to 5:00 P.M. Closed Thanksgiving, Christmas, and New Year's Day. Admission is about $1.50 for adults, half that for children. Phone (706) 678–2226.

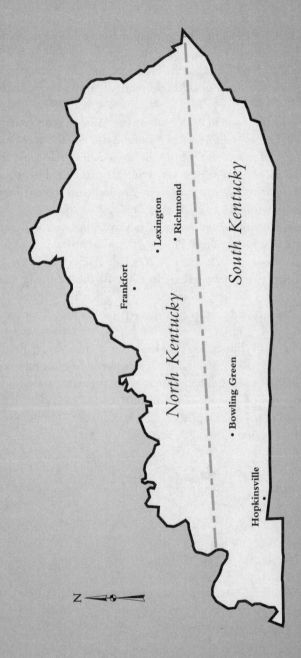

Kentucky

North Kentucky

South Kentucky

Frankfort

Lexington

Richmond

Bowling Green

Hopkinsville

N

Kentucky

Say the word "Kentucky" and people usually think of either bourbon or bluegrass. The 1,600 square miles of green fields and white fences that are known as "Bluegrass Country" will remain in your memory long after you've forgotten the idiosyncrasies of one town or another. But the pastoral air of Bluegrass Country is only part of the state's topography, and not by any means the site of all its history. Kentucky is bounded on the east by the Appalachian Mountains and on the west by the Mississippi River, creating a dramatic contrast between the rugged mountains and the rich flood plain. To the north, Kentucky borders Ohio and thus, as a border state, struggled with great contrasts of ideology and lifestyle during the antebellum and Civil War years as well. Kentucky became a state in 1792, and even though slave owners controlled the state's politics during the 1800s many farmers in the state never owned slaves, so Kentucky never seceded from the Union.

NORTH KENTUCKY

The north-central section of Kentucky is enriched with a cluster of interesting antebellum attractions, all within easy distance of one another. If you start in **Frankfort,** the state capital, you can get a good look at some of the Bluegrass Country, see some fine old buildings, and taste some

Southern cooking so popular that the restaurant that serves it has a what's-for-lunch? hotline. The **Frankfort Visitor Center,** downtown at 100 Capitol Avenue, is your source for an annotated historical walking-tour map with more than fifty historical attractions. Ask for the "Old Frankfort Walking Tour." The center is open year-round, Monday through Friday 9:00 A.M. to 5:00 P.M. from April through October, it is also open Saturday 10:00 A.M. to 2:00 P.M. and Sunday noon to 4:00 P.M. Phone (800) 960–7200 or (502) 875–8687.

The old part of town is on the north side of the city. Some of the buildings included in the walking tour are open to the public, including the **Old State Capitol** and the **Kentucky History Museum,** both at Broadway Street at St. Clair Mall. The Greek Revival capitol building, designed by Gideon Shyrock, was finished in 1831. Its most notable feature is a self-supporting staircase; essentially, it holds itself together by pressure and precise fit. Located next to the old capitol, in the annex, the museum features exhibits tracing Kentucky's social history from its settlement to the 1900s. Displays begin with prehistoric artifacts, then move into room settings representing settlers and Victorian homes. Displays of silver and china and a slide show round out the offerings. Both buildings are open Monday through Saturday 9:00 A.M. to 4:00 P.M.; Sunday noon to 4:00 P.M. Closed major holidays. Admission is free. Phone (502) 564–3016.

The **Kentucky Military Museum** is in this part of town, too, about 4 blocks away, in the old state arsenal at the corner of Main Street and Capital Avenue. Here you will find the requisite uniforms and weapons, including a collection of Kentucky rifles, photographs, and some Civil War items. The museum focuses on the Kentucky militia and National Guard. The museum is open Monday through Saturday 9:00 A.M. to 4:00 P.M.; Sunday noon to 4:00 P.M. Closed major holidays. Admission is free. Phone (502) 564–3265.

About 6 blocks west of the military museum, stop at **Liberty Hall Historic Site,** 218 Wilkinson Street. Two buildings stand on the site. Liberty Hall was the home of Kentucky's first U.S. senator, John Brown. Construction began on the building in 1796 and was not completed until 1801. The bricks were made on the property; the wood was cut and dried there. A local resident says that the home makes her think of the Sugarbaker home in the television show *Designing Women.* The Federalist-style home was occupied by four generations of Browns; the furnishings are family and local Georgian antiques. As you stand in the wide hall, looking through its lovely arch, you can see a pleasing balance of a stairway, a door, and a corner cupboard at the hall's end. The lines are simple; the accessories are spare. The impact is peaceful rather than ornate and cluttered. The first-floor guest room is furnished with Kentucky-made antiques, including a four-poster canopy bed and a wingbacked chair. In the kitchen, a display of Canton blue china flanks a wide fireplace. Old cooking utensils are set out on a simple wood table.

Next to Liberty Hall, the **Orlando Brown House** was built by Senator Brown for his son in 1835. This building remains pretty much the same as when it was built. It is furnished with original family pieces, including china and family portraits. This house was built according to a floor plan similar to the senator's home. There is a similar balance between the door and stairway as you look through the wide arch in the hall. The furnishings, however, produce quite a different effect. Duncan Phyfe tables original to the Orlando Brown house face each other across the hall, with formal portraits of Orlando and his wife, Mary Watts, above the tables, also facing each other. This house is known for having changed very little over the years and therefore accurately reflecting the tastes of the people who lived in it in the 1800s. In the double drawing room, a vibrant green carpet sets off more formal family portraits, one of them including the family dog, Judge. The piano in this room was brought from New York in 1836 as a gift to the Browns.

Outside, the largest formal boxwood garden in Kentucky covers nearly three acres, extending all the way down to the Kentucky River, which snakes through town. A grassy walkway is flanked with azaleas, dogwood, old roses, and boxwood. Liberty Hall Historic Site is open Tuesday through Saturday 10:30 A.M. to 4:00 P.M., with tours beginning at 10:30 A.M., noon, 1:30 P.M., and 3:00 P.M. Sunday tours begin at 2:30 P.M. Closed January and February. Admission is about $4.50 for adults, with discounts for students, children, and senior citizens. Phone (502) 227–2560.

If you are interested in touring a mansion that is still occupied, visit the **Old Governor's Mansion,** now the home of the lieutenant governor of the state, at 420 High Street. This is the oldest official executive residence still being occupied in the United States. Between 1798 and 1914 some thirty-three Kentucky governors lived in this Federal mansion. Many important people have visited here, including seven U.S. presidents. Some of the original furnishings are still in the house. Tours are offered Tuesday and Thursday 1:30 to 3:30 P.M. Admission is free. Phone (502) 564–5500 for tour information, (502) 564–5500 for the guard desk at the mansion. When you want to break for lunch, two restaurants in the area specialize in real Southern cooking. **Sweet Nectar,** at 205 Steele Street, serves the standards—fried chicken, green beans, roasted meats, mashed potatoes, and the like—for lunch and dinner. Phone (205) 227–4915. Or take a quick drive ¼ mile or so west of town on Louisville Road, to where it intersects with U.S. Highway 127. You'll find some fast-food restaurants here. Mixed in with them, **Blue Bonnet Deli,** a combination greengrocer and restaurant, serves different entrees every day. There's fried chicken, of course, but also homey old entrees such as chicken a la king on corn cakes. For less than $4.00 you receive a serving of meat, two vegetables, and bread. There may be chess pie for dessert. This place is so popular that it has a "what's-for-lunch?" hotline, at (502) 227–7712. The restaurant is open for breakfast and lunch. Go early—state workers break for lunch at noon, and often the food is all gone by 12:30 P.M. To talk to a live voice, phone (502) 223–5200.

After you eat, drive on Highway 127 to the north side of town to visit the **Leestown Company, Inc.,** on Wilkinson Boulevard. This is where Ancient Age Kentucky Straight Bourbon is brewed. The distillery has been producing bourbon since 1869. Tours take you through the production process and into old aging warehouses, a log clubhouse, and an attractive courtyard. A video explains the distilling process and the history of the company. Tours are available on the hour, Monday through Friday 9:00 A.M. to 2:00 P.M. Phone (502) 223–7641.

Next, drive 2 miles north, off U.S. Highway 127 to 1400 Manley-Leestown Road, where **Luscher's Farm Relics Museum** displays a collection of early farming tools and machines, all in working order, dating from the early 1800s. Some of the displays, the broad ax and treadmill, for instance, give you some insight into how hard farming was in the Old South. Other machines include reapers, threshers, and assorted pieces of household equipment. The museum is open Memorial Day through Labor Day, Monday through Saturday 10:00 A.M. to 4:00 P.M.; Sunday 1:00 to 4:00 P.M. Admission is about $3.00 for adults, with discounts for senior citizens, children, and families. Phone (502) 875–2755 or (502) 227–7936.

Now, on to **Lexington,** the geographic center of the bluegrass region, where horses are wishes and everyone rides. In a sense, there was a Lexington before there was a Kentucky. The city was founded in 1775, seventeen years before Kentucky achieved statehood. During the antebellum years it was one of the wealthiest communities west of the Alleghenies. Back then it was sometimes called the "Athens of the West." These days Lexington likes to advertise itself as having "More Taras than Atlanta"—a reasonable situation when you remember that General William Tecumseh Sherman burned Atlanta, not Lexington. The people of the region have developed and promoted their antebellum attractions so well that you understand their claim that Lexington "looks more like the Old South than any place farther south." Nor are these people retiring about other accomplishments. Lexington is also called the "Horse Capital of the World," and it is one of the largest burley tobacco markets in the world. The University of Kentucky is here, as well as Transylvania University.

To immerse yourself deeply into the region's culture, you should stop at the **Convention and Visitors Bureau,** 301 East Vine Street, downtown, or at one of the two information centers on I–75 just north and south of the city. All these places will provide walking and driving tour guides with maps, along with the usual brochures. The downtown location is open Monday through Friday 8:30 A.M. to 5:00 P.M.; Saturday 10:00 A.M. to 5:00 P.M. The information centers are open daily 10:00 A.M. to 6:00 P.M. Phone (800) 845–3959.

In the downtown area, see at least the **Mary Todd Lincoln House, The 1848 Lexington Cemetery,** the **Hunt-Morgan House,** the **St. Paul African Methodist Episcopal Church,** and the **Loudoun House.** Each of these places tells a unique part of Lexington's story.

What a Difference a Couple of Centuries Make!

Before the Civil War Lexington's most important crop was hemp, a coarse plant with fibers that were used to make rope for sailing ships. The hemp plant is also the source of the drugs marijuana and hashish. In the South, steam power soon eliminated sailing as an economical form of transportation, and tobacco soon outpaced hemp as Lexington's most important cash crop.

Since southerners didn't smoke rope, hemp ceased to be grown.

The Mary Todd Lincoln House, 578 West Main Street, is where the wife of Abraham Lincoln lived as a child, along with fifteen siblings, beginning in 1832. The Georgian-style house was built in 1803 as a tavern. In 1830 Robert Todd, Mary's father, renovated it to serve as a residence. It has been restored and furnished with period antiques, including personal items and some furnishings that belonged to the Todd and Lincoln families. Some pieces of Mary Lincoln's Meissen and Old Paris china are on display. According to tour guides, Abraham Lincoln visited the home at least three times. This is the first site restored in America to honor a first lady. The house is open from April 1 through December 15, Tuesday through Saturday 10:00 A.M. to 4:00 P.M. Closed holidays. Guided tours take about an hour; the last tour begins at 3:15 P.M. Admission is about $4.00 for adults, with discounts for children. Phone (606) 233–9999.

Farther west, at 833 West Main, The 1848 Lexington Cemetery is the burial spot for Mary Todd Lincoln and members of her family, Henry Clay, a number of local leaders, and 500 Confederate soldiers. It is interesting for several reasons. Not only are people important in American history buried here, but it is also considered a good example of a "rural cemetery," as opposed to the familiar, unlandscaped, city burial grounds. The cemetery is known nationally as an excellent arboretum. If you love the way trees grow in the Southern climes, do visit here even if you haven't much interest in burial grounds. Finally, the cemetery holds a fascinating collection of monuments, ranging from classical Greek and Egyptian Revival columns and urns to ornate Victorian pieces, with fully costumed figures carved into the marble. Brochures are available for self-guided walking tours that include a map of the cemetery and identify the spots where various important people are buried. Grounds are open daily 8:00 A.M. to 5:00 P.M.; the office is open Monday through Friday 8:00 A.M. to 4:00 P.M.; for information only, Sunday 1:00 to 4:00 P.M. Admission is free. Phone (606) 255–5522.

Southeast of the cemetery and the Mary Todd Lincoln House, Main Street crosses Mill Street. At 201 North Mill, the Hunt-Morgan House was built in 1814 by General John Wesley Hunt, the first millionaire west of the Alleghenies. The house and gardens have been restored. Many of the furnishings are old family pieces. There is a collection of Civil War artifacts as well. The museum has six Civil War uniform coats, plus Morgan's sword, important letters, and photographs. One small room is dedicated entirely to General John H. Morgan and his men. Artwork depicts significant events in the Civil War. An interesting aspect of this collection is that items from private collections are rotated through the displays.

The Hunt-Morgan House is owned and operated by the Blue Grass Trust for Historic Preservation, a private, nonprofit organization founded in 1955 to save the house from demolition. The house is open for guided tours March through December 22, Tuesday through Saturday 10:00 A.M. to 4:00 P.M.; Sunday 1:00 to 4:00 P.M. Closed Thanksgiving. Admission is about $4.00 for adults, half that for children. Phone (606) 253–0362.

Walking distance from the Hunt-Morgan House, at 251-252 North Upper Street, is the area's oldest A.M.E. church, St. Paul African Methodist Episcopal Church, founded in 1830. Phone (606) 255–7945.

Another interesting building is the **Loudoun House,** 209 Castlewood Drive, where the Lexington Art League offers studio tours and rotating exhibits. It has the distinction of being one of only five remaining Gothic villas built like castles under the design of architect of A. J. Davis. It is open Tuesday through Friday noon to 4:00 P.M.; Saturday and Sunday 1:00 to 4:00 P.M. Phone (606) 254–7024.

Moving out of the downtown area, driving out East Main Street (which becomes Richmond Road) to the 1400 block, brings you to **Ashland, the Henry Clay Estate.** Clay, a politician known as "The Great Compromiser," lived on this estate from 1811 until he died in 1852. Apparently, compromising was a pretty effective political technique back then: Clay was a U.S. senator, speaker of the house, secretary of state, and several times a presidential candidate. When he failed to get elected, he said, "I'd rather be right than be president."

Tours of his estate include the house, furnished with family heirlooms, several outbuildings, and formal gardens on twenty wooded acres. None of these things is ordinary. The house was built in 1806, enlarged in 1811, and, after Clay's death, torn down and rebuilt on the same foundation. This happened between 1853 and 1857. Clay's son, James, kept the same floor plan but added decorative features popular at the time. The house stands as an example of Italianate style on a Federal floor plan. Most of the furnishings are those of the Clay family going back five generations. The outbuildings include a washhouse and privy, a smokehouse and coach wing, and dairy cellar and icehouses. The icehouses are round, with pointed roofs, resembling two shingled tents side by side. The formal garden has roses, boxwoods, some annuals, perennials, and herbs. It is maintained by the Garden Club of Lexington. Many unusual old trees grow on the property. An easy one to spot is a ginkgo imported to Kentucky by

Never Underestimate the Power of a Woman

L exington produced some colorful women in the 1800s. Perhaps the most notorious was Belle Brezing, famous for starting a "bawdy house" right across the street from the campus of Transylvania University and developing a red-light establishment in Lexington, until World War I took away most of her customers. She was the model for the character Belle Watling in *Gone With the Wind*.

Henry Clay. The estate is open February through December, Saturday 10:00 A.M. to 4:30 P.M.; Sunday 1:00 to 4:00 P.M. Tours begin on the hour; the last tour leaves at 4:00 P.M. Admission is about $5.00 for adults, less for children. Phone (606) 266–8581.

From Ashland you can take the State Highway 4 beltway west to U.S. Highway 27, then drive 5 miles south to **Waveland State Historic Site.** The Greek Revival manor house, on a ten-acre plot, was built in 1847 by a grandnephew of Daniel Boone. The site is a good example of how Kentucky's landed gentry lived in the antebellum years. The manor is furnished with period antiques. In addition to the main house, you may tour the restored antebellum brick servants' quarters, an icehouse, a smokehouse, and an herb garden. Waveland is open from March 1 to mid-December, Monday through Saturday 10:00 A.M. to 4:00 P.M.; Sunday 2:00 to 5:00 P.M. The last tour begins one hour before closing. Admission is about $3.00 for adults, with discounts for senior citizens and children. Phone (606) 272–3611 or (800) 255–PARK.

After touring Waveland, get back onto I–75, where a drive of less than 20 miles south brings you to **Richmond.** On the way stop at **Fort Boonesborough State Park,** which is about 6 miles north of I–75 on State Highway 627, and at **White Hall State Historic Site,** just a couple of miles west of I–75, following signs from the Winchester-Boonesboro exit.

Fort Boonesborough is in the state park on the Kentucky River. It's a replica of the fort that Daniel Boone built in 1775. The settlement was first called Boonesborough. It was expected to be the hub of the colony, but settlers soon began leaving, partly because of Indian attacks and partly because the Kentucky River kept flooding them out. By 1830 there was nothing much left of the settlement. An archaeological dig in 1987 revealed the physical remains of the fort, which served as a starting point for reconstructing the blockhouses and cabins where costumed artisans now demonstrate making eighteenth-century crafts with antique equipment. A series of museum displays and films develop the history and demonstrate the daily details of Kentucky's second settlement. In addition to its history-related attractions, the park offers camping, an Olympic-size pool and a waterslide, miniature golf, a playground, and a grocery store. The Pioneer Forage Trail, in the park, is a ½-mile trail with a self-guided tour detailing the native plant and animal life along the way—the same vegetation that explorers Lewis and Clark and, later, Daniel Boone wrote about. The fort is open April 1 through Labor Day, daily 9:00 A.M. to 5:30 P.M. From Labor Day until October 31, it is open Wednesday through Sunday at the same hours. Admission is about $4.00 for adults, less for children. Phone (606) 527–3131 or (800) 255–PARK.

Continue on to White Hall State Historic Site, notable for being the home of Cassius Marcellus Clay—that's the abolitionist, not the much-later-born boxer, though the two share the quality of having been flamboyant characters. Clay was a newspaper publisher who campaigned vigorously in favor of abolishing slavery. He had a rebellious childhood, a lot of political ambition, and an eye for the ladies, however, leaving historians to debate the sincerity of some of his abolitionist speeches. In any case, he was a friend of Abraham Lincoln, and his activities earned him the nickname "The Lion of Whitehall."

The mansion was built in 1798 in Georgian style by Clay's father. Cassius's wife, Mary Jane, added an Italianate section, built in 1860 above and around the house, making it a house within a house. An interesting feature of the house is an indoor bathroom that is divided into three small rooms—one for a washbasin, another for a commode, and the third for a bathtub made of a hollowed-out poplar log lined with copper. The bathroom had running water of sorts: A storage tank on the top floor collected rainwater from the roof to flow through pipes down to the bathroom.

Some of the furnishings are original to the house. The fact that they remain and that the house can be toured is a triumph for preservationists because after Clay died in 1903, the house was occupied by tenant farmers who stored tobacco and hay in the ballroom. After they moved out, vandals broke the staircase banister, lit fires in the hall, and smashed win-

As the Twig Is Bent, So Grows the Tree

Laura Clay, the daughter of Cassius Clay, became a national figure in the suffragist movement. She was the president of the Kentucky Equal Rights Association for twenty-four years. She also worked to improve the lives of poor people and immigrants in the area and supported the temperance movement. Her causes were different, but her passion for them was like her father's.

dows. The Commonwealth of Kentucky eventually bought the land around the house, and the great-grandchildren of Cassius Marcellus Clay donated the buildings. Restoration began in 1968. The mansion is open April through October, daily 9:00 A.M. to 4:30 P.M. Admission is about $3.50 for adults, less for children. Phone (606) 623–9178.

The welcome center in downtown Richmond, the **Richmond City Hall,** 359 Main Street, offers an excellent tour guide and map of old buildings. The public buildings, such as City Hall, and the **Madison County Courthouse,** also on Main Street, are open for inspection during normal business hours. Others are private homes, but you can still enjoy them from outside.

Richmond was also the location of an important Civil War battle. For a free guide, write ahead to P.O. Box 250, Richmond, KY 40475, or phone (606) 623–1000, extension 210. If you choose instead to stop at the visitors' center in the City Hall building, you can pick up not only the guide but also a driving-tour map and tape cassette for the **Battle of Richmond Tour.** This is an outstanding guide, complete with a solidly researched summary of the battle.

The tour begins at the bottom of Madison County and works through eight specific stations back to the city. Markers and important sites along the way are colorfully explained. At each point you have the option of simply driving by or getting out to walk around at such places as the Confederate cemetery and the Mount Zion Church, which was used as a Union hospital. According to the tour guide, arms and legs amputated from wounded soldiers were stacked up in a heap outside the windows. The tour takes at least two hours. The $5.00 rental fee for the tape cassette will be returned when you turn in the cassette.

Pottery aficionados should take a side trip of about 15 miles on Highway 52 east, from Richmond to **Bybee,** to look around **Bybee Pottery,** built about 1809. This is said to be the oldest existing pottery west of the Alleghenies. It still operates in the old log building where it has been for more than a century. The central building is built of logs with solid walnut beams. Accumulated clay dust has raised the floor level several inches since the 1800s. Potting here is still done by hand, on a wheel. The clay comes, as it always has, from pits nearby. The pottery produced here is for sale. Bybee Pottery is open Monday through Friday 8:00 A.M. to noon and 12:30 to 4:00 P.M. The kiln is opened Monday, Wednesday, and Friday at 8:00 A.M. The best time to visit this kind of pottery, if you are hoping to choose from a good selection, is shortly after the kiln opens. Phone (606) 369–5350.

South of Richmond, via I–75, is the college that Cassius Marcellus Clay helped found in 1855, **Berea College.** In the words of the Reverend John G. Fee, who established the institution on land donated by Clay, the school was intended to be "Anti-slavery, anti-caste, anti-rum and anti-sin giving an education to all colors, classes, cheap and thorough."

What was going on here stands in fascinating contrast to plantation life and reflects the fact that antebellum Kentucky was of divided opinion about slave labor. The school is still known as being set up to provide a liberal arts education and to help students learn marketable skills, such as furniture building, weaving, hotel administration, food preparation, and farming. Berea was the first interracial college in the South. In a reversal of the usual pattern, classes at Berea were *not* segregated until the 1904 Day Law forbade integrated classrooms. In 1950, the school went back to its earlier integration.

Most of today's 1,500 students come from Appalachia. They are chosen for their academic ability and financial need. They all work at least ten hours per week, and they pay no tuition. For visitors, it all comes together at **Boone Tavern Hotel and Dining Room,** where instructors and hired professionals provide management and direction for an inn and restaurant staffed mostly by students. The fifty-nine rooms contain furniture handmade by students. Students also make the craft items in the gift shops and conduct tours of the historic campus. Tea is served daily in the Lincoln Lobby, a comfortable room dominated by a striking portrait of Abraham Lincoln without a beard. The restaurant's signature items are fluffy spoon bread, made with white cornmeal, and chess pie. The dining room serves three meals a day. Hotel rates begin at about $52 for one person, $57 for two people in a room. Phone (606) 986–9358 or (800) 366–9358.

Also on the campus, the **Log House Craft Gallery** displays a century of craft tradition, including the Wallace Nutting Collection of Early American furniture. Phone (800) 347–3892. And the **Berea College Appalachian Museum,** on Jackson Street, displays artifacts from the Southern highlands. The museum operates according to the motto "In Appalachia, we do not live in the past, but the past lives in us." Exhibits cover everything from farming to cooking. Students dye yarn, play dulcimers, spin, and so on. A combination of art, photography, videos, antique tools, and the actual crafts suggest how the mountain people used to live. The museum is open Monday through Saturday 9:00 A.M. to 6:00 P.M.; Sunday 1:00 to 6:00 P.M. Closed Thanksgiving, Christmas, Easter, and the month of January. Admission is about $1.50 for adults, less for senior citizens, students, and children. Phone (606) 986–9341, extension 6078.

Tours of the campus are available Monday through Friday at 9:00 A.M., 10:00 A.M., 1:00 P.M., and 3:00 P.M.; Saturday 9:00 A.M. to 6:00 P.M.; Sunday noon to 6:00 P.M. To get to the campus, take exit 76 at Berea and follow Kentucky Highway 21 to the inn, which makes a good starting point.

The easiest way to get to the next cluster of attractions is to continue south on I–75 about 20 miles to Mount Vernon, where you pick up U.S. Highway 150 and head northwest to **Danville.** A walking-tour brochure from the **Danville-Boyle County Tourist Commission,** 304 South Fourth Street (phone 606–236–7795) guides you to a number of restored antebellum buildings, including **Old Centre,** Main Street, on the campus of Centre College (open weekdays, phone 606–236–5211), and **Jacobs Hall,** a restored Italianate dormitory on the campus of the Kentucky School for the Deaf (open weekdays, phone 606–236–5132).

Also explore the log structures of picturesque **Constitution Square State Historic Site,** 105 East Walnut Street. This is a reproduction of the first courthouse square in Kentucky, where the state's first constitution was written and adopted in Grayson's tavern. A painting on display in the Old Log Courthouse in the square depicts the last-minute debates before the constitution was signed. The site is open daily 9:00 A.M. to 5:00 P.M. Admission is free. Phone (606) 236–5089 or (800) 255–PARK.

Constitution Square State Historic Site in Danville is a reproduction of the first court-house square in Kentucky, where the state's first constitution was written in a tavern.

Across the street, it's a little gory but nevertheless interesting to stop in the **McDowell House & Apothecary Shop,** 125 South Second Street. On Christmas morning in 1809, Dr. Ephraim McDowell made medical history by becoming the first surgeon to successfully remove an ovarian tumor. (Presumably, the patient also made history, being the first person to have same removed.) The site comprises a farmhouse, with a smaller attached brick building for the apothecary, and herb gardens that provided curatives for the doctor's practice. Guided tours show the lifestyle of an early Kentucky family. Open Monday through Saturday 10:00 A.M. to noon and 1:00 to 4:00 P.M.; Sunday 2:00 to 4:00 P.M. Admission is about

$3.00 for adults, with discounts for senior citizens and children. Phone (606) 236–2804. Closed major holidays.

You'll get a good taste of how one family earned money to pay their surgeons back then by visiting **Penn's Store,** at the junction of State Roads 37 and 243. The store, the oldest general store in the United States, has been run by the same family since 1850. As you would expect, it's an unprepossessing, weathered little wooden building with a tin roof. Depending on the season, you might find a few watermelons or pumpkins on the porch, which is guarded, of course, by a sleeping dog. Open Tuesday through Saturday 9:00 A.M. to 5:00 P.M.

Ten miles west of Danville, on U.S. Highway 150, the **Perryville Battlefield State Historic Site,** at **Perryville,** commemorates the worst Civil War battle in Kentucky. About 17,000 Confederate soldiers, outnumbered by at least 5,000 Union troops, lost the battle, ultimately giving Union troops control of the entire state. You can walk around the battlefield and see burial grounds and monuments for the men on both sides. A museum displays artifacts, and a gift shop sells souvenirs. The museum is open April through October, daily 9:00 A.M. to 5:00 P.M. Admission is about $1.50. The park is open April through October, daily 9:00 A.M. to 9:00 P.M. Admission is free. Phone (606) 332–8631.

West on U.S. Highway 150, continue about 20 miles more to **Lincoln Homestead State Park,** north of Springfield on State Road 528. The park is on 150 acres of land originally settled by the Lincoln family. A replica log cabin stands where the original home of Abraham Lincoln's father stood. Copies of the blacksmith and carpenter shops in which Abraham apprenticed are here, too, along with the restored cabin in which Lincoln's mother, Nancy Hanks, lived before her marriage. The park has fishing, picnic areas, a playground, a museum, and a gift shop. It has an eighteen-hole golf course, too, but somehow that seems out of place and time. The park is open May through September, twenty-four hours a day. Buildings are open 8:00 A.M. to 6:00 P.M. In October the buildings are open on weekends only. Admission to the park is free; admission to the buildings is about $1.00 for adults, about half that for children. Phone (606) 336–7461 or (800) 255–PARK.

After you spend some time at the park, continue on U.S. 150 to **Bardstown,** the second-oldest city in Kentucky, where another state park, **My Old Kentucky Home State Park,** commemorates the life and music of Stephen Foster. He wrote "My Old Kentucky Home" at Federal Hill mansion here in 1852. This, of course, is the song for which Foster is best known in Kentucky, but it is by no means his only contribution to the world of music. You've probably sung other songs he wrote without even realizing it.

Your visit to Foster's Old Kentucky Home will include a tour of the mansion, which is furnished with family antiques and portraits. The Greek Revival mansion was built in about 1851; it is where the first Confederate flag was raised in Kentucky. Costumed guides conduct tours of the antiques-filled mansion, the formal gardens, and the outbuildings. Part of this whole experience is the **Stephen Foster Outdoor Drama,** a professional outdoor production held in the park in which the hillside comes alive with more than fifty of Foster's songs—everything from "Camptown

He Was Born in Pennsylvania! Does that Make Him a Yankee?

Stephen Foster was born near Pittsburgh, on the Fourth of July in 1826. He attended many Negro camp meetings, which inspired him to write the old songs described in *The Golden Book of Favorite Songs* as "tender." Among his songs are "Old Black Joe," "Old Folks at Home," and "Massa's in the Cold, Cold Ground."

His themes were homesickness and longing for past times. In "Old Folks at Home," he laments:

Way down upon de Swanee River, far far away
Dere's wha my heart is turning ever, Dere's wha de old folks stay.
All the world am sad and weary, everywhere I roam
Oh, darkies, how my heart grows weary, far from the old folks at home.

His chorus in "My Old Kentucky Home," goes:

Weep no more, my lady, O weep no more today.
We will sing one song for the old Kentucky home,
for the Old Kentucky home, far away.

Races" to "Jeanie with the Light Brown Hair"—sung and danced by an exuberant cast in bright and billowing antebellum-style costumes. Performances begin at 8:30 P.M. from June to Labor Day, except Monday. The Saturday 2:00 P.M. matinee is presented in an indoor theater on the grounds. In bad weather the evening performance is taken indoors as well. Tickets for the show are about $10 for adults, half that for children. Phone (502) 348–5971 or (800) 626–1563.

The park is open daily from June through Labor Day, 8:30 A.M. to 6:30 P.M.; shorter hours the rest of the year. Park admission is about $4.00 for adults, with discounts for senior citizens and children. Phone (502) 348–3502.

In downtown Bardstown, not far from the courthouse square, **Spalding Hall,** 114 North Fifth Street, was a school in the 1800s. It was used as a hospital during the Civil War. Now it houses the **Bardstown Historical Museum,** where displays range from Indian relics and Civil War artifacts to Stephen Foster collectibles. Also in Spalding Hall, the **Oscar Getz Museum of Whisky History** displays everything from early advertising to a moonshine still. One item is the liquor license that Abraham Lincoln had for a tavern in Illinois in 1833. Some other memorabilia relate to Carrie Nation, the Kentucky-born woman who attacked demon rum with an ax. The museums are open May through October, Monday through Saturday 9:00 A.M. to 5:00 P.M.; Sunday 1:00 to 5:00 P.M. November through April they are open Tuesday through Saturday 10:00 A.M. to 4:00 P.M.; Sunday 1:00 to 4:00 P.M. Admission is free. Phone (502) 348–2999.

On the courthouse square, Bardstown has a couple of lodging places that fall in a category somewhere between unique and quirky. **Old Talbot Tavern,** 107 West Stephen Foster Avenue, has been in continuous operation since 1779. It gets you to thinking about all the people who've slept and eaten and done heaven knows what else here—everyone from Abraham Lincoln and Andrew Jackson (not together) to Stephen Foster. Even if you don't spend the night, you are invited to browse through the building. The first thing you will see upstairs at the tavern is a roomful of murals that are said to have been painted in 1797 by members of the entourage of Louis Philippe of France, who later became king, when he stayed at Bardstown while in exile from his country. The murals are full of gunshot holes. They say that Jesse James shot them for target practice when *he* stayed in Bardstown, in exile from practically everywhere. The rooms, which all have private baths, are furnished with antiques. Downstairs, the inn has a pub with stone walls and several dining rooms. By far the most popular item on the menu is the fried chicken, though many people also like the rabbit. The restaurant serves lunch and dinner every day. The tavern has just come under new management, so if you decide to stay or eat here, it would be a good idea to call ahead to inquire about what, if anything, has changed. Rates begin at about $50. Phone (502) 348–3494 or (800) 4–TAVERN.

Next to the tavern, **Jailer's Inn,** 111 West Stephen Foster Avenue, invites you to spend the night in the Nelson County Jail, built about 1797. The stocks and pillory are still out front. Inside, things have changed. A lot. Even if you stay in the room that was a former women's cell and is done entirely in prison black and white, it won't feel like punishment. In addition to the two original bunks, the room has a waterbed atop a black and white tile floor laid in a geometric pattern. The other rooms, such as the Garden Room and Victorian Room, are theme-decorated and pretty. All the rooms have private baths. Rates, including continental breakfast, begin at about $55 per room. Phone (502) 248–5551.

From Bardstown, take the Bluegrass Parkway east to loop back toward Lexington. When you get to U.S. Highway 127, go north to **Harrodsburg,** back in Bluegrass Country. Established in 1774, this was the first permanent English settlement west of the Alleghenies.

Downtown, the **Old Fort Harrod State Park** re-creates the community that lived within the fort in 1775, to illustrate what life was like here at the time. Costumed guides play the role of the early settlers and demonstrate their craft making. Animals in the corral are kept as they would have been back then. The replicas of a schoolhouse and pioneer cabins, furnished with handmade implements and furniture, help you to understand the simple lives of the people who lived here. The park also contains the cabin where Abraham Lincoln's parents are believed to have been married. The 1830 mansion museum in the park displays Indian and Civil War artifacts. More than 500 pioneers are buried in the cemetery in the park. The park is open year-round. Days and hours of operation vary seasonally for the attractions. Phone (606) 734–3314 or (800) 255–PARK.

An outdoor drama, "The Legend of Daniel Boone," is performed in the amphitheater behind the park. Daniel wasn't exactly Dixie, but his kind of life, with its fighting and roughing it, led to the next phase, after culture calmed down a bit. The show includes songs and narrative about his life, as well as choreographed fighting. Performances are held mid-June through August, Monday through Saturday at 8:30 P.M. Admission is about $12 for adults, half that for children. Phone (606) 734–3346.

You could plan a side jaunt to **Hodgenville,** south of Bardstown on U.S. Highway 31 East, to see the **Abraham Lincoln Birthplace National Historic Site.** This 116-acre park is about 3 miles south of Hodgenville on U.S. 31 East. The memorial has fifty-six steps, one for each year of Lincoln's life. An audiovisual presentation depicts his years in Kentucky. The park is a nice place for a picnic. It is open daily from 8:00 A.M. Phone (502) 358–3137.

It is also interesting to see the simple cabin reproduction, **Lincoln's Boyhood Home,** at the site of the original cabin. It's 7 miles northeast of Hodgenville on U.S. 31 East. You'll actually pass it on your way to the National Historic Site if you're driving down from Bardstown, and you can stop before you go the rest of the way if you want to. Lincoln lived here from 1811 to 1816. This is where the young boy first saw slaves being transported along the road, one of the experiences that helped shape his attitudes on the subject. Tours are offered from Memorial Day to Labor Day, daily 9:00 A.M. to 7:00 P.M. The rest of the time, the site closes at 5:00 P.M. Admission is about $1.00 for adults, half that for children. Phone (502) 358–3163.

One more tribute is paid to Lincoln with the **Lincoln Museum,** downtown in Hodgenville at 66 Lincoln Square. Exhibits show scenes from his life, along with an art collection and Civil War artifacts. The museum is open Monday through Saturday 8:30 A.M. to 5:00 P.M.; Sunday 12:30 to 5:00 P.M. Closed Thanksgiving, Christmas, and New Year's Day. Admission for adults is about $3.00, with discounts for senior citizens, children, and military personnel with identification. Phone (502) 358–3163.

After studying the lives of Lincoln and the settlers, drive east on the Bluegrass Parkway, then take U.S. Highway 127 south to Harrodsburg. Visit **Shaker Village of Pleasant Hill** for a fascinating glimpse of a lifestyle that produced some of the best furniture design, tools, and food in the country. This is the most completely restored Shaker community in the country. The restoration has more than thirty of its original buildings, on 2,700 acres surrounded by about 20 miles of stone fence. This site is worth at least a day of your time; you could spend much longer without running out of things to learn and experience. For the village to make sense, you need to know that the Shakers were members of a religious utopian society who called themselves "The United Society of Believers in Christ's

Costumed interpreters at Shaker Village of Pleasant Hill demonstrate daily activities of the Shakers in the 1840s.

Second Appearing." In the 1840s nearly 6,000 Shakers lived in communities not just in Kentucky but across the country. Their name derived from the "shaking" that was part of their religious dancing. Remember as you learn about them that in the South, they were developing their unique community and way of life at exactly the same time as the mountain people of Appalachia and the plantation dwellers of the Deep South were building quite different societies.

Like the Quakers and the Moravians, the Shakers were plain people who eschewed unnecessary ornamentation and dressed simply. They were also celibate. The absence of lots of little Shakers, of course, is one of the reasons for the demise of this community. But they were tremendously talented in their pursuit of efficiency and their elimination of excess. Antique Shaker furniture and reproductions are prized as much as the simple, delicious recipes from which they prepared their ample meals. Shakers invented the flat broom, the clothespin, the circular saw, and water-repellent fabric. When you visit Shaker Village of Pleasant Hill, you have the opportunity to see their tools being used, to walk through their gardens, to eat their food, and to sleep in one of their rooms. You can buy some of their crafts and herbs in the gift shop.

In the guest rooms you find a strip of heavy pegs on the wall. The Shakers hung everything from clothes to chairs on such pegs. When you stay at Shaker Village, you will do the same. The rooms are furnished with their simple, functional furniture, rag rugs, and plain linens. The guest rooms do, however, have modern bathrooms, telephones, and television. The Shakers wouldn't have approved of television because they wanted to live apart from the secular world, but if they had been around long enough, they probably would have invented modern bathroom appurtenances themselves—and probably better ones.

At table, in the **Trustees House Restaurant,** you discover that the Shakers always adopted the food of the area in which they lived. In Kentucky, this means fried chicken and country ham, fried fish, and beef. The fresh vegetables from the village garden are passed at the table in bountiful quantity. You will know that the bread is fresh from the kitchen because you will have smelled it baking much of the day. The Shaker lemon pie reflects the Shakers' unwillingness to waste anything, even lemon peels. The pie is made with whole lemons, very thinly sliced, and baked with eggs and sugar in a double crust. Breakfast, lunch, and dinner are served to guests and to the public by reservation. Room rates begin at about $49 single, $56 double. The village is open for tours daily from 9:30 A.M. to 5:00 P.M. Admission is about $8.50 for adults, with discounts for teenagers and young children. To get to Shaker Village, go 7 miles northeast of Harrodsburg on U.S. Highway 68. Signs mark the drive. Phone (606) 734–5411.

In Harrodsburg proper, another inn reflects more typical life in the Old South. **Beaumont Inn,** 638 Beaumont Drive, is well known for its Southern cooking and hospitality. This is a family operation; the Dedman family is into its fourth generation of innkeepers. The inn is filled with family antiques and pictures of family ancestors. The Greek Revival–style brick building was completed in 1845 to replace a log school for young ladies after it burned down. The Dedmans publish a walking tour and history of the building, including such notes as the fact that the original window panes in the bedrooms have names and dates of engagements etched into them by the students who once lived at the school. The brochure also gives a history of some of the most interesting antiques and pictures in the inn.

Most people come to Beaumont Inn to eat. The food is basic country cooking done very well and offered in great variety and quantity. Standard entrees might include roast beef, aged country ham, and roast turkey. Such dishes as mashed potatoes and gravy, corn pudding, green beans, limas, and mock scalloped oysters (which may be salsify) accompany the entree. The service is efficient and down-home friendly. The restaurant serves lunch and dinner for guests and the public. The room rates, including a full breakfast, begin at about $75 for a double room, $15 less for a single. Phone (606) 734–3381 or (800) 352–3992.

SOUTH KENTUCKY

In the 1830s **Bowling Green** was the most prosperous town in the area, because of its river trade. The Louisville and Nashville Railroad Company built tracks through Bowling Green in the 1850s, giving the local economy yet another boost. The population was an unusual mix of Protestants, with families originally from Virginia and Pennsylvania, plus Irish Roman Catholic and German immigrants who came to work on the railroad.

The mixed population also had mixed views on the issues underlying the Civil War. Bowling Green tried to stay neutral, though most people opposed secession. At the time the war began, people in the area favored the Union by about three to one; but local families often saw their men, in disagreement, go to both armies. Because the town was a key passage between Confederate Tennessee and Unionist Kentucky, both sides wanted to control it. Eventually, about 20,000 Southern troops moved into the area, and in November 1861 Bowling Green was named the Confederate capital of Kentucky. After the war Union troops came into town. As town historians tell it, Bowling Green was a long time recovering from the divisive presence of soldiers from both sides in the community.

Some of this story is told through exhibits in the **Kentucky Museum and Library,** on the campus of Western Kentucky University. In addition to changing exhibits, there is a permanent collection of photographs showing downtown Bowling Green as it used to be. The exhibit "Growing Up Victorian" gives you a look at what it was like to be a child in the late nineteenth century. Apparently, it was not fun. Children's activities were all shaped to teach them to be pious and polite, in keeping with the values of their parents. Parents wanted to produce and show off children who were supposed to be more like perfect little adults than real children. A Victorian girl's diary and a short audiovisual presentation explain the displays, which include furniture, clothes, and toys. In a reproduced family sitting room, formal parlor, and child's bedroom, you see examples of how parents orchestrated such training through pictures of grandparents, open Bibles, and sheet music such as "God Bless the Loved Ones at Home" left on the piano. The parlor is decorated as it would have been for a child's funeral—a realistic recognition of the fact that few families got by without losing a child. In another display, there is a large collection of Kentucky crafts and tools.

The Felts House, an 1830s log house with wood plank floors, is filled with reproduction furniture, household items, and clothing, giving you a sense of what it would have been like to live in a log house. And in the library, books, original manuscripts, family letters, photographs, newspapers, and local records document Kentucky history and Bowling Green's place in it.

The museum is open Tuesday through Saturday 9:30 A.M. to 4:00 P.M.; Sunday 1:00 to 4:00 P.M. The Felts House is open during regular museum hours in summer, but weekends only May through October. Admission is about $2.00 for adults, $1.00 for children, $5.00 for families. Admission is free on Sunday. Phone (502) 745-2592.

To get to the museum from I-65 South, take exit 28 to Bowling Green. Follow 31 West and Highway 68-80 (Adams Street) to Western Kentucky University. Just past Fourteenth Street, turn left. The museum is 5.5 miles from exit 28. From I-65 North, take exit 20 to Green River Parkway. From Green River Parkway, take exit 4. Turn right onto 31 West. Turn left onto University Boulevard and follow it to the museum, 4 miles from exit 4.

Two miles west of Bowling Green's town square, **Riverview,** 1100 West Main Avenue, overlooks the Barren River. This Victorian building has been restored to recall its years as a center of social life after the Civil War. Guided tours explore not only about the architecture and furnishings but also the lives of the family that lived here. One of the most interesting tours is "The Other Victorians: 19th Century Servant Life," presented the third Saturday of each month at 10:00 A.M. Riverview is open for guided tours from February until the Saturday before Christmas, Tuesday through Saturday 10:00 A.M. to 4:00 P.M.; Sunday 1:00 to 4:00 P.M. The last tour begins promptly at 4:00 P.M. Admission is about $3.50 for adults, $1.50 for students, $6.00 for families. Phone (502) 843–5565.

Ten miles west of Bowling Green, **Shakertown at South Union,** another restored Shaker community, this one begun in 1807, is a place to learn more about the Shaker way of life. It is especially interesting to compare what you see here with what you found at Shaker Village at Pleasant Hill (see page 112). Of course, the underlying principles of the communities were the same: communal ownership of property, living apart from the world, and celibacy.

Incidentally, the founder of the Shakers was Mother Ann Lee, who claimed that she was the female manifestation of Christ. Her motto was "Put your hands to work and give your hearts to God."

Shakers at South Union did that by saving, packaging, and selling garden seeds and making and selling fruit preserves. They earned a national reputation for producing high-quality products. South Union also produced handmade silk.

Several of the original buildings here have been restored. In the forty-room 1824 Centre House, the Shaker Museum displays examples of Shaker craftsmanship in boxes, baskets, fabric, tools, and furnishings. Reproductions of these items are for sale in the museum shop, along with books about Shaker society. The built-in cabinets and pegs on the walls are similar to those at Pleasant Hill. The architecture of Centre House, with its twin stairs and separate sleeping quarters, makes a clear visual representation of the Shaker policy of separating men and women.

The Shaker Tavern offers lunch and bed-and-breakfast accommodations in a Victorian-style building. The worldly atmosphere seems inconsistent with Shaker ideas, but the Shakers built the inn to attract customers, not to live in themselves. The museum is open March 15 through November 15, Monday through Saturday 9:00 A.M. to 5:00 P.M.; Sunday 1:00 to 5:00 P.M. Admission is about $3.00 for adults, with discounts for children. The Tavern is open the same months, Tuesday through Saturday, for lunch and overnight accommodations. Phone (502) 542–4167 for the museum, (502) 542–6801 for the tavern. To get to Shakertown from I–65, take exit 20 onto the Green River Parkway. Take exit 5 from the parkway onto U.S. Highway 68-80. Turn left and follow the signs.

About 64 miles south of Bowling Green via U.S. Highway 68, the **Hopkinsville** area reflects the difficult Civil War division and the equally tragic Cherokee Trail of Tears in 1838. On your way there, stop at the **Jefferson Davis Monument State Historic Site,** about 10 miles before Hopkinsville. The Davises lived here until 1889. Jefferson Davis was the only president of the Confederate States of America, which lasted from 1861 to 1865. The site is marked with a 351-foot-tall obelisk. An elevator takes you to the top for a great view of the surrounding countryside. The park includes picnic shelters, a playground, and a gift shop.

In Hopkinsville proper, the **Pennyroyal Area Museum,** 217 East Ninth Street, has exhibits about the forced relocation of the Cherokees as well as artifacts from the Civil War. Other exhibits pertain to agriculture (Hopkinsville is a tobacco town) and railroading. While you are at the museum, ask for a brochure for a self-guided walking tour of the downtown area. The museum is open April through November, Monday through Friday 9:00 A.M. to 4:00 P.M.; Saturday 10:00 A.M. to 3:00 P.M. Admission is about $1.00 for adults, half that for children. Phone (502) 887–4270.

Just north of Hopkinsville on U.S. Highway 41, at Ninth Street and Skyline Drive, the **Trail of Tears Commemorative Park** is located on what was a campground during the tribe's brutal forced march to Oklahoma. The campground is now a well-landscaped park, with life-size bronze statues of Chiefs Whitepath and Fly Smith, and the graves of some other chiefs. An information wall and a bronze plaque give some of the historical details and show the route of the march, and a courtyard of flags identifies the nine states involved in the relocation. The Heritage Museum, in a restored log cabin on the grounds, emphasizes Cherokee art. An intertribal powwow is held in September, the first weekend after Labor Day. The museum is open April through September, Monday through Saturday 10:00 A.M. to 4:00 P.M. Admission is free, but donations are accepted. The park is always open. Phone (502) 886–8033.

Louisiana

LOUISIANA REFLECTS THE INFLUENCE of its earliest settlers—the Spanish; the French; the French-speaking Cajuns, who came from Nova Scotia—and, of course, the Creole and Choctaw Indians, who were already here when the Europeans arrived. Louisiana entered the Union in 1812, just in time to be invaded by the British at the end of the War of 1812. The pirate Jean Lafitte helped a ragtag collection of American troops defeat the British and, as a consequence, became enough of a hero to attach his name permanently to many things in Louisiana, from buildings to streets to bridges.

The state has lots of bridges because water spreads everywhere from the Gulf of Mexico, lakes, and the Red and Mississippi Rivers. The region's soil is rich with the fertile silt carried from the north and deposited at rivers' end. The state is almost half wetlands; south Louisiana has more wetlands than Holland. New Orleans is enough below sea level to require burying the dead in tombs above ground level.

The fertile land encouraged vast plantations, while the abundance of water in tidal bays and bayous created the swamps—the two main geographic features of the state. Both the plantations and the swamps played a role in shaping antebellum Louisiana. Before the Civil War began, the state had several thousand plantations, growing mostly indigo, sugar, and cotton. The Louisiana planters were some of the richest in the country, and they lived extravagantly, ostentatiously, in a slave-supported economy.

Louisiana

N

Mississippi River

Southeast Louisiana

• St. Francisville

⊙ Baton Rouge

New Iberia
•

• Franklin

New
Orleans

Mississippi R

South Central
Louisiana

The Civil War destroyed much of the state economically; marching and marauding soldiers destroyed fine homes and fields. Still, about a thousand of the splendid old plantation homes remain. Many are restored, and quite a few are open for public tours.

As for the swamps, they supported another, simultaneous, way of life. It stands to reason that in a land consisting nearly of half water, not everyone could be a planter. Many people made a living harvesting the bounty of the swamps—crayfish, alligators, and birds. To experience antebellum Louisiana in all its diversity, therefore, you need to tour not only the plantations but also the swamps.

SOUTHEAST LOUISIANA

Beginning on solid land, a good place to start exploring Louisiana is in one of its oldest towns, **St. Francisville,** established in the early 1800s on a narrow ridge above the Mississippi River. If you are driving south from Natchez, Mississippi, St. Francisville is an easy drive down U.S. Highway 61. Incidentally, local historians estimate that about two thirds of the known American millionaires before the Civil War had plantations on the stretch of road from Natchez to New Orleans. St. Francisville, located in about the middle of that stretch, had a generous share of them.

The town started out as not much more than muddy lanes. Then a hotel, a newspaper, the second library in Louisiana, a Masonic lodge, and a courthouse all sprang up in less than two decades. In the National Register Historic District today, 146 structures stand, most intact since they were built. This makes an excellent orientation to the area. The **West Feliciana Historical Society,** in its museum at the corner of Baton Rouge and Ferdinand Streets, offers a four-page tour guide and map detailing the main sites and their histories. The museum includes exhibits about local history and provides tourist information and guidebooks. It is open Monday through Saturday 9:00 A.M. to 4:00 P.M.; Sunday 1:00 to 4:00 P.M. Closed holidays. Phone (504) 635–6330.

Barrow House, 524 Royal Street, toward the river, is an 1809 saltbox with a Greek Revival wing added in the 1860s. It has cast-iron–railed balconies, much as you'd find in New Orleans. Barrow House operates as a bed-and-breakfast inn and also serves dinner by reservation. The main house is furnished with fine antiques, including a Prudent Mallard rosewood armoire and a queen-size (believe it or not) bed with a Spanish moss mattress. (For 200 years people in Louisiana traditionally filled their mattresses with Spanish moss; no one has found a better use for it.)

Part of the same inn, the Printer's House, next door, was built about 1780 for the Spanish Capuchin monks who first settled here. The cottage is a restored post-and-beam structure. The Victorian and Empire rooms and suites in this building are especially private.

Altogether, the inn has five rooms and three suites in two buildings, all with private bath. The innkeepers, Lyle and Shirley Ditloff, dispense Southern hospitality with remarkable insight into each guest's temperament and inclination toward sociability. In other words, they help you if you want help, chat if you want to talk, and leave you alone if you want privacy. Rates begin at about $90. Phone (504) 635–4791.

About 4 miles north of St. Francisville, on U.S. Highway 61, the twenty acres of **Afton Villa Gardens** reflect the Southern love of formality and flowers. The original plantation dates back to 1849. Its villa took eight years to construct, but when it was finally finished, it had everything—towers, turrets, stained glass, marble, ornate plaster, even Dresden china doorknobs. The first owner, David Barrow, considered building a moat, but decided that it would attract mosquitoes. You enter the property through a wrought-iron entrance with a brick Gothic gatehouse next to a pond and fountain, then continue through an archway canopied with live oaks, Spanish moss, and huge old azaleas. Because Union soldiers assumed that the Gothic gateway opened onto a cemetery and thus walked on past without entering, this villa survived the Civil War. But in 1960, the house burned down. What's left are the entrance, the gardens, terraces, trees, and, now, a cemetery. The house has been replaced by Italian statues. The landscape was originally designed by a French landscape artist, whose influence is still evident in the brick paths that lead through formal boxwood mazes softened with seasonal flowering plants. Grassy terraces create a transition into the wooded perimeter. The gardens are open March through June and October through November, daily 9:00 A.M. to 4:30 P.M. Closed Thanksgiving. Admission is about $4.00 for adults; children under age twelve are admitted free. Phone (504) 635–6773.

Just east of Highway 61, on State Highway 10, **Rosedown,** a major tour plantation, has not only gardens but also a restored mansion furnished with Federal, Empire, and Victorian antiques. This plantation demonstrates what antebellum Southerners with good taste could accomplish when money and labor were no object. The main part of the house is of cypress, painted white. It has Doric columns and double galleries, plus three brick-and-stucco wings that were added later. Daniel Turnbull, an Englishman descended from George Washington, built the home. Then he and his wife, Martha Barrow, traveled to Europe to find pieces suitably elegant to furnish it. Because the plantation stayed in the family until 1956, when it was bought to be restored and opened to the public, most of Rosedown's original furnishings are still in the house. You will also find some fine works of art still in place, most notably several original Audubons—not just birds, but also the portrait of a young girl Audubon had come to West Feliciana Parish to tutor.

The soil at Rosedown was fertile and the climate conducive to horticulture. Moreover, Mrs. Turnbull was a knowledgeable gardener who liked to experiment—easy to do when she had all the money and all the labor she needed to develop her plans. Mrs. Turnbull's gardens have been restored from detailed diaries that she kept to record the progress of her horticultural experiments. Some of the plantings are more than one hundred years old. As you admire the gardens, remember that although Mrs.

"A Little Bit of Heaven Right Here on Earth"

In her book *A Tourist's Guide to West Feliciana Parish,* Anne Butler Hamilton writes that Mrs. Martha Turnbull's diaries record thirty years of daily gardening observations, followed by her accounts after the Civil War of weeds taking over, even though she tried to keep the gardens up by working alongside helpers whom she paid in produce from the plantation. Subsequent generations of women in the family struggled to keep the property from deteriorating entirely when the boll weevil dealt another blow to their economic base, already nearly destroyed by the Civil War.

In 1956 Catherine Fondren Underwood, of Houston, Texas, bought the property and began a restoration that was notable for saving not only the house and furnishings but also the gardens and outbuildings.

Turnbull would have directed the digging and planting, she probably would not have had her own hands in the ground during the plantation's good years. Rosedown is open March through October, daily 9:00 A.M. to 5:00 P.M.; November through February, daily 10:00 A.M. to 4:00 P.M. Closed December 24 and 25. Admission is about $10 for adults, half that for children under age twelve. Phone (504) 635–3332.

South of St. Francisville, still on State Highway 61, in the **Audubon State Commemorative Area,** is **Oakley,** the tall plantation house in which the painter John James Audubon lived while he was working on his famed book *Birds of America*. The house, built in 1799, reflects the West Indies influence rather than the more elaborate Greek Revival style that became popular for plantation homes in the 1800s.

Oakley was designed for comfort in a hot, humid climate. The building sits on a brick basement and rises unusually high, with an attic on top of two stories. Both the basement and the attic help insulate the house from the sun's radiant heat, while the position and shape of the house make the most of prevailing breezes. The top floors have galleries to catch the breeze, with jalousies to keep out the sun. The home is much more simple than later plantation structures in the area—just two rooms deep inside, with no hallways. The staircases are on the outside of the building.

Although the place is famous now because Audubon lived here, he did not own the home. It was built by Ruffin Gray and passed through the generations in that family. The State of Louisiana acquired and restored Oakley in 1947. It is furnished in Federal style, as it would have been when Audubon lived in it. In addition to works by Audubon, displays include a collection of lighting fixtures dating from the late 1600s and early housekeeping artifacts. The outside kitchen and a barn have been reconstructed. Formal gardens with roses and crape myrtles set among large old live oaks approximate what would have been growing originally, and nature trails winding through the one hundred acres give you a chance to enjoy the wildlife that appealed so much to Audubon. The area is open daily 9:00 A.M. to 5:00 P.M. Closed Thanksgiving, Christmas, and New Year's Day. Admission is about $2.00 for adults, free for senior citizens and children. Phone (504) 635–3739. To get to Oakley, go south from St. Francisville on U.S. Highway 61 to Louisiana Highway 965. Turn left and drive 2.9 miles.

Another plantation in the area, **Greenwood,** north of St. Francisville a few miles off Louisiana Highway 66, differs from Oakley in every way imaginable. A Greek Revival–style mansion built in 1830, Greenwood is anything but simple. It was built on a 12,000-acre plantation where 750 slaves toiled in cotton and sugarcane fields. The mansion has twenty-eight exterior brick columns; a 70-foot central hall flanked by large, high-ceilinged rooms; and doors adorned with silver doorknobs and hinges. Outside, a reflecting pond dug by slaves to make bricks for the columns blends peacefully into the landscape, shining with the muted grays and greens of live oak trees draped in Spanish moss. Some of the trees are more than 150 years old.

The mansion isn't. Although it survived the Civil War because Federal troops used it as a hospital, it was struck by lightning in 1960. Everything burned but the twenty-eight brick columns. Since then the house has been reconstructed, without the original plans, from information provided by old photographs and interviews with people who had been at Greenwood. The reconstruction project proceeded almost like an archaeological dig, using remains from the fire as clues to how the house had been designed. The research and reconstruction took more than fifteen years. This is the house where the television miniseries about the Civil War, "North and South," was filmed. Greenwood is open March through October, daily 9:00 A.M. to 5:00 P.M.; November through February, daily 10:00 A.M. to 4:00 P.M. Admission is about $5.00 for adults, with substantial discounts for children. Phone (504) 655–4475. To get to Greenwood, take Highland Road from Louisiana Highway 66 and drive 3 miles.

The plantations discussed so far cluster around St. Francisville and are near U.S. Highway 61. Another series of plantations south of St. Francisville dots the Great River Road along the Mississippi, running roughly from Baton Rouge to Destrehan, outside New Orleans.

You can find some important sites in Baton Rouge. You might want to check them out before continuing on your plantation tours. The **Baton Rouge Visitor Information Center,** in the new state capitol building, has brochures and information about the city and nearby attractions. The center is open daily 8:00 A.M. to 4:30 P.M. Phone (504) 383–1825 or, outside Louisiana, (800) LA–ROUGE.

Now the second-largest city in Louisiana and a major industrial port, Baton Rouge was a prize that seven different nations struggled to win and keep. The influence of all of them, from the French Bourbons to the Confederacy, shows in the architecture, politics, traditions, and cuisine of the city. It shows also in the mannerisms of the citizenry: You will still encounter many people in Baton Rouge who practice the old ways—women who speak in soft voices and sweet accents, men and women who are routinely courteous, and folks who offer any kind of help you might need.

The old capitol building, overlooking the Mississippi River, served as the center for the Louisiana legislature until occupation by Union troops forced the citizens to move their government activities. The Union troops burned the original capitol building; it had to be rebuilt in 1882, when the state's government came back to Baton Rouge again. Louisiana's **Old State Capitol,** 100 North Boulevard at River Road, will make an impression on you whether or not you actually visit it. A white Gothic Revival–style castle, its designer, architect James Harrison Dakin, said in 1849 that he had "endeavored to adopt such a taste of style and architecture as would at once give the edifice a decided distinctive, classic, and commanding character as is appropriate to its purpose." But in 1855, a traveler from Natchez wrote that at a distance, the capitol's "white appearance and bulk . . . give it the look of an iceberg." (He also wrote that Baton Rouge was a fine-looking town and that its capitol was stately, but once you've called something other than an iceberg an iceberg, the damage is done.)

The huge Gothic building, with turrets on either side of the entrance and stained-glass windows above it, has an 1882 cast-iron staircase, stained-glass windows from the same date in the house and senate chambers, and, also dating from 1882, a cathedral dome and marble floors. The building was designated the Center for Political and Governmental History in 1994. In addition to film and video archives, interactive exhibits, and a multimedia presentation, the building, now a National Historic Landmark, has a museum devoted to local history. There is also a gift shop, specializing in Louisiana political memorabilia, books, maps, and artifacts. The museum is open Tuesday through Saturday 10:00 A.M. to 4:00 P.M.; Sunday noon to 4:00 P.M. Closed Christmas, New Year's Day, and state holidays. Admission is about $4.00 for adults; discounts are offered to senior citizens and students. Phone (504) 342–0500.

Magnolia Mound Plantation, 2161 Nicholson Drive, near the campus of the Louisiana State University, preserves the Creole heritage of the region. The authentically restored French Creole home was built about 1791 on a plantation of 950 acres, where first tobacco and indigo and then cotton were the cash crops. The front gallery of the house is 80 feet wide, with wooden balustrades. Square wooden columns support the roof. The house is constructed with hand-hewn, pegged timbers. Inside, a central chimney joins two back-to-back fireplaces, and the parlor ceiling is cov-

In with the New

L ouisiana's governmental offices moved to a new state capitol building that was built during the Great Depression. Then-governor Huey Long convinced the public and the Louisiana legislature that even though times were bad, an efficient new building would eventually save money; he resorted to a little arm-twisting from the rear of the house chamber during the voting to get approval. The building took only fourteen months to complete. It is the tallest state capitol in the United States—thirty-four floors of exterior limestone and interior marbles. Statues and friezes depict the stream of Louisiana history and commerce, from its pioneer days through the Civil War into contemporary times. Huey Long was assassinated in the building in 1935, just three years after it was finished. He is buried on the grounds. His statue faces the building and, inside, a bronze relief of his image, donated by the United Confederate Veterans, hangs over the elevators.

ered with a striking blue material. The furnishings are Louisiana- and Federal-style antiques from the 1800s.

Outside, an overseer's house, pigeonnier, detached kitchen, gardens, and carriage house re-create other aspects of the plantation's life. Costumed guides demonstrate open-hearth cooking, using mostly ingredients grown on the site. Some of the live oaks that surround the house are more than two centuries old. Magnolia Mound is open Tuesday through Saturday 10:00 A.M. to 4:00 P.M.; Sunday 1:00 to 4:00 P.M. Closed major holidays and Mardi Gras Day. Admission is about $3.50 for adults, with discounts for senior citizens and children. Phone (504) 343–4955.

While you are in the area, you might stroll the **Louisiana State University** (LSU) campus, established in 1850. The landscaping, with stretches of grass and paths lined with live oaks, seems quintessentially Southern. The campus is 1.5 miles south of downtown Baton Rouge, between Highland Road and Nicholson Drive. Phone (504) 388–3202.

The **LSU Arboretum,** on twelve landscaped acres at 11855 Highland Road, provides an opportunity to learn about trees and plants native to Louisiana, all of them labeled for identification. The arboretum is open daily in March, April, May, October, and November from 8:00 A.M. to 3:00 P.M. Guided tours are available by appointment. Admission is free, but donations are welcomed. Phone (504) 769–2363.

Another project of LSU, the **Rural Life Museum,** on the 450-acre Burden Research Plantation, gives you a detailed view of life and culture in preindustrial Louisiana. The museum takes up five acres of the plantation and includes more than twenty buildings. Some of them were moved from other sites in the state; some are copies of typical plantation buildings. The museum complex comprises three areas: the barn, the working plantation, and folk architecture. In the barn, you will find hundreds of farm tools and home implements that were part of daily rural life until the early twentieth century. Exhibits are devoted to logging, medicine, lighting, textiles, slavery and African interests, wood crafts, toys, Indian items, and the Civil War. In the folk architecture division, seven buildings represent the various aspects of early Louisiana life—a church, a pioneer's cabin with corncrib and potato house, a shotgun house, an Acadian house, and a dogtrot house. An outdoor oven stands behind the Acadian house; there are a syrup house and sugarcane grinder next to the dogtrot house. The working plantation complex includes a commissary, overseer's house, kitchen, slave cabins, sick house, schoolhouse, blacksmith's shop, sugar house, and grist mill. They are all furnished as they would have been to accommodate the basic activities of life on a nineteenth-century working plantation in Louisiana. The small outhouses behind the slave cabins and the "four-holer" near the overseer's house and schoolhouse introduce a note of unromantic reality into the scene.

Next to the museum, paths lead you through the **Windrush Gardens,** twenty-five acres of lakes and semiformal gardens where crape myrtles, azaleas, camellias, and other plants typical of nineteenth-century plantation gardens grow. The museum and gardens are open daily 8:30 A.M. to 5:00 P.M. Closed major holidays. Admission is about $5.00 for adults, with discounts for senior citizens and children. Phone (504) 765–2437. To get to the museum and gardens, take exit 160 from I–10. The complex is at the intersection of Essen Lane and I–10.

As for food, it is hard to find a bad meal in Baton Rouge. The restaurants reflect not only the rich diversity of the city's early settlers but also the eclectic tastes and love of food that typify the local population. Possibilities range from Indian, Lebanese, and Mediterranean to Italian and Chinese.

Many restaurants also offer Cajun and Creole cuisines. But for regional cooking emphasizing regional ingredients, you might try the well-established restaurant **Mike Anderson's Seafood,** at 1031 West Lee Drive in Baton Rouge. The restaurant has been in business for more than twenty years, during which time it has established a reputation for creative treatments of fresh gulf shrimp, lump crabmeat, crawfish, and many kinds of fresh fish—all the fish and seafood indigenous to the area. For people who don't eat anything with shells or fins, Mike Anderson's also serves USDA. prime steak. Cocktails are available. The restaurant is open for lunch and dinner every day. Closed major holidays. Phone (504) 766–7823.

Downtown, **Phil's Oyster Bar,** 5162 Government Street, serves fresh Louisiana oysters on the half shell, as well as seafood po'boys, practically a dietary staple in south Louisiana. The restaurant is open Monday through Saturday 10:30 A.M. to 9:30 P.M. Phone (504) 924–3045.

On the campus of the Louisiana State University, the **LSU Faculty Club,** Highland Road at Raphael Semmes, serves Southern lunches, including seafood, daily specials, sandwiches, and salads. The restaurant welcomes the public as well as faculty members. Open Monday through Friday 11:30 A.M. to 1:30 P.M. Phone (504) 388–2356.

Outside the city, **The Cabin Restaurant** serves traditional Louisiana fare such as po'boys, chicken gumbo, and fried seafood in a group of restored slave cabins. The restaurant serves lunch and dinner daily. Closed Christmas and New Year's Day. Large enough to handle bus tours, this is a high-volume, friendly place. Phone (504) 437–3007. To get to the restaurant, take Sorento exit 182 from I–10 and go west on State Highway 22 to where it intersects with State Highway 44.

The following suggestions take you to some of the major plantations on the roads that hug both sides of the Mississippi, in the order that you would reach them if you were floating down the river on a raft. This means crossing the river several times as you move from Baton Rouge toward New Orleans. If you prefer, you can look at a map and simply drive down one side of the river and up the other. This listing covers some of the better-known operations as well as some more recent discoveries, but it is by no means an encyclopedic guide to plantations on the Mississippi. New restorations and businesses constantly appear. Stop at any place that is open to the public that catches your eye, old or new, whether it is mentioned here or not.

Overload Warning!

Visiting more than two or three plantations in a day will blur their characteristics in your mind, make your feet swell, and send you screaming to the nearest chain motel begging for a room with chrome or plastic or fake pine paneling—anything, anything at all without history, significance, or character. If you try to see all the plantations in one trip, you won't enjoy any of them because you simply can't absorb so much information in a short time. The details soon begin to run together.

At **Whitecastle,** on the west side of the Mississippi River, the largest plantation home in the South, **Nottoway,** offers an astonishing tour, overnight bed-and-breakfast accommodations, and Cajun and Creole cuisines. Built by a sugar planter, John Hampden Randolph, Nottoway is a product of the days when fabulously wealthy planters strove to outdo one another in the splendor of their mansions. The standard spiel about Nottoway notes that the building is a blend of Greek and Italian architecture built from the period 1849 to 1859, with 200 windows and 165 doors, constructed as part of a 7,000-acre sugar plantation. But there's much more to say about Nottoway. In addition to its elaborate columns and ornamentation, the mansion had a ten-pin (bowling) alley, running water, indoor bathrooms, gas-burning fireplaces, and a communications system—all installed well ahead of the times. Moreover, it is hard to communicate the sheer size of the place. Its sixty-five rooms occupy nearly 65,000 square feet. You enter the mansion through 11-foot-high front doors into a hall with a 16-foot-high ceiling. The main staircase leading from the entrance hall has a mahogany railing and stairs so wide that it is possible for a tour group going up to pass another coming down without anyone's having to scrunch.

Six of Randolph's eight daughters were married in the 65-foot-long white ballroom, where silver bellpulls for calling servants still hang near fireplaces with white marble mantels. Here the Randolph daughters were presented to society and participated in much of the plantation's extravagant entertainment. (You can rent this same ballroom for your wedding!)

Across the hall, in the gentleman's study, a curved mirror fit into the

Nottoway was built between 1849 and 1859, when wealthy planters tried to outdo one another with their extravagant mansions. The house is nearly 65,000 square feet in area.

wall made it possible to keep an eye on the festive daughters of the household. Green velvet drapes puddle luxuriously on the floor. Every room on the tour, from the master bedroom to the music room, has examples of good (though extravagant) taste, careful planning, and the money to have them properly executed.

Except for some damage to outbuildings and the grounds, Nottoway survived the Civil War in pretty good shape. Although Yankees came up from their boats on the Mississippi to camp on the grounds, a Union gunboat officer who had once been a guest in the home intervened to protect the building. It has been restored and furnished in period with many of the original antiques.

Nottoway is open for guided tours, which take at least an hour and a half, every day from 9:00 A.M. to 5:00 P.M. Closed Christmas. Admission is about $8.00 for adults, with substantial discounts for children.

You can stay overnight at Nottoway in one of thirteen guest rooms, divided between the mansion and the overseer's cottage. Rates, which include sherry, the mansion tour, wakeup breakfast (sweet potato muffins, juice, and coffee), full plantation breakfast, and use of the pool, range from about $95 to $250 per room or suite.

A meal in the restaurant at Nottoway is also a grand experience. The cuisine, which is basically Creole and Cajun, concentrates on the crab, shrimp, fish, game, and vegetables of the area. One reviewer raved over an appetizer of fresh crab cake served on eggplant and covered in a spicy seafood sauce. A typical dinner entree might be quail with pasta in a sauce containing gulf shrimp. Desserts are extravagant, and the wine list includes domestic and imported choices. The restaurant overlooks the mansion and courtyard of the plantation. Open for lunch daily 11:00 A.M. to 3:00 P.M., for dinner 6:00 to 9:00 P.M.

For information about Nottoway tours, bed-and-breakfast accommodations, and restaurant reservations, phone (504) 545–2730 or (504) 545–2409. In Baton Rouge, phone (504) 346–8263.

To get to Nottoway from Baton Rouge, take I–10 west to the Plaquemine exit and follow State Highway 1 for 18 miles south to the plantation.

On the east side of the Mississippi, **Tezcuco Plantation,** at **Burnside,** represents an entirely different kind of plantation experience, because the old home is not the most important feature on the grounds. Tezcuco offers tours, bed-and-breakfast accommodations, and a restaurant. And here, more than at many plantations, you will feel that walking around the grounds is a natural and comfortable part of your visit.

The main house, finished in 1855, is now restored and open for tours. Actually, though it is called a raised cottage, the building has many features usually associated with larger plantation mansions. The house is built of brick made on the plantation by slaves and of cypress cut from swamps on the plantation. It has dormer windows on all four sides of the roof, a wide stairway in the front leading up to the gallery, and six square wood pillars supporting the roof entablature. Inside, the house is notable for a wide central entrance hall and large rooms with 16-foot-high ceilings. The ceiling cornices and center rosettes are made of intricately detailed plaster. The interior doors and window sashes have the original hand-painted faux-bois

Ordinary People. Sort of.

John Hampden Randolph, born in Virginia on March 24, 1813, married Emily Jane Liddell either in 1837 or 1841, depending on which of her notes you believe. Randolph received $20,000 and twenty slaves from her family as her dowry. The couple had eleven children, eight of them girls. In a family photograph with two of their young daughters, John and Emily appear comely but not extraordinary in any way, except that John's dark hair is charmingly curly and his trousers seem a bit tight, even for the period.

According to a thoroughly researched little book by E. J. Bourgeois II and P. T. Stuyck, *Nottoway: History of the Grand Manor* (copies are available at the plantation), Randolph was an intelligent, canny businessman who kept meticulous, minutely detailed records of his transactions. His records show that he protected his investment in his slaves by bringing an Episcopalian priest to the plantation once a month and a doctor every week, thus maintaining both the physical and spiritual health of all who lived there.

Apparently he was also considerate of his family and relatives. His records include praiseful letters from them and show that he spent generous sums on his children's education and music lessons.

Mrs. Randolph turned out to have a good head for business, too. At one point she tried to recover the sum of her dowry. After Randolph died she not only kept running Nottoway but also bought Victoria Plantation from another widow. In 1889 she sold Nottoway for $100,000.

(false grain) finish popularized by the French. The furnishings—fine antiques of the period—include Charles Eastlake and Prudent Mallard pieces as well as Meissen porcelains and Limoges china dating from about 1850. Guides in antebellum dress, hoop skirts and all, take you through the rooms and point out their important features. In the little girl's bedroom, for instance, you learn that girls were taught to embroider samplers to help

The bed-and-breakfast accommodations at Tezcuco are in renovated and improved slave cabins.

them master color, the alphabet, religious ideas, and stitches. You can see the kinds of dolls with which such a young girl would play and the sort of bed in which she might sleep.

Other structures on the property, a chapel, a life-size dollhouse, and the blacksmith shop, for example, are equally interesting. Most of the out-buildings are not original to the property but have been brought in from other locations. The slave cabins have been refurbished and improved. Now usually called "cottages," they house most of the bed-and-breakfast accommodations. Most have kitchens, and all have air-conditioning and television. They are furnished with a mix of furniture that is both antique and just old. The pecky cypress–paneled walls set off the work of Louisiana artists. Most of the cottages have front porches with rockers, inviting guests to sit chatting back and forth from one cottage to another. If you spent the night, a full Creole breakfast is delivered to your door.

The impressive old live oaks festooned in Spanish moss, without which one simply cannot have a Louisiana plantation, surround the house and help integrate the buildings.

Also on the plantation grounds, the restaurant, serving breakfast and lunch, emphasizes regional entrees and appetizers ranging from a traditional chicken andouille gumbo (andouille is a sausage) to fried alligator and catfish. Side orders of fried okra and dirty rice fit the cuisine style. Of the desserts, bread pudding with praline rum sauce is the most "Southern" choice. In the sandwich category, po'boys of fried shrimp or catfish practically scream "authenticity." The restaurant serves beer and wine. It is open every day 8:00 A.M. to 3:30 P.M.

A new feature at Tezcuco, **River Road African American Museum and Gallery,** was established to collect, preserve, and interpret artifacts that "provide positive information about the history and culture of African Americans." The museum honors all those slaves who were bought and brought to Burnside in 1858 to work the sugar and rice plantations. Many of their descendants still live along the Mississippi, and the museum's records provide an opportunity to research African-American ancestry. The artwork in the museum reflects the art, music, dance, stories, cooking, and crafts that African Americans have passed down through generations, from before the time of slavery to the present. Some of the exhibits, such as of African masks, help demonstrate practices in Africa that remain part of the African-American heritage. Other exhibits include contemporary art, information about black musicians, photographs of famous African Americans and sports figures, donations from families in the area, and a registry of African-American Civil War army veterans from 1890. The museum is open Wednesday through Sunday 1:00 to 5:00 P.M. Donations are welcomed. Phone (504) 644–7955.

The plantation is open for tours daily 9:00 A.M. to 5:00 P.M. Closed Thanksgiving, Christmas, and New Year's Day. House tours cost about $6.00 for adults, with discounts for children and senior citizens. Bed-and-breakfast accommodations, including a house tour, complimentary wine, coffee, and tea, and a full breakfast, begin at about $60 for a double room. For information about tours, accommodations, and the restaurant, phone (504) 562–3929. To get to Tezcuco, take exit 179 from I–10 onto L.A. 44 south to Burnside. The plantation is 1 mile north of the Sunshine Bridge on State Highway 44.

Still at Burnside, close to Tezcuco, **Houmas House Plantation** offers guided tours by appropriately costumed guides. Like Nottoway, Houmas House stood at the center of a large sugar plantation and belonged to a wealthy planter, John Burnside, but that's where the similarities end. Houmas House was built in two stages—a four-room French- and Spanish-style house was built in the late 1700s, while a Greek Revival front was added in 1840. The house is elegant in its symmetrical simplicity. It has fourteen doric columns, dormer windows, a three-story spiral staircase, and two hexagonal garconniers flanking the main house outside. Burnside, who bought the house from the Prestons of South Carolina in 1857, entertained lavishly here. The mansion has been restored and furnished with antiques of the early 1800s. Appropriately, since Burnside never married, it gives no sense of family life. Outside, formal gardens and live oaks continue the symmetry of the architecture. Houmas House is open for tours by guides dressed in antebellum costume every day 10:00 A.M. to 5:00 P.M.; open November, December, and January, 10:00 A.M. to 4:00 P.M. Closed Thanksgiving, Christmas, and New Year's Day. Admission is about $7.00 for adults, with discounts for children. Phone (504) 473-7841.

Now, crossing the Sunshine Bridge to the west side of the river again, follow State Highway 18 to **Vacherie.** Here is **Oak Alley Plantation,** another place where you can tour, shop, eat, and sleep. Oak Alley is especially noted for its live oaks, which form a living green "alley" from the Mississippi River to the plantation house. These trees are older than the house. A French settler planted twenty-eight oaks in two rows 80 feet apart, sometime in the early 1700s or possibly even before that. They apparently were moved there from their natural site along the riverbank to form the long alley from the river to the settler's cabin. When Jacques Roman built the mansion in 1836, he deliberately set it at the same site. His idea was that the alley of trees would set off the mansion; over time, however, the trees have stolen the show. Twenty-eight columns surrounding the house, and twenty-eight slave cabins beyond it, echo the twenty-eight trees.

The restaurant on the plantation serves Cajun and Creole food, often from recipes that originated in local family kitchens. Overnight accommodations are provided in cottages on the grounds. Rates begin at about $85 per cottage and include a continental breakfast.

The plantation is open for tours: November, December, January, and February daily 9:00 A.M. to 5:00 P.M. Closed Thanksgiving, Christmas, and New Year's Day. Admission is about $6.50 for adults, with discounts for children. The restaurant is open daily 9:00 A.M. to 3:00 P.M. Phone (504) 265-2151.

Oak Alley is a large operation, geared up for everything from bus tours to corporate retreats. The place exudes the kind of Scarlett-and-Rhett glamour long associated with old Dixie. Just 3 miles away, **Laura,** a Creole plantation built in 1895, offers an entirely different kind of experience, illustrating again the fascinating diversity of the South even in its plantation days. Laura provides a glimpse of plantation life that never had anything to do with hoop skirts or mint juleps.

Originally the working sugarcane plantation of two Creole families, Laura is one of the oldest and largest plantation complexes on River Road. It has twelve buildings, including two manor houses, slave quarters, and Creole cottages. It was here, in the 1870s, that the West African folktales of Compair Lapin, or Br'er Rabbit, were first recorded in America in Creole French, about ten years before Joel Chandler Harris published them. Laura is one of the last surviving Creole plantations. The French language and traditional customs were still in use as recently as 1984. For eighty-four years the plantation was run by Creole women, who were known as sharp businesspeople and skilled managers, so it is appropriate that the restoration and documentation focus on the lives of the women, children, and slaves.

The plantation tours, emphasizing not only authenticity but also anecdotal detail, are based on 5,000 pages of documents from the National Archives in Paris, France, and on diaries of Laura Locoul, who lived there and for whom the plantation was named. The tours give you a realistic, rather than a romanticized, view of 200 years of life on the plantation. One notable display is the largest collection of family artifacts original to any Louisiana plantation. It includes clothing, photo albums, and business and slave records. There are personal items, too—even such sentimental things as baby teeth saved by the family. Life-size cutout pictures of family and slaves positioned strategically around the house add another element of realism. All the pieces on display were recovered from various places in the United States and France.

The renovation at Laura left places where you can see the brick-between-post construction of the walls, Civil War cannonballs embedded in the walls, and penciled lines marking the ages and heights of plantation children. Unretouched paint reflects the Creole taste for bright colors—yellow, green, red—as well as more subdued mauve and gray.

Laura is open for guided tours daily 9:00 A.M. to 5:00 P.M. Closed major

Laura, a Creole plantation built in 1895, shows you a kind of plantation life that had nothing to do with hoop skirts or mint juleps.

holidays. Admission is about $5.00 per person. Phone (504) 265–7690. Laura is located on the west side of the Mississippi River, at 2247 Highway 18 in Vacherie.

From Vacherie, you can zip back over the Sunshine Bridge or take the ferry to **Reserve** and **San Francisco Plantation.** In the book of photographs *Louisiana's Plantation Homes* (photos by Dick Dietrich, text by Joseph Arrigo), it is noted that this mansion looks like "the ornate steamboats that plied the Mississippi in the 1800s." It certainly doesn't look like any other plantation home in the area, or anywhere in the South for that matter.

The architecture of the mansion is a mix of Victorian, Classic, and Gothic. It has an outsize ventilated roof; ornate grillwork and gingerbread trim decorate the exterior. Two huge, peaked cisterns, painted bright blue, rise nearly as high as the roof on either side of the house. Water could be piped from these into the house. Inside, the restored mansion is painted in bright colors, as the salons of riverboats were, and there are murals on the ceilings and faux marbling and graining on the woodwork and mantels.

The name of the plantation has nothing to do with the city in California. It is a derivation of a French phrase, *sans fruscins,* that means "without a penny in my pocket"—a reference to the financial state of the owner after construction. The plantation is open for tours daily 10:00 A.M. to 4:00 P.M. Closed Thanksgiving, Christmas, New Year's Day, Mardi Gras, and Easter. Phone (504) 535–3213.

Your next stop is on the same side of the river, less than 10 miles from the New Orleans airport, at **Destrehan.** Built in 1787 in West Indies style, **Destrehan Manor** is the oldest-documented plantation house remaining in the Lower Mississippi Valley. The plantation first produced indigo, corn, and rice, but it soon switched to sugarcane because it was more profitable. Brick garconniers were added to both sides of the house to accommodate Jean Noel Destrehan's growing family. The pirate Jean Lafitte often visited Destrehan; his ghost is said to appear from time to time to indicate where he hid his treasure in the walls. During the Civil War Union troops seized the house and used it to house freed slaves in a "freedman's colony." Costumed guides take you through the house and explain its history. Tours are available daily 9:30 A.M. to 4:00 P.M. Closed major holidays. Admission is about $5.00 for adults, with discounts for children and senior citizens. Phone (504) 764–9315. Destrehan Plantation is at 9999 River Road State Highway 48), 8 miles from the New Orleans International Airport, in Destrehan.

Destrehan also has a less-well-known plantation, where people actually live in the mansion. The tour guides are taught to think of the place as their home and the visitors as their personal guests. **Ormond Plantation** is located at 13786 River Road (State Highway 48). This home was built in the Louisiana Colonial style, modeled on the sugar plantations in the West Indies. It was once known for entertaining members of the Louisiana and Spanish governments. The handcarved furnishings from the 1850s are Spanish. Like Laura, the Ormond Plantation mansion's construction was brick between posts (bricks between cypress studs).

This is an unusual tour home in that guests who come for tours or lodging have the opportunity to move at will through the rooms. Displays are not roped off, although signs do request that you not pick up the china. Collections of antique dolls and antique slot machines are especially novel displays. The bed-and-breakfast guest rooms, furnished in period style but with the modern comforts of private baths and air-conditioning, are in the main house. The restaurant, which offers a gourmet Louisiana-style buffet lunch menu that changes every day Monday through Friday, is in two garconniers, or bachelor's quarters. Room rates, including a full breakfast, a tour of the plantation, and evening wine, cheese, and fruit, begin at about $125 per room. Because the guest rooms are also part of the mansion tour, you take possession at 4:30 P.M., after the last tour, and check out at 9:30 A.M., before the first morning tour. Phone (504) 764–8544.

Travelers often compare visiting **New Orleans** to visiting a foreign country. The first thing you have to do is learn to pronounce it properly: "N'arlins," or "New Or-yee-ans," but never, ever "New OrLEEns." Writers have produced some very fat guide books to this city that is famous, above all else, for its Mardi Gras festivities and its food.

Until you have seen it yourself, it is hard to believe how seriously old New Orleans society takes Mardi Gras specifically and parties generally. The very first thing the local citizens did after the Civil War ended was to bring back the Mardi Gras parade, almost as though it had never been interrupted. Mardi Gras peaks on Fat Tuesday (the last Tuesday before Lent), but the carnival season begins early in January and gains intensity in the two-week period before Ash Wednesday. Although people flock into the city from everywhere for Mardi Gras, in many ways it is a series of parties that natives of New Orleans keep for themselves alone. The parades are public spectacles, but the balls are private and invitations are coveted, and the crews who put together the floats and parades are basically secret societies. Local people sometimes go so far as to rent tenements along the parade routes, where they hold huge parties with amazing amounts of alcohol and the traditional Mardi Gras food, red beans and rice.

While it is all colorful and fascinating, Mardi Gras is not a particularly good time to visit New Orleans. The town is sufficiently overwhelmed with tourists to make people who work in hotels and restaurants surly; and prices go up, as does crime. Moreover, most of the city's attractions close on Mardi Gras Day.

But whenever you go to New Orleans, your activities will probably be concentrated in the French Quarter. Notable for its many fine old buildings and remarkable ironwork on balconies and gates, this was where New Orleans began. Technically, though, the French Quarter really isn't French any more. The earliest buildings were French structures, but fires in the late 1700s burned most of them; those that have replaced them are, for the most part, Spanish. The names of the streets, however, remain mostly French.

The French Quarter is the district between Canal Street, Rampart Street,

Julie Smith, in her mystery novels *New Orleans Beat* and *Jazz Funeral*, describes the small-town gossipy nature of old New Orleans society going back for generations. She also talks about the climate, including a comment about the air, which most people perceive as humid, being thought of as "soft" by locals. Hard as it may be to believe, people long accustomed to high humidity come to feel comfortable with it.

Esplanade Avenue, and the Mississippi River. The best way to see it is by walking. Brochures to guide you are available at the **Greater New Orleans Tourist and Convention Commission,** 529 St. Ann Street, New Orleans, LA 70130. Phone (504) 566–5031. It's common to begin a tour at Jackson Square, the heart of the Quarter from the earliest days of the city, but you can be sure of finding interesting architecture no matter where you set off.

If you would like to tour a New Orleans mansion, go about 3 blocks southeast of Jackson Square on Chartres Street to the **Beauregard-Keyes House,** 1113 Chartres Street, where Confederate general Pierre Beauregard lived for a couple years in the late 1860s. The Greek Revival house was built in 1826 and was restored later by Frances Parkinson Keyes. Costumed guides take you through the house, the furnishings of which include General Beauregard's bed. The house is open Monday through Saturday 10:00 A.M. to 3:00 P.M. Admission is about $4.00 for adults, with discounts for children and senior citizens. Phone (504) 523–7257.

Also on Chartres Street, the **New Orleans Pharmacy Museum,** 514 Chartres, displays not only old medical and pharmaceutical equipment but also a collection of voodoo cures and curses and a medicinal herb garden. The museum is open Tuesday through Sunday 10:00 A.M. to 5:00 P.M. Admission is about $2.00. Phone (504) 565–8027.

In the opposite direction, at 820 St. Louis Street, the **Hermann-Grima House,** a restored mansion built in 1831, will give you a close look at how an old New Orleans household operated. You can tour the slave quarters and also the Creole kitchen, where demonstrations of Creole cooking are held on Thursday (except in summer, when, especially in New Orleans, it's too hot to cook). The house is open Monday through Saturday 10:00 A.M. to 3:30 P.M. Admission is about $4.00 for adults, with discounts for children and students. Phone (504) 525–5661.

What's Cajun and What's Creole?

Good question. It is getting harder and harder to tell these cuisines apart. Historically, Creole cooking is the product of generations of mixed national influences—black, French, Spanish, and Southern—emphasizing regional seafood and produce, often using butter or cream sauces.

Southern writer John Edgerton, in his book *Southern Food,* called Cajun cooking "Creole's country cousin." Generally, Creole cooking used to be more complicated and rich, set upon the tables of the urban well-to-do by people whose main responsibility in the household was planning and preparing meals, while Cajun cooking was the home cooking practiced by rural folk making a meal of whatever they could fish, forage, or shoot. Their food was heavily spiced (Tabasco sauce was created in Louisiana in the 1860s), and it contained more beans, sausages, and vegetables than Creole dishes.

You will see another kind of household in **The Lower Pontalba 1850 House,** at 523 St. Ann Street. The Pontalba buildings were built in 1849 by the Baroness de Pontalba to encourage people to keep living in the area. All the rooms in this house, including the slave quarters and kitchen, are furnished with New Orleans antiques dating from the mid-1800s. The house is open for guided tours Wednesday through Sunday 10:00 A.M. to 5:00 P.M. Admission is about $3.00 for adults, with discounts for senior citizens and students. Children under age twelve are admitted free. Phone (504) 568–6968.

Gallier House Museum, 1118 Royale Street, is interesting because the architect James Gallier, Jr., who, like his father, designed many important buildings in Louisiana, designed this house for himself. The building has been restored and furnished in antiques of the 1860s. It is open for tours Monday through Saturday 10:00 A.M. to 4:30 P.M.; Sunday noon to 4:30 P.M. Admission is about $4.00 for adults, with discounts for students, children, and senior citizens. Phone (504) 523–6722.

To enliven the history of the various sites in the city, you might stop at **Musee Conti Wax Museum,** 917 Conti Street, to see the life-size wax figures in scenes representing New Orleans history. Napoleon Bonaparte is there, as well as the pirate Jean Lafitte and President Andrew Jackson. There are also many more contemporary materials.

When it comes to restaurants, you can stop at virtually any eating place in the French Quarter and expect good gumbo, barbecued shrimp, and étouffées. The most famous old restaurant in New Orleans is **Antoine's,** 713 St. Louis Street, about a block away from the Hermann-Grima House. Even if you don't eat here, the restaurant is fun to know about. It was founded in 1840 and has long been one of the spots for old New Orleans society. Antoine's is where the recipe for oysters Rockefeller was created. The recipe remains a secret; what you get under that name anywhere else is an approximation. The menu is French Creole and expensive.

The best way to eat at Antoine's is to get yourself invited by a native who can book into one of the smaller private dining rooms. In that situation, you will probably be treated to elaborate service, including after-dinner drinks and flaming desserts, which are served in a ring of fire that briefly seems to cover the entire table. Otherwise, the restaurant can be hard to get into (you must have a reservation), and in the main dining room, you are pretty much just another face in the crowd. Open for lunch and dinner except Sunday and major holidays. Phone (504) 581–4422.

Another French Quarter restaurant known for French Creole cuisine is **Galatoire's,** 209 Bourbon Street. The entrees here tend to be less expensive, and the dining room is almost always very busy. Reservations are not accepted, so you will probably have to wait to get in, but many knowledgeable local people feel that this restaurant captures the taste and atmosphere of the old city very well. The restaurant is open Tuesday through Sunday 11:30 A.M. to 9:00 P.M.; Sunday noon to 9:00 P.M. Closed major holidays. Phone (504) 525–2021.

Among the many lodging possibilities in New Orleans, the pirate surfaces again, at least in name, at **Lafitte Guest House,** 1003 Bourbon Street. The house was built in 1849 as a single-family home, and though it is now an inn with fourteen guest rooms, it retains something of its homey feeling, with Victorian furniture and oriental carpets. Some of the guest rooms in the main house still have the original black-marble mantels over the fireplaces. Some smaller rooms, in what used to be the slaves quarters, have exposed brick walls. Rates, including continental breakfast and evening wine with hors d'oeuvres, begin at about $80 per room in the off-season, higher during peak times. Phone (504) 581–2678 or (800) 331–7971.

Lamothe House, 621 Esplanade Avenue, another inn with an old-time feel in the French Quarter, was the home of a Louisiana sugar merchant in the late 1830s. The place is full of good-quality Victorian antiques. There are twenty guest rooms. Rates, including continental breakfast and evening libations, begin at about $75 per room. Phone (504) 947–1161.

At the edge of the Lower Garden District, **Terrell House,** 1441 Magazine Street, reflects the New Orleans party spirit in an unusual way. It was turned into an inn by the late Freddy Nicaud, who loved dining at Antoine's, collecting fine antiques for Terrell House, and Mardi Gras. Once, when a serious illness in the family made it necessary to cancel a birthday party that was to have been held on a riverboat, Nicaud insisted on at least taking a group to dinner in one of the private dining rooms at Antoine's. "We have to have *some* party," he said. Freddy died in 1994, just three weeks after having participated in all Mardi Gras activities.

Terrell House is glorious, with twin parlors, marble fireplaces, and guest rooms that open onto balconies. The antique furnishings, many from the Nicaud family, include New Orleans pieces, some by Prudent Mallard. Incidentally, Magazine Street is an excellent place to find antique shops away from the bustle of the French Quarter. The neighborhood sometimes looks a little rough, but it is probably safer than the French Quarter, and taxis are inexpensive and easy to find. Rates, including continental breakfast and evening cocktail, begin at about $70. Phone (504) 524–9859 or (800) 878–9859.

When you have finished viewing plantations and city sites, be sure to try a swamp tour. Most of these can be arranged from New Orleans or at the departing sites. Close to the city, the **Jean Lafitte Swamp Tours** leave from Lafitte Highway, about 15 miles away. The narrated tours of the history of the bayou take about two hours and feature wildlife from alligators to white-tailed deer. You can arrange to be picked up at your hotel. Phone (504) 689–4186. Rates begin at about $35, including transportation from your hotel, less if you don't need to be picked up, with discounts for children and senior citizens.

Cypress Swamp Tours, leaving from the little town of Westwego, near New Orleans, offer a variety of possibilities. Narrated by Cajun guides, the choices range from two-hour tours to see alligators and other waterlife, to a longer Cajun Stories Excursion, to a daylong "Cajun and Plantation Stories Excursion," which includes lunch and a tour of San Francisco Plantation (see page 138). Rates vary from about $20 to $50, depending on the tour, with discounts for children. Phone (504) 581–4501.

You will find more chances for swamp tours as you move into south-central Louisiana and the Bayou Lafourche in Cajun country.

SOUTH CENTRAL LOUISIANA

They call **Bayou Lafourche** "the longest 'street' in the world." Although it is only 45 miles southwest of New Orleans, the wetlands area reflects an entirely different way of life. The Cajun culture focuses on fish, water birds, alligators, and small game, and boats are the vehicles of choice.

Traveling west on Highway 90 from New Orleans and the Mississippi River brings you close to the little town of **Kraemer,** home of some excellent swamp tours. **Torres' Cajun Swamp Tours** features the Cajun guide Captain Roland Torres, who has made his living in the local swamps, lakes, and bayous since he was a young boy. He has taught the same skills to his three sons. As you float through the swamp in a flat-bottomed pontoon-style boat, you will see turtles, snakes, herons, owls, egrets, and alligators. Tours take about two hours. Rates begin at about $10 per person, with discounts for children and senior citizens. You must make a reservation; phone (504) 633–7739.

Zam's Bayou Swamp Tours and Restaurant gives you a chance to see swamp life in the wild and also a collection of live alligators and local animals, plus some preserved creatures. You can taste alligator and turtle meat in the restaurant. Tours are available every day starting at 10:30 A.M., 1:30 P.M., and 3:30 P.M. Reservations are not necessary. Rates are about $12.50 for adults, $6.00 for children. Phone (504) 633–7881. To get to Kraemer, go north from Highway 90 on Highway 307.

After your swamp tour, head into **Thibodaux,** which is nearby at the juncture of Louisiana Highways 1 and 20, to visit **Laurel Valley Village,** a rural-life plantation museum. With more than sixty structures still standing, this is the largest surviving nineteenth-century sugar plantation in the country. Among the buildings you can tour are a country store and schoolhouse from the early 1900s, plus some dwellings dating as far back as 1815. A store on the grounds sells items made by people who live in the Bayou

Lafourche area. Because many of the buildings on the property are under repair, you may not walk around at will but must take a guided tour. The entire operation is run by a nonprofit public group and volunteers. The village is open weekdays 10:00 A.M. to 4:00 P.M.; Saturday and Sunday 11:00 A.M. to 5:00 P.M. Closed holidays. Donations are welcomed. Phone (504) 447–2902 or (504) 446–7456. The village is 2 miles east of Thibodaux on State Highway 308.

In Thibodaux proper, the **Wetlands Acadian Culture Center,** run by the National Park Service, illustrates Cajun culture dating from the 1600s. The center is part of the Jean Lafitte National Historical Park and Preserve. Craft demonstrations and media presentations are part of the program. The center is open Tuesday through Thursday 9:00 A.M. to 6:00 P.M.; Friday through Sunday 9:00 A.M. to 5:00 P.M. Closed Christmas. Admission is free. Phone (504) 448–1375.

Thibodaux has an important old church, **St. John's Episcopal Church,** 718 Jackson Street. It is one of the oldest Episcopal churches west of the Mississippi River. The parish was organized in 1843; the building was consecrated in March 1845. The oldest Episcopal church building in Louisiana, St. John's is an example of Georgian church architecture rare in America. It is on the National Register of Historic Places. Holy communion is offered Sunday at 8:15 A.M. and 10:30 A.M. To arrange building tours, phone (504) 447–2910.

Another important Episcopal church stands just 18 miles away, in **Napoleonville,** on State Highway 1. **Christ Episcopal Church,** consecrated in 1854, is considered an excellent example of American Gothic architecture. Built of locally made Louisiana cypress and brick, the building has been damaged several times by storms and war, but has been restored each time. Holy communion is offered Sunday at 7:00 A.M. To arrange a building tour, phone (504) 447–2910.

These days, Napoleonville's main claim to fame is **Madewood Plantation,** a restored plantation home offering tours, bed-and-breakfast accommodations, and authentic Cajun dinners featuring such delicacies as shrimp pies, gumbos, and bread pudding. The mansion has an unusually homey feel, despite its Greek Revival style and white columns. Upstairs, one room is set up as a dressing room; its scoop-shaped bathtub would be filled and emptied with a bucket. In some of the other tour bedrooms, old clothes are laid out, apparently ready for someone to put them on. Madewood got its name because all the timber for the structure was cut on the property—the workers "made wood."

Newspaper stories about Madewood often include the information that its builder, Thomas Pugh, died of yellow fever shortly before the project was finished, in 1848. His wife, Eliza, took over and saw that the house was completed. She stayed on the plantation, married off her children, and, according to one account, "then used her skills to save the home from the ravages of the Civil War."

The current owners, Keith and Millie Marshall, continuing to develop the property, have moved some other old buildings onto the grounds, so your choices for guest rooms include five rooms in the mansion, one slave cabin, and three suites in the Charlet house. Overnight rates begin at about $165, single or double, and include full breakfast and dinner. Tour rates are about $5.00 for adults, with discounts for children and senior citizens. Closed Thanksgiving, Christmas, and New Year's Day. Phone (504) 369–7151. The plantation faces State Highway 308.

Now you will have to backtrack a little to get west of Napoleonville and drive north on U.S. Highway 90 to **Franklin, New Iberia,** and **St. Martinville,** along the Bayou Teche. These towns, all close to the highway, offer special notable plantations and gardens.

Unlikely as it sounds, Franklin was named for Pennsylvanian Benjamin Franklin, by an admirer who settled the town. Some settlers also came from "up north," and their Yankee connections probably kept Franklin from being ruined by Union troops during the Civil War. **Oaklawn Manor,** built in 1837, stands at the end of a long, winding drive through a huge grove of live oaks. Alexander Porter, who established the plantation to farm sugar, lost his wife and one of their two daughters after just four years of marriage. Porter stayed on the estate and, after retiring from politics, concentrated on improving his property, building the manor, and developing the grounds, even pruning the trees himself. Some of the live oaks are believed to have been growing since Christopher Columbus's era. The Greek Revival mansion has walls 20 inches thick, six Tuscan columns, and a ballroom that fills the entire third floor. One of the highlights of the mansion tour is a collection of prints and original oils by John James Audubon. The mansion is open for tours daily 10:00 A.M. to 4:00 P.M. Closed major holidays. Admission is about $6.00 for adults, with discounts for children. Phone (318) 828–0434. To get to Oaklawn, take exit 3211 off State Highway 90.

Next, New Iberia, a French Acadian–Spanish town dating from the late 1700s, has two popular attractions, Live Oak Gardens, and Shadows-on-the-Teche.

As the property's name implies, at **Live Oak Gardens,** 5505 Rip Van Winkle Road, the grounds are an important attraction. Not that anything is wrong with the house. A Victorian home built in 1870 by Joseph Jefferson, the third-highest-paid actor of his time, the house has been restored and appropriately furnished for tours. But it is especially lovely outside, and the grounds include a nature preserve. Twenty-five acres of gardens, where crape myrtles and other flowering plants scattered among live oaks are accented with fountains, make up another part of the tour.

In small, separate buildings, one art gallery features local works, and another gallery displays the largest public collection of duck decoys—both functional and ornamental—in Louisiana. Then you may get to see the real McCoy decoy, which is to say a live duck or two, if you take the narrated boat cruise on Lake Peigneur, which is included in the price of admission. A cafe on the property serves light meals (nothing unusual, though the guide does allow as how the catfish platter seems to impress Yankee tourists). Live Oak Gardens is open daily 9:00 A.M. to 5:00 P.M. Closed Thanksgiving, Christmas, and New Year's Day. Admission is about $10 for adults, with discounts for senior citizens and children. Phone (318) 365–3332. To get to Live Oak Gardens, go 6 miles southwest on State Highway 675/14.

Shadows-on-the-Teche, 317 East Main Street, is a plantation house built in 1834 in Greek Revival style, with overtones of French-Creole, Anglo-American, and Georgian architecture thrown in. The balance and symmetry of columns, chimneys, and so on, are classical. But the dormers in the gabled roof reflect the Anglo-American influence, and the chimneys are set in interior walls, in Creole fashion. The family owned several sugar plantations, but the house is a "town" house, apart from all of them. The mansion originally was lavishly furnished and landscaped, characteristics that were honored when the house was restored. The child's bedroom, for instance, features a full testered bed dressed in lacy white, a porcelain doll in her own cradle, and a dollhouse with its own balanced columns, dormers, and chimneys.

The people who lived in the house—four generations of the Weeks family—were as interesting as the building itself. Joseph Arrigo, in the text for the book *Louisiana's Plantation Homes* (photographs by Dick Dietrich), writes that David Weeks, like many other plantation masters, died just about the time his house was finished. His widow, Mary Clara, like so many planter's widows, ran the family's several plantations with notable success. During the Civil War, Union forces occupied the house and Miz Mary Clara kept to the attic, where, according to Arrigo, she died in 1863. The National Trust for Historic Preservation owns and operates the property. It is open for guided tours daily 9:00 A.M. to 4:30 P.M. Closed Thanksgiving, Christmas, and New Year's Day. Admission is about $5.00 for adults, with discounts for senior citizens and children. Phone (318) 369–6446.

Still traveling north, you will come to **St. Martinville,** which was settled in 1760. St. Martinville was notable as the place where Evangeline came to find her lover and discovered that he had already married someone else. The **Longfellow-Evangeline State Commemorative Area,** on the Bayou Teche, focuses on the Oliver Plantation house, built about 1836 with mud and moss chinked between cypress beams and shored up with brick. The area has an outdoor kitchen and an Acadian reproduction cabin. Kitchen gardens and an orchard demonstrate the kinds of food that would have been grown for families in the region. The area is open daily, 9:00 A.M. to 5:00 P.M. Closed Thanksgiving, Christmas, and New Year's Day. Admission is about $2.00 for adults; children and senior citizens are admitted free. Phone (318) 394–3754. The area is on State Highway 31.

Finally, near the intersection of Interstates 49 and 10, is **Lafayette.** Part of the area known as Acadiana, settled by a polyglot of peoples in the 1700s, this restored and re-created town offers a look at how the Acadians on the bayou lived in the early 1800s. Some of the buildings have been brought to the site from other places in Louisiana to create a balance among homes, barns, and such service structures as stores. The village is open daily 10:00 A.M. to 5:00 P.M. Closed major holidays. Admission is about $5.50 for adults, with discounts for senior citizens and children. Phone (318) 981–2364.

Mississippi

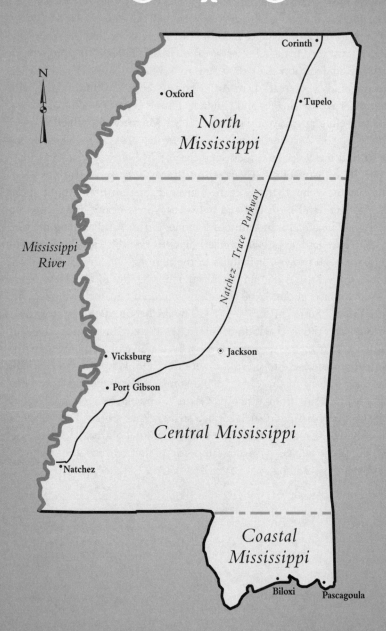

N

Corinth

Oxford

Tupelo

North
Mississippi

Natchez Trace Parkway

Mississippi
River

Vicksburg

Jackson

Port Gibson

Central Mississippi

Natchez

Coastal
Mississippi

Biloxi

Pascagoula

Mississippi

MISSISSIPPI IS A STATE OF FIRSTS, LASTS, BIGGESTS, and bests. It was the home of the first heart transplant, the first can of condensed milk, and the first rayon fibers. One Mississippi town is called the "Cotton Capital of the World." A Mississippi man, Hiram Revels, was elected during Reconstruction as the first African American to serve in the U.S. Senate. These days the people of the state like to boast that they have "the South's warmest welcome." Drive through the foothills in the north of the state, the rolling countryside in the center and south, and shoreland along the Gulf, passing through both small towns and good-sized cities—regardless of the size of the community, you will find people with an abiding interest in the history of their place and an enthusiasm for sharing it with travelers.

Mississippi became a territory in 1798 and a state in 1817. Native Americans—Chickasaw, Choctaw, and Natchez—still lived in the state, but they had given up their lands by 1840. Mississippi was the second state to secede from the Union, and the second to be readmitted in 1870. The Civil War took a huge toll on the state's towns and cities, economy, and population. About 78,000 Mississippi men entered the Confederate military; by the end of the war, 59,000 of them were dead or wounded.

Many of the finest antebellum mansions were burned during the war. When you travel here, you find reminders of those horrors: a single marker

151

A War By Any Other Name

The people of the North dubbed the Civil War "The War of the Rebellion," while Southerners referred to the conflict as "The War for Southern Independence." Slavery may have taken center stage as the catalyst issue, but the average soldier was neither slave-holder nor abolitionist. "Billy Yank" fought to preserve the Union; "Johnny Reb" to ensure states' rights. The Civil War was not an action of conquest, but a conflict of principles. Union or Confederate, the volunteers who marched into battle in 1861 believed their cause was just.

— From "Civil War Guide," by the Mississippi Department of Economic and Community Development, Division of Tourism Development; compiled with the research assistance of the Mississippi Department of Archives and History. The publication includes a complete listing of Civil War battle reenactments held in the state. To request a free copy of this excellent account, write the Mississippi Department of Economic and Community Development, P.O. Box 1705, Ocean Springs, MS 39566-1705; phone (800) 927-6378.

or a huge preserved battlefield, a mansion with a cannonball still embedded in an interior wall. Mississippians have not forgotten.

NORTH MISSISSIPPI

The foothills of the Appalachian Mountains begin in the northeastern part of Mississippi, creating a rugged terrain entirely different from the image of flat land and cotton fields that people tend to have about the state. You get a more accurate impression of this part of Mississippi if you remember that it borders Tennessee. Although the peace of the countryside now contrasts dramatically from the violence that Civil War fighting brought to the area in the 1800s, this part of the state has many reminders of those years. The little town of **Corinth,** just across the border from Tennessee, was the site of the Battle of Corinth, in 1862, in which 2,000 men were killed and 7,500 wounded. This was an important battle because Corinth was located at the junction of two railroads, and both sides regarded occupying it as key to their ultimate victory. In the Battle of Corinth, the Confederates tried to retake the town, which they'd been forced to evacuate earlier. The fighting got down to hand-to-hand combat in most of the downtown area; the Confederate forces eventually lost.

The easiest site to get to is **Battery Robinett,** on West Linden Street; but you'll find other reminders of the war—battery sites, rifle pits, and important buildings—all over town. More than 7,000 Union soldiers killed in twenty battles in Mississippi and Tennessee are buried at the **Corinth Battlefield and National Cemetery,** on Horton Street, mostly in graves marked UNKNOWN SOLDIER. Confederate soldiers, having died closer to home, stood a better chance of being identified, but they could not be buried in a national U.S. battlefield since at the time they would have been considered enemies of the nation. At the Corinth Chamber of Commerce, 810 Tate Street, you can pick up a brochure and a tape narrated by a local historian describing the Civil War history of the area. Phone (601) 287–5269.

Two Confederate generals and one Union general headquartered at the **Curlee House,** 301 Childs Street. Built about 1857 and furnished in period antiques, the house is open for tours Thursday through Monday 1:00 to 4:00 P.M. Admission is about $1.50 for adults, less for children. Phone (601) 287–9501.

The **Northeast Mississippi Museum,** Fourth Street at Washington, exhibits Civil War artifacts as well as remnants of earlier times—Chickasaw Indian artifacts. Local artists also exhibit here. Admission is free. Phone (601) 287–3120.

The Generals' Quarters bed and breakfast, at 924 Fillmore Street in the historic district, continues the Civil War theme. The 1872 Victorian house has four guest rooms and a suite, furnished with good-quality antiques that are sturdy enough not to make you uncomfortable. In the suite, for instance, there is a solid-cherry four-poster bed with an upholstered canopy, built in the 1800s. The atmosphere is homelike. Innkeepers Charlotte Brandt and her husband, Luke Doehner, live in the building, too. Luke, who is a chef, prepares the full breakfasts. Rates begin at about $75. Phone (601) 286–3325.

At **Tupelo,** about 50 miles south of Corinth on U.S. Highway 45, Confederate troops, led by General Nathan Bedford Forrest, routed Union soldiers in a battle at **Brice's Cross Roads** in June 1864. This enraged General Sherman, who ordered his troops to "follow Forrest to the death, if it costs 10,000 lives and breaks the Treasury." Brice's Cross Roads bat-

Come Out, Come Out, Wherever You Are

Federal forces numbering 126,315 inched their way toward Corinth in May of 1862, erecting earthworks every step of the way for twenty miles. The Union troops were eventually entrenched so close to Corinth that they could hear the clatter of trains and the beat of Confederate drums inside the fortified city. Vastly outnumbered and facing a shortage of supplies, Beauregard decided to retreat to Tupelo. The evacuation was conducted with the utmost secrecy. Dummy cannons guarded the lines, campfires burned, and buglers serenaded the deserted works. As the empty train cars returned to the station, the Confederates cheered as if being reinforced. When Halleck's men cautiously entered the city at daybreak on May 30, they discovered only a deserted town and abandoned earthworks.

— From "Civil War Guide," Mississippi Department of Economic and Community Development, Division of Tourism Department

tlefield is 15 miles northwest of Tupelo. Admission is free. Phone (601) 680–4025.

Tupelo National Battlefield, on West Main Street, and **Tupelo Museum,** on State Highway 6 west, tell the story of the subsequent battle in which Union General A. J. Smith engaged Confederate forces commanded by Lee and Forrest. Because of a wounded foot, Forrest had to command from a carriage instead of a horse. The men misunderstood one of his commands, causing the Confederates to lose the battle. But although they had won, the Federals were exhausted and out of supplies; they retreated to Memphis so fast that they left their wounded behind. The national battlefield marks the position of the Confederate offensive line with a memorial honoring both sides. The museum exhibits artifacts recovered from the fields, and a diorama explains the action. The Battle of Tupelo was the last major battle of the Civil War fought in Mississippi.

Also at Tupelo is the **Natchez Trace Parkway Visitors Center** (see page 170), where you can watch a short audiovisual program on the history of the Trace and pick up literature related to the history of the area. Phone (601) 680–4025.

While you re in the area, stop at **Chickasaw Village Site,** northwest of Tupelo, between U.S. 78 and State Route 6, at Milepost 261.8 on the Natchez Trace Parkway. Although the Chickasaw Indians predate what we think of as the antebellum South, their presence certainly helped shape it. An exhibit shelter and audio station here tell the story of the Chickasaws, and on the nature trail, you can see some of the plants they used. It helps establish in your mind the continuity of the worlds of the Native Americans and the early Southerners who moved into their territory. Open daily, twenty-four hours. Admission is free. Phone (601) 842–1572.

Oxford, about 50 miles west of Tupelo on State Highway 6 west, was almost completely destroyed by Yankee troops in 1864. Visiting now, you can still find the spirit of the Old South, especially at "Ole Miss," the **University of Mississippi,** founded in 1848, just a little more than a decade after the land Oxford is built upon was acquired from Chickasaw Indians. General Grant occupied the campus in 1862, not deterred by the students and faculty who fought for the Confederacy as the "University Greys." A few buildings on the campus survived the burning of Oxford, including the Lyceum and the Barnard Observatory (which never got the telescope intended to be installed there because of the war). You can pick up a walking-tour brochure on the campus at 200 Lyceum. Closed Sunday. Phone (601) 232–7378. Also on the campus, stop at the **Blues Archive,** in Room 340 in Farley Hall. This museum has the largest collection of blues recordings in the world, along with reference books and memorabilia. The archives include B. B. King's personal collection. The museum is open Monday through Friday. Phone (601) 232–7752.

Five blocks east of the campus, on University Avenue and Fifth Street, the **University Museums** display everything from Greek antiquities to nineteenth-century scientific equipment. The doll collection and the Southern folk art collection of more than 6,000 items give you a view of the South through the crafter's eye. Open Tuesday through Saturday 10:00 A.M. to 4:00 P.M.; Sunday 1:00 to 4:00 P.M. Closed major holidays and university holidays. Admission is free. Phone (601) 232–7073.

Isom Place, 1003 Jefferson Avenue, reflects the cultural changes in Oxford in an interesting way. Opal Worthy, a local woman who used to own the building, spent three years researching its history. She and her husband, Dr. Haley D. Worthy, bought it in 1960 and restored it. Built about 1838, it was originally a three-room log house. It is constructed entirely of timber cut on the grounds and was built by Native American and slave labor. The house, a classic example of planter-type architecture and listed on the National Register of Historic Places, was built for Thomas Isom, the first permanent white resident of Oxford. He had come to the area to open an Indian trading post. In front of the house is a huge magnolia tree, grown from seeds that Dr. Isom's wife, Sarah McGee, brought with her from Abbeville, South Carolina.

Opal Worthy, now in her nineties, has sold Isom Place. The current owners, Palmer and Priscilla Adams, offer bed-and-breakfast accommodations in two suites. The suites have antique poster beds and private kitchens. While guests do not have the run of the entire house, a tour is included in the room rates, which begin at about $100 a night. People who are not staying at the inn may have a tour by appointment. Phone (601) 234–2738.

One more town in North Mississippi, **Holly Springs,** about 50 miles north of Oxford on State Highway 7, flourished during the antebellum years and suffered during the repeated fighting of the Civil War. The town was raided by both armies, for a total of at least sixty-one attacks. According to local historians, victory shifted back and forth between the two sides so often that the first thing citizens in town did when they got up each morning was look out the window to see which flag was flying. In one raid in 1862, Confederate General Early Van Dorn surprised the Union troops in early morning, destroying so many supplies that General Ulysses S. Grant had to delay his march into Vicksburg. Van Dorn Avenue in Holly Springs commemorates that victory.

Despite all the fighting, ninety of the town's antebellum homes survived. Various colorful stories circulate explaining why the homes were spared. General Grant's wife, Julia, was staying in one of these houses, at Walter Place. Van Dorn forbade Confederate troops to go inside as long as Mrs. Grant was there; in gentlemanly response, General Grant forbade his Union troops to enter or harm the building later. At Hamilton Place, the mistress of the house charmed Union Troops by playing the piano for them. And the local woman residing at Wakefield married a Union officer. These and other antebellum homes are open for the annual spring pilgrimage. A self-guided tour brochure, which you can use to study the old homes from the outside, is available any time.

For details on homes and tours in Holly Springs, stop at the **Marshall County Historical Society,** 220 East College Avenue. A special room in the museum contains relics of the Civil War as well as artifacts from other wars. The museum also displays tools and items from daily life in the area, Indian artifacts, quilts, clothing, and textiles, a schoolroom, and a doctor's office. The museum is open every day but Sunday from 10:00 A.M. to 5:00 P.M. Phone (601) 252–3669.

CENTRAL MISSISSIPPI

Moving from north to south, as Sherman and his troops did, you come next to the Mississippi Delta, an area of good farmland, forests, swamps, lakes, and rivers. In this area you will find reminders of the earliest inhabitants—the Mississippi Valley Indians—as well as glimpses of the hard life from which the blues came and a living-history presentation of life on an antebellum cotton plantation.

In **Greenwood,** about 35 miles west of I–55 on U.S. Highway 82, the Civil War caused no physical damage, but it did nearly ruin the economy. Cotton was the heart of commerce here until the war depleted the ranks of able-bodied men. The economy eventually recovered, still with cotton as king. Greenwood is known today as "the Cotton Capital of the World."

Cotton grows all over the delta. When the cotton is in bloom, beginning in late summer, great expanses of fields are blanketed with white. One local person put it, "It's beautiful. Looks like fields of snow." Another resident, though, pointed out, "No farmer wants it out there in the field being pretty very long. They want to get it in and sold." Watching the machines that pick and bale the cotton is fascinating. Of course, in the antebellum years, people picked cotton by hand.

Farmers in this area often let schoolchildren come to the fields to try cotton picking. You will be welcome too, provided you let them know you're coming. To arrange for permission to pick some cotton, phone the **Greenwood Convention and Visitors Bureau,** (800) 748–9064, or write it at P.O. Box 739, Greenwood, MS 38930. The Visitors Bureau can arrange for you to tour a cotton factory to see cotton being graded by hand, just as it was in antebellum years on **Cotton Row,** in downtown Greenwood, on Howard Street. Twenty-four of the row's original cotton companies still function. The area is listed on the National Register. If you visit the first Saturday in August, you'll make CROP day, when the whole town celebrates Cotton Row On Parade, with crafts and food vendors, bands, and games.

To learn more about early cotton culture, visit **Cottonlandia Museum.** Exhibits here represent Delta history, including the lives of lumberjacks, trappers, and Native Americans. There are even photographs of the last chief of the Choctaws. The museum has Civil War artifacts from the ironclad Union gunboat *Star of the West,* which was captured and sunk in the Yazoo River by Confederates who were hoping to block more Union troops. There is also a restored cannon from nearby Fort Pemberton that apparently stood loaded, ready to fire, for 128 years. The museum is open Monday through Friday 9:00 A.M. to 5:00 P.M.; Saturday and Sunday 2:00 to 5:00 P.M. Admission is about $2.50, less for senior citizens and children. Phone (601) 453–0925. The museum is on U.S. Highway 82 bypass, west of the Yazoo River bridge.

Another place to learn about life in cotton country is **Florewood River Plantation.** In this reproduction are both traditional museum displays and living-history presentations showing what it was like to live on an antebellum cotton plantation in the 1850s. A visit begins with a tram ride to "the big house." There an "interpreter" in 1850s costume explains the history and functions of the house and antique furnishings. After that you can use a written guide for a walking tour of the rest of the plantation and its buildings. Guides strategically positioned at various sites explain more of what you're seeing. Craftspersons demonstrate such activities as potting and candlemaking as they would have been practiced in plantation life. Some of Florewood's farm animals—hogs, mules, ducks, chickens, and peacocks—are tame enough to pet and feed. In the museum, displays depict cotton production from the early days to modern times. A model gin press and gin accurately duplicate the real thing in smaller size.

Visiting here at Christmas is a special treat. The Christmas tour, always held the first Friday and Saturday in December, duplicates an 1850s Mississippi plantation Christmas, with decorations, music, and, since there was no electricity, thousands of candles.

The plantation is open Tuesday through Saturday 8:00 A.M. to 5:00 P.M.; closed for lunch from noon to 1:00 P.M. Tours leave every thirty minutes, though fewer are offered from December to March. Admission is about $3.50 for adults, less for children and senior citizens. Phone (601) 453–0925. The plantation is 2 miles west of Greenwood, off U.S. Highway 82.

The Taxman Cometh

The big house at Florewood River Plantation resembles many Mississippi plantation houses in that it has a few very large rooms and halls rather than a greater number of smaller rooms. Under Mississippi law, taxes were levied according to the number of rooms buildings had, so the more rooms, the higher the tax. There are no closets, because they counted as rooms. It was common, therefore, to see a space large enough for two or more rooms used for more than one purpose, dotted with armoires and chests, taxable as a single room.

About 73 miles south of Greenwood on I–55, **Canton** has a preserved pre-Civil War courthouse on Courthouse Square and a preserved jail built in 1870 on East Fulton Street that may interest you. They haven't been changed from their original condition. Admission to both places is free, but you need an appointment to get inside. For information, call the **Canton Convention and Visitors Bureau** at (800) 844–3369.

A little less than 30 miles farther south, still on I–55, you come to Mississippi's largest city and state capital, **Jackson.** Union troops took the city on May 14, 1863. General Ulysses S. Grant celebrated in an elegant hotel while the rest of his troops got drunk and paraded through the streets. In the ensuing pandemonium, local people grabbed what they could carry and ran from their homes without even bothering to lock doors, while convicts in the penitentiary set it on fire. The city was called "Chimneyville" after Sherman burned it in July 1863. Stop at the **Metro Jackson Convention and Visitors Bureau,** 921 North President Street, for a brochure to take a historical walking tour of the city. You can make arrangements in advance by writing P.O. Box 1450, Jackson, MS 39215-1450; phone (800) 354–7695.

One of the buildings to survive Sherman's fire is **Governor's Mansion,** 300 East Capitol Street. Mississippi governors have lived in this Greek Revival structure since 1842. Sherman ate his victory dinner here after the fall of Vicksburg, and the mansion served as a hospital during the war. The building was nearly torn down in the early 1900s, but Jackson's citizenry united to save and renovate it. The mansion is a National Historic Landmark.

Two museums in Jackson also merit a visit. **Mississippi State Historical Museum,** 100 South State Street, in the old state capitol building, is one of the state's better examples of Greek Revival architecture. In the Civil War section of the museum, a "Sherman necktie" is displayed—to make Southern railroads unusable, Sherman would pull up the iron rails, heat them over a fire, and bend them around a tree. The necktie on display was found in the mud of the Pearl River near the museum, next to where the tracks once were. Material for self-guided tours is available. Open Monday through Friday 8:00 A.M. to 5:00 P.M.; Saturday 9:30 A.M. to 4:30 P.M.; Sunday 12:30 to 4:30 P.M. Admission is free. Phone (601) 359–6920.

The **Smith Robertson Museum,** 528 Bloom Street, focuses on the history of African Americans in Mississippi. The building was the first public school for blacks in Jackson. Open Monday through Friday 9:00 A.M. to 5:00 P.M.; Saturday 9:00 A.M. to noon; Sunday 2:00 to 5:00 P.M. Closed holidays. Admission is about $1.00 for adults, half that for children. Phone (601) 960–1457.

While you're in Jackson, you may want to pick up a few craft items at the **Chimneyville Crafts Gallery,** 1150 Lakeland Drive. Professional craftspersons demonstrate and sell native, traditional, and contemporary crafts. Admission is free. Phone (601) 981–2499. The gallery is in the **Jim Buck Ross Mississippi Agriculture and Forestry/National Agricultural Aviation Museum.** This is a complex of exhibit areas showing the history of transportation and farming in Mississippi. A nature walk on the grounds identifies specimens of native plants, while buildings transported here from other areas are grouped to create a representative village. The complex is open Monday through Saturday 9:00 A.M. to 5:00 P.M.; Sunday 1:00 to 5:00 P.M. Closed Thanksgiving, Christmas, and New Year's Day. Admission is about $3.00 for adults, less for senior citizens and children. Phone (601) 354–6113. The complex is east of I–55 off exit 98B. Signs will direct you.

From Jackson, drive west on I–20 about 45 miles to **Vicksburg,** an important stop for serious Civil War students. The forty-seven-day Siege of Vicksburg, in 1863, was the worst fighting of the war in Mississippi. Union troops did tremendous damage during this time. **Vicksburg National Military Park** has a 16-mile driving tour along the battlefields, dotted with interpretive markers. Re-creations of offensive and defensive positions, with forts and artillery, help you grasp the strategy and progress of the battles.

Appropriately enough, the largest Civil War cemetery in existence, the **Vicksburg National Cemetery,** located on the park acreage, has the graves of about 17,000 Civil War soldiers. These are not Confederate soldiers, but Union ones—because the cemetery is a *national* cemetery. The Rebels, who would have been considered Union deserters at the time, were not allowed to be buried there. (Confederate soldiers are buried in the city cemetery, Soldiers Rest.) The Union soldiers buried in the national cemetery died either in battle or later from war-related wounds within a 100-mile radius of Vicksburg. Some were buried elsewhere and were later exhumed to be moved to the national cemetery. Between this shifting of bones and the men's having little recognizable identification to begin with, identities were lost in what seems like shocking numbers by today's standards: Of the 17,000 Civil War soldiers buried in Vicksburg National Cemetery, 13,000 are not identified! Of the memorials in the park, the largest is the Illinois Memorial; that state provided 36,225 Union troops.

Probably the **U.S.S.** *Cairo* **Museum** attracts the most attention in the park. Confederates sank the ironclad gunboat *Cairo* in the Yazoo River in 1862. It was the first ship in history to be sunk by an electrically detonated torpedo. The ship sank slowly, close to the shore, so all the men on board survived. The *Cairo* has been salvaged and restored. Next to it is a museum where objects saved from the ship are exhibited; you can also see a short audiovisual presentation about the gunboat here. The museum is open 9:00 A.M. to 6:00 P.M. in summer, with shorter hours at other times of the year. Admission is free. Phone (601) 636–2199.

The Vicksburg National Military Park covers 1,700 acres. It's thus a good idea to stop at the visitors' center at the park entrance when you arrive. Here you can watch an eighteen-minute film about the Vicksburg campaign, get oriented to the sites within the park, and rent a driving-tour tape for $4.50 (or buy it for $5.95). For more intensive instruction, you can hire a licensed guide for $20. The park is open daily from 8:00 A.M. to 5:00 P.M. Admission is $4.00 per car; people over age 62 and under 17 are admitted free. Phone (601) 636–0583. The park is just east of U.S. Highway 80 at Vicksburg.

To look at the Civil War from a more personal point of view, stop at **Cedar Grove Mansion-Inn,** 2200 Oak Street. John A. Klein built this mansion in 1840 as a wedding present for his bride, and the Kleins lived here during the Civil War. Once a Union gunboat cannonball roared through the door and hit the parlor wall. Mrs. Klein insisted on leaving it where it was to remind people of the war. It's still there. A ragged cannonball hole in the floor also remains, now framed and protected by heavy glass. General Grant stayed in the mansion for three nights after the fall of Vicksburg, turning the servants quarters below the main floor into a Union hospital for his soldiers; you see the rooms through the glassed hole. Virtually every room of the mansion has similar personal stories that you can learn from the innkeepers and guides.

The war obviously took a toll on this mansion, as did the years of poverty following, but the current owner, Ted Mackey, has been working on its restoration and furnishing for years to bring the property to its pre-Civil War splendor. Many of the antique furnishings are original to the house, including an armoire and a baby bed by Prudent Mallard that the Kleins bought while on their honeymoon.

The grounds gleam with formal gardens, gazebos, fountains, and a pond that looks like a goldfish pond but was used in 1885 to hold live catfish until it was time to cook them.

You can partake of the antebellum atmosphere in several ways. Tours are offered daily from 9:00 A.M. to 5:00 P.M., except Christmas. Admission is about $5.00 for adults, less for children. Bed-and-breakfast accommodations are offered in some of the mansion rooms, a pool house, the carriage house, and five small cottages across the street. Rates, ranging from about $75 to $160, include a tour of the house and a full plantation breakfast. Finally, you can dine any evening but Monday in the elegant Cedar Grove Restaurant.

For information on all options, call (601) 636–1000 or (800) 862–1300. To get to Cedar Grove, take the Washington Street exit from I–20. Proceed north, then turn left onto Klein Street.

Another inn on Klein Street, **The Corners,** at 601 Klein, overlooks the Mississippi and Yazoo Rivers. The inn's 68-foot verandas are a great place to watch sunsets. This two-story Victorian Greek Revival mansion was built about 1872. Public and guest rooms are furnished with period antiques. The house is listed on the National Register of Historic Places. The inn has eleven rooms, three with fireplace. Rates begin at about $75, including a full plantation breakfast and a tour of the house. Phone (601) 636–7421 or (800) 444–7421.

Another important mansion in Vicksburg is **Anchuca,** an 1830 Greek

Revival–style mansion at 1010 First Street, where you will feel like the old antebellum life never stopped. It's furnished with eighteenth- and nineteenth-century pieces that look as though they are used, not just polished for show. Small artifacts add life to the scene—a pair of wire-rimmed eyeglasses next to an open book, a player piano open and ready to go, an epergne of Waterford crystal heaped with fresh flowers at the center of the formal dining table. Slave quarters stand next to formal gardens across brick courtyards. Confederate president Jefferson Davis once spoke from a small balcony on the front of the house. In recent years Anchuca has offered bed-and-breakfast accommodations and still does occasionally, although the telephone numbers for Anchuca now ring and are answered at Cedar Grove Mansion-Inn. Anchuca is available for tours by appointment. Phone (601) 636–4931 or (800) 631–6800. To inquire about bed-and-breakfast offerings, phone the innkeeper, May Burns, directly, at (601) 631–6800.

In addition to its bed-and-breakfast mansions, Vicksburg has some important homes that offer tours but not overnight accommodations. **Duff Green Mansion,** 1114 First East Street, for instance, was used during the Siege of Vicksburg as a hospital for both Union and Confederate troops at the same time. Even though men from both sides were inside the house, it was attacked five times, forcing Mrs. Green, who was pregnant at the time, to deliver her son in a nearby building instead of at home. She named him Siege.

McRaven, at 1445 Harrison Street, is remarkable not only for having survived the Civil War but also because it is built in three sections, each from a different era and representing a different architectural style. Here you see in microcosm the evolution of a Mississippi dwelling from Early American days through the late antebellum period. Because of heavy fighting in the vicinity of the house, tremendous numbers of Civil War artifacts and weapons have been found on the grounds. They are displayed along with antique tools and furnishings.

Slaves built the **Old Court House,** on the spot where Cherry, Jackson, Monroe, and Grove Streets come together. The courthouse has been restored and now serves as a museum for regional antebellum items. The museum is open in summer Monday through Saturday 8:30 A.M. to 5:00 P.M.; Sunday 1:30 to 5:00 P.M. It closes at 4:30 P.M. in fall and winter. Admission is about $2.00 for adults, less for senior citizens and children. Phone (601) 636–1663.

A good place in Vicksburg for old-time Southern cooking is the **Wal-**

nut Hills Restaurant, where food is served family style in great variety and quantity at round tables. At one meal your table might hold chicken and dumplings, stuffed pork chops, half a dozen vegetables, rice, gravy, slaw, biscuits, corn bread, and fruit cobbler. Open Monday through Friday 11:00 A.M. to 9:00 P.M.; Sunday 11:00 A.M. to 2:00 P.M. Closed Saturday. Phone (601) 638–4910.

Like Natchez, Vicksburg has spring Pilgrimage tours during which many of the city's antebellum homes and buildings are open to visitors. Dates run from the third Saturday in March through the first Sunday in April. For details, contact the **Vicksburg-Warren County Convention and Visitors Bureau,** P.O. Box 110, Vicksburg, MS 39180. Phone (601) 636–9421 or (800) 221–3536.

Natchez and Vicksburg are about 70 miles apart on U.S. Highway 61. Halfway between them is the little town of **Port Gibson,** which Grant passed on his way to Vicksburg and found too beautiful to burn. One such place is **Oak Square Plantation,** now an inn, at 1207 Church Street, right beside the highway. This mansion was built in 1850. It is furnished with family antiques, including canopied beds in the twelve guest rooms. Rates start at about $70. You may take a guided tour of the house without spending the night. Phone (601) 437–4350 or (800) 729–0240.

While you're in town, take a look at the 1859 **First Presbyterian Church,** Church Street, on Highway 61 south. A 12-foot gold-leaf hand points toward heaven from atop the steeple. Inside the church, you'll see chandeliers from the steamboat *Robert E. Lee.* The church is open daily 8:00 A.M. to 5:00 P.M. Admission is free. Phone (601) 437–4351.

Port Gibson has a two-day spring Pilgrimage. For details, contact **Port Gibson Chamber of Commerce,** P.O. Box 491, Port Gibson, MS 39150. Phone (601) 437–4351.

About 7 miles northwest of town, the 400-acre **Grand Gulf Military Park** has restored buildings and forts marking the site where Union gunboats shelled Forts Cobun and Wade. The museum contains Civil War artifacts. It is open Monday through Saturday 8:00 A.M. to 5:00 P.M.; Sunday 9:00 A.M. to 6:00 P.M. Closed Thanksgiving, Christmas, and New Year's Day. Admission for the park and museum is $1.50 adults, less for children.

A jaunt of approximately 30 miles down Highway 31 brings you to where the romantic tradition of the Old South flourishes—in **Natchez.** It is a town with magnolia blooms, mint juleps, hoop skirts, Southern cooking, and elegant mansions.

In its heyday, Natchez was a place where cotton earned people fabulous amounts of money. Being a port town also swelled the local coffers. That prosperity was reflected in the mansions that filled the town. The Civil War marked the end of those days; in the years following the war, people struggled financially, which allowed for little upkeep on the buildings. As times improved, people once again turned their attention to their fine old mansions, gradually making the repairs, renovations, and restorations necessary to return them to their early grandeur.

These days it is the old mansions—some 500 of which remain—for which Natchez is best known. Visiting the antebellum homes of this Mississippi town is like attending a ball for a bevy of aging belles. Some of them have kept in shape and look wonderful. Some show signs of the years of wear and tear, but you can still see the basic lines of their earlier beauty. And some have had spectacular makeovers that look almost too good to be true.

The interest in these mansions has spread prodigiously, thanks to the "Pilgrimage tours," begun by the Natchez Garden Club in 1932. The women of the club had been looking for ways to encourage tourism, to bring money into their faltering local economy, and to preserve the fine old mansions of the community. The tours turned out to be an inspired idea that helped keep Natchez going during hard times by bringing in tourist dollars. The idea of Pilgrimage tours has since been adopted by many other Southern towns with fine mansions, but it originated in Natchez. The success of Pilgrimage tours has been widely regarded as yet

Women Only. Well, Maybe a *Few* Good Men

The garden club that started Pilgrimage eventually divided. Now Pilgrimage is sponsored by the Natchez Garden Club and the Pilgrimage Garden Club. These clubs used to be exclusively for women, but as men have become increasingly interested in restoring and preserving old homes, they have been allowed to participate . . . to a degree. As one club member said, "You know how everything has changed. We had to be flexible, so we have a few honorary men." The men are mainly in situations, such as dances, where men are traditionally a necessary part of the scene.

another example of Southern women doing what had to be done to keep hearth and home together.

Pilgrimages are held twice a year, from early March to early April, and again in October. It takes a full three days to do all the tours available. In addition to the house tours, which cost about $20 per person, per tour, the event also features pageants, concerts in historic churches, and stage entertainment in the antebellum South theme. For a broader view of the town, you can arrange for tours by horse-drawn carriage. For full Pilgrimage details, phone (800) 647–6742.

Although the greatest number of mansions are open to the public during Pilgrimages, you may prefer to visit during a less frantic time of year. Many homes are open year-round for touring, and some of them offer bed-and-breakfast accommodations. Each provides a different view of the good life in the antebellum years and is on the National Register of Historic Places.

Dunleith, at 84 Homochitto Street, has especially lovely grounds. The 1856 Greek Revival mansion sits surrounded by forty acres of landscaped park, with formal garden areas. With galleries and colonnades on all sides, it looks like a Greek temple. Behind the house, you can sit on a park bench under the branches of an ancient magnolia tree to survey the property. The lower floor is open for public tours, with three bed-and-breakfast rooms on the second floor of the main house and eight more in a courtyard wing. All the rooms have working fireplaces. Breakfast is served in what used to be the poultry house, which has been renovated into a great brick-walled room with a bright country decor and highly polished wood floors. The breakfast is classic Mississippi: scrambled eggs, bacon, sausage, cheese grits, biscuits, and pancakes. Dunleith is a National Historic Landmark. Room rates begin at about $90 per room. Phone (800) 433–2445 or (601) 448–8500. To get to the mansion, take State Highway 81 heading south into Natchez. It becomes Homochitto Street. The plantation is on the left.

Monmouth Plantation, 36 Melrose Avenue, does everything on a grand scale. It is open year-round for tours. Its staff includes three hostesses who are fully versed in the history, architecture, and antiques of the mansion. The house was built in 1818 and is a National Historic Landmark. This is a nice stop if you are interested in antiques. The table in the formal dining room, for example, is an Empire piece from New York, and the water pitchers are made of coin silver.

The twenty-seven acres of grounds include a Civil War museum, a

In addition to gardens, a gazebo, and a footbridge, the grounds at Monmouth Plantation in Natchez include a croquet course.

pond, and a croquet course that calls to mind graciously clad ladies giving the croquet balls a genteel tap with their mallets. In addition to a full Southern breakfast, five-course candlelight dinners, served with ornate silver, are available. Guest accommodations include nineteen rooms and suites in three buildings on the plantation. Rates begin at about $100. Phone (800) 828–4531 or (601) 442–5852. To get to Monmouth, take the Melrose Avenue exit from the 61/84 bypass just outside Natchez. Follow Melrose to where it intersects with the John A. Quitman Parkway. The mansion sits on a hill.

Weymouth Hall, 1 Cemetery Road, represents yet another kind of Natchez mansion. This is an 1855 Greek Revival mansion that stands alone on a bluff overlooking the Mississippi River. The owner/innkeeper personally supervised the restoration of this building, paying attention to its fine millwork and bridge work. He furnished the house with an impressive collection of antiques handmade by John Belter, Charles Baudoine, and Prudent Mallard. The Rococo furniture in the double parlor looks like a perfect matched set, but it was assembled one piece at a time. The five guest rooms here are in the main house, not in adjacent buildings or added wings. Rates, including a full plantation breakfast and house tour, begin at about $85 a room. Phone (601) 445–2304. To get to Weymouth, take Canal Street from State Highways 65 and 84 on the south side of Natchez. Go north to the end of Canal, then take Linton Avenue to Cemetery Road.

If you're one of those people who saw *Gone With the Wind* every time it came around, be sure to go to **Linden,** 1 Linden Place. The front door-way of this 1800 Federal plantation home was the model for the one used in the film. This was the family home of the innkeeper, Jeanette Feltus, who still lives here. The home is furnished with canopied beds and other heirlooms that have been in Jeanette's family for generations. While you're here, check the famous punkah—a huge, wooden paddle hinged from the ceiling over the dining room table. In pre-Civil War days a slave pulled a rope to move the punkah back and forth across the table to keep away flies. Rooms start at about $85 a night. Make reservations and receive full details through Natchez Pilgrimage Tours, (800) 647–6742 or (601) 446–6631. To get to the inn, exit Highway 61/84 onto Melrose Avenue. The inn is just off Melrose.

The Burn, at 712 North Union Street, an 1832 Greek Revival-style mansion, was once used as a headquarters for Union troops. It was later used as a hospital for Union soldiers. The home is known for a spiral stair-case in the central hall and for its gardens, which grow 125 different kinds of camellias. The house is in downtown Natchez, but its gardens give it a somewhat secluded feel. Guest accommodations are six rooms and a cot-tage. Rates begin at about $80. For reservations, phone (800) 647–6742. To get to The Burn, drive into the downtown area from Highway 61 North, turning right on Union Street. From 61 South, go right on Homo-chitto to Union, then right on Union.

Two other mansions in Natchez, **Ravenna** and **Ravennaside,** have an interesting connection. Ravenna, built about 1835 as a family home for Mr. and Mrs. James S. Fleming, stands amid three acres of old-fashioned gardens. It has three guest rooms in the house and a one-bedroom guest house by a swimming pool. Close to that property stands Ravennaside at 601 South Union Street. This imposing structure used to be the guest

Family Ties

The novel *Pilgrimage: A Tale of Old Natchez*, by Louise Willbourn Collier, describes life at The Burn in believable detail. The author is the great-great-granddaughter of John and Sarah Walworth, who first owned The Burn in the 1800s; she has incorporated family history into the fiction, including relationships between the Walworths and the people at Linden. One scene describes a dinner at Linden during which one of the servant's children was called in to pull the punkah. Such descriptions, including references to the heat and such activities as taking tea on the gallery (porch) to catch a breeze in summer, make you realize that a good many physical discomforts went along with living in grand Southern mansions before the era of window screens and air-conditioning. Reading this novel while you're in Natchez will contribute to making its history come alive.

house for visitors to Ravenna—Mrs. Fleming designed Ravennaside not as a home but as an elaborate place to entertain and accommodate guests. Today, beautifully restored, it has a glorious music room, with the original parquet floors and a white grand piano. The social center of the opulent house was the Trace Room, which has hand-tinted wallpaper of the Natchez Trace. In this room, you will find Wedgwood plaques in the fireplace and a musicians' balcony. Photographs more than a hundred years old show you that much of the original furniture still stands where it has always stood.

Between the early days and today, the uses of the buildings changed. Ravennaside became the home of the late Mrs. Roan Fleming Byrnes, daughter of the original owners. Known in Natchez as "Sweet Annie," she was famous for working to get the Natchez Trace completed. The map she used to track its progress still hangs in the little kitchen that people used to call her "war room." Rooms at Ravenna are booked through Natchez Pilgrimage Tours, (800) 647–6742 or (601) 446–6631. Rates begin at about $85. Rates at Ravennaside begin at about $75. Phone (601) 442–8015. From the John R. Junkin Drive (State Highway 61), turn onto Homochitto Street, then turn left on Union.

These bed-and-breakfast tour homes represent just a sampling of two dozen or so operating in Natchez. Call Natchez Pilgrimage Tours (phone numbers page 169) for more information.

At the corner of Pearl and High Streets, **Stanton Hall,** one of the largest antebellum mansions in the country, does not operate as a bed-and-breakfast, but it does have a restaurant, **Carriage House Restaurant,** on the same grounds, across the courtyard. The restaurant, open for lunch (and for dinner, only during Pilgrimage), is known for authentic Southern fried chicken. (Phone 601–445–5151.) Stanton Hall was built in 1857. Covering an entire city block, the mansion is a preservation project of the Pilgrimage Garden Club and is furnished with antiques from Natchez. Stanton Hall is open for tours every day 9:00 A.M. to 5:00 P.M. Closed Christmas. It is a Pilgrimage tour home and does not have separate tours during that time. Admission is about $4.00 for adults, half that for children. Phone (601) 446–6631.

Another tour home does not offer bed-and-breakfast accommodations; in fact, it doesn't even have bedrooms. **Longwood,** 140 Lower Woodville Road, is the largest remaining octagonal house in the United States. Construction was begun about 1856, but because of the war, it was never finished inside. As soon as the war started, the Yankee builders quit. The fact that Dr. Haller Nutt, for whom the house was being built, sympathized with the Yankees didn't stop Union troops from wiping out most of his holdings in Louisiana. Dr. Nutt hurried to Vicksburg to try to convince

Sweet Annie's Passion

The Natchez Trace Parkway is a 450-mile scenic road running from Mississippi, through Alabama, into Tennessee. The parkway follows the original "trace," a route that began as a buffalo and Indian trail said to be more than 8,000 years old. Later it became a pioneer road. The parkway is now a project of the National Park Service, with history markers, living-history exhibits, picnic and camping areas, and nature trails at close intervals along the way. The route is popular with bicyclists. For more information on the Natchez Trace, phone (601) 842–1572.

Longwood is the largest remaining octagonal house in the United States. It has no bedrooms because all the Yankee construction workers fled when the Civil War started. The ghosts of the couple who were having it built are said to wander about the house. Building a house can be a very trying experience.

General Grant not to destroy any more of his property, but he got caught in bad weather and had to go back to Longwood, where he came down with pneumonia and died. Longwood has never been finished. Builders have a reputation for being slow, but really!

Local lore has it that the ghosts of Haller and his wife, Julia, wander the property at twilight, probably trying to figure out how to get the builders on the ball. On the tour you will see the first-floor rooms, elegantly furnished with family heirlooms. And in the corridors you'll see the tools that the Yankee workmen left when they fled at the beginning of the war. If you tour in the right spirit, maybe you'll see the ghosts, too. Longwood is open daily 9:00 A.M. to 5:00 P.M. Closed Christmas and during Pilgrimage. Admission is about $4.00 for adults, half that for children. Phone (601) 446–6631 or (800) 647–6742.

Other homes are open for Pilgrimage and Christmas tours but do not keep guests. It is also possible to tour a bed-and-breakfast mansion without spending the night there. The cost is usually about $4.00 for adults, less for children. For listings and descriptions of all the bed-and-breakfast homes and the tour homes, write Natchez Pilgrimage Tours, P.O. Box 347, Natchez, MS 39121; phone (800) 647–6742 or (601) 446–6631.

Other area activities available through Natchez Pilgrimage Tours include a Mississippi Riverboat ride and a forty-minute narrated carriage tour of the town. Also take some time to visit **Natchez Under-the-Hill,** on Silver Street. This part of Natchez sits under a bluff, by the river. In the 1800s it was an unsavory place where crime, saloons, gambling, and hotels of questionable purpose flourished. It is now more reputable, although one of Mississippi's permanently anchored gambling ships is moored just offshore. Its main ambience, though, comes from its quaint collection of shops, bars, and restaurants. The **Magnolia Grill,** at 29 Silver Street, sits next door to the **Under-the-Hill Saloon.** Lunch and dinner are served at the restaurant seven days a week. Phone (601) 446–7670. Also on Silver Street, **Natchez Landing** is open for dinner, specializing in catfish and barbecue. Phone (601) 442–6639. Still under the hill, 15 Ferry Street, the **Wharf Master,** with a rustic atmosphere in an old cypress house, is open from 11:00 A.M. to 11:00 P.M. The specialty at these and many other restaurants in Natchez is catfish. Once it would have been pulled from the muddy river and have been considered poverty fare. Now it's raised on catfish farms, has become downright trendy, and probably tastes a whole lot better.

South about 30 miles on U.S. Highway 61 is **Woodville,** an early Mississippi town with a graceful Southern atmosphere. It has some nice antebellum homes and churches as well as Rosemont Plantation, the early home of the president of the Confederate states, Jefferson Davis. The plantation house is on the outskirts of town, on State Highway 24 East, a mile east of U.S. Highway 61. You may decide to look around town first. Request a brochure for a self-guiding walking tour and information about historic buildings elsewhere in the county by writing the Woodville Civic Club, P.O. Box 814, Woodville, MS 39669; phone (601) 888–6809.

After looking around town, you can drive on out to **Rosemont Plan-**

tation. Built about 1810, the house contains many of the original furnishings of the Davis family. A windowsill carved with the names of the Davis children reminds you that even great men play childhood pranks, roses planted by the porch by Mrs. Davis remind you that their lives were about more than war, and a family cemetery on the grounds reminds you of our common destiny. Rosemont is open Monday through Friday 10:00 A.M. to 5:00 P.M. Closed January and February. Admission is about $6.00 for adults, half that for children. Phone (601) 888–6809.

COASTAL MISSISSIPPI

That stretch of Mississippi that you see while driving along the coast of the Gulf of Mexico differs in many ways from the rest of the state. In earlier times the little towns along the coast—Ocean Springs, Long Beach, Pass Christian, and Bay St. Louis, especially—were resorts for the affluent, as was the larger city of Biloxi. To a considerable extent, they still draw vacationers. Pascagoula, being close to the shore and on the Pascagoula River, was important in the past not only for vacationing but also as an industrial and shipping center. As gambling boats have come onto the scene here, the area has become more glitzy, with more nightlife, particularly in Biloxi.

The gambling is controversial among local residents. Some welcome the additional travelers; some worry about the kinds of people who will be attracted. One sure result of the proliferation of gambling casinos along the shore is that you can't expect to stop on the spur of the moment on a weekend and find a place to stay. Lots of people come from other parts of the state to spend a coastal weekend, with days spent on a fishing boat and nights aboard a gambling boat. If you plan to explore this area on a weekend, be sure to call ahead and make reservations.

I–40 covers this coastal stretch from Alabama to Louisiana, but sometimes it's fun to get off and take the short jaunt down to U.S. 90, which runs so close to the water that parts of the road are awash during stormy weather. From this vantage point, you will find that all the towns along the gulf are in a string, with one town nearly running into the next.

Closest to the Alabama border, **Pascagoula,** named for the river, is the Indian word for "Singing River." After dark, in late summer and early fall you may hear a sound that sounds like a continuous hum or whir. Local lore says that this is the death song of Pascagoula Indians who drowned themselves in the river to avoid being conquered by Biloxi Indians. Whether river or ocean, water figures in almost every activity here.

Gambling boats aren't the only floating attraction. The **Scranton Floating Museum** gives you insight into the importance that fishing has had for Mississippi culture. Aboard this 70-foot commercial shrimp boat, you can see what the shrimper's life is like on the deck and in the galley, bunk room, and wheelhouse. Down below, a museum has exhibits about the Gulf Coast. The museum is open Tuesday through Saturday 10:00 A.M. to 5:00 P.M.; Sunday 1:00 to 5:00 P.M. Admission is free. Phone (601) 762–6017.

Also in Pascagoula is one of the oldest structures in the United States. The **Old Spanish Fort and Museum** isn't Spanish, and it isn't a fort. It is, however, an interesting museum. The building was built in 1718 as a carpenter's shop, one of about a dozen buildings that once were enclosed by a stockade. This is the only building left. The actual fort still stands, however, and has been restored. In places you can see the original building material—a mix of clay, Spanish moss, and ground oyster shells. The museum, located on the three-acres property, displays Indian artifacts and other items from early Mississippi life. The grassy grounds go all the way down to the river and are nicely set off with huge azaleas and a few picnic tables. Three cannons that Andrew Jackson captured elsewhere add a bit of drama, too. The site is open Monday through Saturday 10:00 A.M. to 5:00 P.M.; Sunday noon to 5:00 P.M. Closed holidays. Admission is about $2.00 for adults, less for children and senior citizens. Phone (601) 769–1505.

Moving just a few miles west, you could stop at **Gautier** to spend some time in the **Mississippi Sandhill Crane National Wildlife Refuge.** This has officially been a refuge for only about twenty years, but its 19,000 acres will give you a chance to appreciate how the shore must have looked, undeveloped, in earlier times. The center is open for hiking, photography, and birding Monday through Friday 8:00 A.M. to 5:00 P.M. A visitors' center is located a half mile north of I–10 at exit 61. Phone (601) 497–6322.

Enjoy lots more unspoiled land in the **Gulf Islands National Seashore,** a string of islands stretching from Florida to Gulfport, harboring native flora and fauna. Wilderness camping is allowed on Horn Island. For less strenuous exploring, exit U.S. 90 just east of Ocean Springs into the Davis bayou area, where you'll find standard facilities such as a campground, bathrooms, and an information center. Phone (601) 875–0821.

Another part of the Gulf Islands National Seashore, **Ship Island,** sits 12 miles out in the Gulf of Mexico. **Fort Massachusetts,** on the island, first belonged to the Confederates but was captured by the Union early in the war. Union troops used the fort as a staging ground for their attack on New Orleans. Later the fort was a POW camp for captured Confederates; one inmate was a housewife from New Orleans who taught her children to spit on Yankee officers. You can take a ferry from Biloxi or Gulfport to get to Ship Island. For details from Biloxi, phone (601) 432–2197; from Gulfport, (601) 864–1014.

You can find more details about Ship Island at the interpretative center back on the mainland. The main headquarters of the Gulf Islands National Seashore is at 3500 Park Road in **Ocean Springs.** The visitors' center has programs and exhibits about the park as well as information about hiking trails, beaches, camping, and specific islands. Phone (601) 875–9057.

The town of Ocean Springs looks more like a movie set for the perfect old Southern beach town than like a real place. The first permanent French settlement in the Mississippi Valley was begun here in 1699 by Pierre LeMoyne d'Iberville. In 1854 a doctor opened a sanitarium based on the springwaters that the Indians called "healing waters." He named the place Ocean Springs.

It's fun to walk the streets of this little town, with its quiet streets and picturesque live oaks. Under one of these oaks, **Oak Shade Bed and Breakfast,** 1017 La Fontaine, offers accommodations a block from one of the springs. The building was once the home of the Ocean Springs harbor master. It's a modern brick building, but it *is* under that great old oak in a great old town and is notable for welcoming children. Rates begin at $65 to $85, depending on the day of the week and the season. Phone (601) 872–8109.

After you explore Ocean Springs, visit **Biloxi,** one of the first permanent white settlements in the Mississippi Valley. The town was important in the past for oysters and shrimp. These days, however, shrimp boats are overshadowed by the floating casinos that line the waters just off the shore. The city has been glitzed up accordingly.

You can still find important historic sites here, of course. Notably, Jefferson Davis, president of the Confederacy, lived the last twelve years of his life at **Beauvoir,** 2244 Beach Boulevard, a mansion overlooking the Gulf of Mexico. In this setting, he entertained many friends and soldiers—even the Union soldier who captured him at the end of the war. Davis loaned

175

the soldier money to go home; in exchange, he asked that the soldier help any Confederates in trouble who he might encounter up north. Davis wrote *The Rise and Fall of the Confederate Government* here. For years after Davis's death, Beauvoir was a home for Confederate veterans and their families, including several former slaves who fought for the Confederacy. More than 2,500 had people registered in the home at some time before Beauvoir became a museum in 1940.

The furnishings and personal items belonging to the Davis family are still in place. The home is on fifty-four acres, with outbuildings, an old Confederate hospital, and a Confederate cemetery. In the hospital, weapons, uniforms, and personal items of Confederate soldiers are exhibited. A film interprets the site and its history. This is where the Tomb of the Unknown Soldier of the Confederate States of America was dedicated. Beauvoir is open every day 9:00 A.M. to 5:00 P.M. Closed Christmas. Admission is about $5.00 for adults, less for children and senior citizens. Phone (601) 388–1313.

The Father Ryan House Bed and Breakfast is nearby, at 1196 Beach Boulevard. The house, built in about 1841, was visited often after the war by Father A. J. Ryan, the poet laureate of the Confederacy. He was a close friend of Jefferson Davis. According to letters and references, Father Ryan restored this house himself. The poetry that he wrote while in residence is copied in calligraphy and displayed throughout the house. Books about Father Ryan, his letters, and his poetry, as well as Margaret Mitchell's book *Gone With the Wind,* opened to where she mentions Father Ryan's visit, are arranged in the entry hall and library for the perusal of guests. After you study the memorabilia, stroll the gardens and enjoy the peaceful ocean view. The suites and rooms are furnished in period antiques. Rates begin at about $65. Phone (601) 435–1189.

For a meal in one of the oldest houses in America, try **Mary Mahoney's Old French House and Cafe,** 138 Rue Magnolia. The house was built about 1737. In the backyard grows a live oak believed to be 2,000 years old! The restaurant menu is a la carte, specializing in seafood. In its sidewalk cafe, which is short-order, you can sample such regional specialties as po'boys and red beans and rice. The restaurant is open Monday through Saturday for lunch and dinner. The cafe is open Sunday as well. Phone (601) 374–0163.

Also on Rue Magnolia, at 119, the **Magnolia Hotel and Mardi Gras Museum** is interesting for two reasons. First, it is the only hotel dating

The Conquered Banner

Furl that Banner, for 'tis Weary;
Round its staff 'tis drooping dreary;
Furl it, fold it, it is best;
For there's not a man to wave it,
And there's not a sword to save it,
And there's not one left to lave it
In the blood which heroes gave it;
And its foes now scorn and brave it;
Furl it, hide it—let it rest!

—The first stanza from the poem by Father A. J. Ryan

from before the Civil War left on the Mississippi Gulf Coast. Next, it displays all the trappings of local Mardi Gras festivities. Admission is free, but donations are accepted. Phone (601) 432–8806.

The Old Biloxi region has many old homes that you can study with a self-guided walking tour from the **Biloxi Visitor Center** at the Town Green, 710 Beach Boulevard. The tour includes more than twenty buildings, from Greek Revival to French Colonial. The center is open Monday through Friday 8:00 A.M. to 5:00 P.M.; Saturday 9:00 A.M. to 5:00 P.M.; Sunday noon to 4:00 P.M. Phone (601) 374–3105.

In addition to the downtown sites, you'll find some interesting places to look at along the beach, including the **Biloxi Lighthouse,** at State Highway 90 and Porter Avenue. This lighthouse is 65 feet high, built of cast iron. It was built in 1848. You need an appointment to see the inside. Admission is free, but donations are accepted. Phone (601) 435–6293.

You may be able to arrange to take the **Biloxi Shrimping Trip,** which leaves from the Small Craft Harbor, off Highway 90 at Main Street. These tours, aboard a reconditioned shrimp boat, take about seventy minutes. During this time you will learn about the shrimping industry, sail into the gulf, and watch the entire shrimping process, beginning with the casting of the nets. The boat only leaves when at least a dozen people are aboard. It doesn't go at all in bad weather or during winter months. You should definitely phone ahead to make arrangements (601–374–5718).

Another possible shipboard experience is a trip on the *Glenn L. Swetman,* moored in the Point Cadet Marina. The boat is a replica of Biloxi seafood schooners in the late 1800s. For about $15, it takes you on a two-and-a-half-hour trip along the harbor; however, you have to be there at a time when it's not out on charter. For full details, phone (601) 435–6320.

Even if you can't manage a shrimp trip, you can still learn a lot about the seafood industry at the **Seafood Industry Museum,** Cadet Point Plaza, 115 First Street, just west of the Ocean Springs Bridge off State Highway 90. Exhibits tell the story of the growth and changes in the Mississippi seafood industry, with displays of antique tools, photographs, and artifacts explaining boat building, and information about the predominant local food—seafood. Open Monday through Saturday 9:00 A.M. to 5:00 P.M. Admission is about $2.50 adults, less for children. Phone (601) 435–6320.

From Biloxi you pass through Gulfport, a planned city that didn't have much activity at all until railroads came to town at the beginning of the twentieth century. The history here begins mostly with post-World War II influences, so move on to **Long Beach.** This area used to be an Indian village, with a trading post for a number of Native American tribes that lived in the gulf. It is also reputed to be where a pirate named Pitcher hid his treasure; so far, no one has found it. You'll stop here mainly to see a tree: **Friendship Oak,** on campus of the University of Southern Mississippi, Gulf Park, stands 50 feet high and has a trunk 17 feet around.

Several pleasant restaurants on Beach Boulevard specialize in seafood prepared with a Southern touch. Any one of them makes a nice stop in your travels. You may find that you eat shrimp with even more enthusiasm now that you know what goes into catching it.

You're no sooner out of Long Beach than you're into **Pass Christian.** Indians used to live here, too, but the town's fame came primarily from its popularity as a summer resort. During the 1800s the Gulf Coast was called the "American Riviera," and Pass Christian was known as "The Pass." Incidentally, you do not pronounce this the way it sounds; the proper pronunciation is *paw crist-ee-AN.* Wealthy planters and six different presidents vacationed here, all pronouncing it correctly, no doubt. This community has a small historic district, an inn, and an outstanding restaurant as well as crafts, specialty, and antiques shops. In the historic district are some good examples of old architecture marked with plaques explaining the significance of each building. One typical such plaque, on the **Union Quarters** house on Scenic Drive, explains that the home was used as quarters for Union officers in April 1862, during the Yankee occupation of the city. To show good faith, the Yankees asked the lady of the house, Mrs. Mary K. Walker Saucier, to play the Confederate song "Bonnie Blue Flag." You can't go inside, but you can get a good sense of the place by looking at its white iron fences and studying its exterior.

Overlooking the harbor and beach on West Scenic Drive, **Harbour Oaks Inn** offers bed-and-breakfast accommodations. The inn was built about 1860, then called The Crescent Hotel. After years of popularity it

Spanish Moss

You will find Spanish moss anywhere in the South where the climate is warm and the humidity is high. A popular legend about Spanish moss is recounted in the self-published 1993 book *Coasting: An Insider's Guide to the Gulf Coast,* by Judy Barnes, Jolane Edwards, Carolyn Lee Goodloe, and Laurel Wilson. It seems that on her wedding day, an Indian princess cut her long hair, as was traditional, and hung it over an oak. But the bridal couple were killed that same day and buried under that same tree. The princess's hair turned gray and started to grow, and it has been spreading among the trees ever since.

There is so much of the moss that people have been trying to find a use for it ever since. Spanish moss has been tried as a packing material, bagged as a decorative item for florists, and tied with ribbons and sold for plant lovers to take home and hang in their showers. Perhaps most unusual, it was used to stuff a mattress that is still in place in a bed in Louisiana (see page 122). When Spanish moss is alive, it is soft and pliable, gray-green in color. When it dies it becomes brittle, dusty, and turns a dull gray. If you want to take some home with you, keep it damp as you travel, then, once home, keep it hanging in the shower to provide the moisture it needs to stay alive.

fell upon hard times and is now being restored, a floor at a time, by the owners, Tony and Diane Brugger. This place has the quintessential Southern elements—a veranda with rockers for watching boats in the harbor, ancient live oak trees dripping with Spanish moss out back, and, inside, easy hospitality, including a guest kitchen where you can make coffee or serve yourself wine from the refrigerator. Rates begin at about $80. Phone (601) 452–9399.

The next town you come to as you drive along the beach road, U.S. Highway 90, is **Bay St. Louis.** This area was occupied by the French at the end of the 1600s, then by the Spanish. Finally, in the early 1800s, it was made part of the United States. Like Pass Christian, the town was a resort for wealthy planters and merchants from New Orleans. Although the many fine old hotels are gone, many of the Victorian homes still stand. You can pick up material for a walking tour of the historic sites at the **Historical Society Home,** 108 Cue Street. The tour takes you past a number of old buildings in the area called "Old Towne," where some of the little houses still have tin roofs. On Main Street, a series of specialty shops sell antiques and collectibles, art, and gift items.

If you enjoy Creole and Cajun foods, stop at the **Creole Kitchen,** 207 Main Street, to buy some take-home packages of the picante sauces, seasonings, sausages, and pralines that typify these spicy cuisines. The shop is open Monday through Saturday.

North Carolina

 ONE OF THE GREAT SURPRISES ABOUT NORTH CAROLINA is how little, beyond the name Carolina, it has in common with South Carolina. Not that there aren't some similarities; both states claim that milk is the state beverage, for instance. More seriously, North Carolina also was one of the original Thirteen Colonies and figured heavily in the Revolutionary War. But when it came to the Civil War, the two states took separate paths. Where South Carolina was passionately secessionist and remains to this day self-consciously and deliberately Southern, North Carolina developed a different character.

One reason was that North Carolina had not been shaped so much by the English-style aristocracy of the other Southern seaboard colonies. More often, this state attracted subsistence farmers and small tradespeople. While the cotton and rice culture of the Deep South supported a lifestyle rather like that of England's landed gentry, North Carolinians were mostly yeoman farmers who worked alongside their slaves, if they had any, and tradespeople who practiced their skills and taught them to their sons. Manufacturers in the state developed strong relationships with Northern markets, so it is not surprising that when secession became an issue, many North Carolinians did not want to leave the Union. Being completely surrounded by secessionist states, however, they had little choice.

North Carolina thus seceded on May 20, 1861. The war took a heavy toll. According to Barbara Ryan, an innkeeper in Durham and a longtime

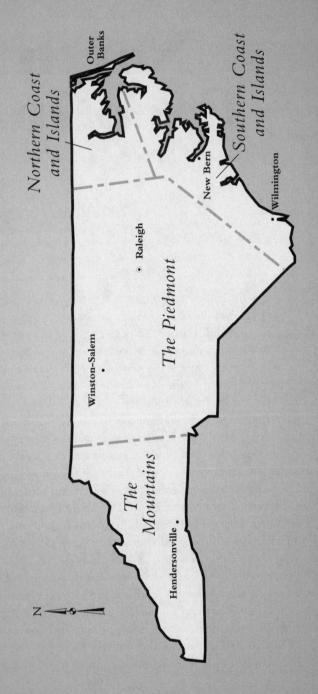

student of the state's history, ten Civil War battles occurred in North Carolina. North Carolina troops counted for more than a quarter of the casualties in the entire South; more troops came from here than any other state. General William Tecumseh Sherman's march destroyed farms, and Reconstruction ruined businesses. But commerce, science and technology, education, medicine, and tourism helped the state survive and thrive. Its good-natured people helped, too.

THE NORTHERN COAST AND ISLANDS

To get a taste of the antebellum South, North Carolina style, start in the northern coastal area, the site of the earliest attempts at European colonization. In the extreme northeast corner, visit North Carolina's first town, **Bath,** established in 1705. Back in those days it must have seemed like a good place to put a town. The spot was close to both the Pamlico River and the Ocracoke Inlet of the Atlantic Ocean. Some French Protestants came down from Virginia to settle; some English colonists were also attracted to the area. Within three years the town had a dozen houses and about fifty inhabitants. They lived on naval trade, furs, and tobacco. In just a few more years, they added a grist mill and a shipyard, then a public library, and a free school for Indians and blacks.

But all was not calm. Blackbeard the pirate kept sailing in and hanging around. Political rivals fought. Indians attacked. Yellow fever and drought struck. It was some years before things settled down enough for the citizens to build a courthouse (1723) and a church (1734). Then they started ferry service across the Pamlico River and built a postal road between Bath and New Bern and Edenton.

A merchant built what in 1751 was the largest home in Bath. During these years governors and politicians lived and met in Bath and considered the town the colony's capital. But, fickle as politicians are wont to be, they shifted their interest to the town of Washington, about 15 miles up the Pamlico River, in 1776. The Beaufort County government settled in Washington in 1785, and that changed everything. Although the Marsh and Bonner families came as merchants and built homes, and Jacon Van Der Veer manufactured rope at the edge of town and operated a steam sawmill along with Joseph Bonner, no new spurts of growth ever took hold. Even today Bath remains a tiny village with a population of only a few hundred people. But it has the distinction of being one place *not* occupied by Union troops during the Civil War, so the early buildings remain intact, giving you a glimpse of one kind of antebellum South—the sedate, seaside village where not too much of anything happens.

The North Carolina Department of Cultural Resources operates the **Historic Bath Visitor Center** on Carteret Street (drive in on State Highway 92). It offers tours of the **Palmer-Marsh House,** the **Van Der Veer House,** and the **Bonner House.** You may also go into the **St. Thomas Church.** In the Palmer-Marsh House, you'll find the original colonial kitchen in the cellar. The Van Der Veer House functions as a museum, with exhibits relating to village history. And the Bonner House contains period furnishings. All these restored old buildings are part of a National Register historic district marked by the boundaries of the original town.

The Historic Bath Visitor Center is open April through October from 9:00 A.M. to 5:00 P.M.; Sunday 1:00 to 5:00 P.M. Closed Monday, and with operating shorter hours in winter. Admission to tour homes is about $1.00 per building for adults, half that for children. Phone (919) 923–3971.

Moving south, along the coast, at Albemarle Sound, **Elizabeth City** and **Edenton,** two communities about 30 miles apart on Highway 17, offer a lot of romantic history. In Elizabeth City, the thirty-three-block historic district has the largest number of pre-Civil War commercial buildings in North Carolina. A map for a self-guided walking tour is available from the **Chamber of Commerce,** on Ehringhaus Street, open Monday through Friday 9:00 A.M. to 5:00 P.M. Phone (919) 335–4365. About 2 miles south of Elizabeth City on State Highway 17, the **Museum of the Albemarle** commemorates the importance of Native Americans in the region with displays of Indian artifacts. It is open Tuesday through Saturday 9:00 A.M. to 5:00 P.M.; Sunday 2:00 to 5:00 P.M. Admission is free. Phone (919) 335–1453.

Farther south, Edenton is 90 miles east of I–95 at the junction of Highways 17 and 32. Broad Street runs through the center of town. Edenton, located directly on the Albemarle Sound, has done a wonderful job of preserving its historic heritage, appealing to travelers, and cultivating the natural beauty of the area. The town was settled in 1685 and was incorporated in 1722 as the first capital of the province of North Carolina.

Blackbeard frequented this area, which makes sense when you realize that this was a busy port town in the eighteenth and early nineteenth centuries. It was an important point during the Revolutionary War for shipping in supplies to transport north to George Washington's army. Early leaders in the town included men who signed the Declaration of Independence, defied the British blockades, and helped ratify the United States Constitution. Female activists held forth, too. In 1774 fifty-one women signed a declaration in the courthouse square vowing not to drink tea or wear clothing from England. Many of the people who live here descend directly from those early leaders and take visible pride in sharing their heritage with visitors.

This is one of those places where everything just seems to work. Much of the waterfront area is devoted to public park areas, which are nice for strolling and enjoying the Albemarle Sound and Edenton Bay. Even the courthouse, **Chowan County Courthouse,** on East King Street, a 1767 building in fine condition, sits facing the water. It is believed to be the oldest courthouse in continuous use in North Carolina.

Buildings in the historic district date from the eighteenth and nineteenth centuries. They include the **Cupola House,** 408 South Broad Street, built in 1758; **St. Paul's Episcopal Church,** on the corner of Broad and Church Streets, built about 1736; and **James Iredell House State Historic Site,** 105 East Church Street, built in 1773. Walking tours leave daily from the Visitor Center, 108 North Broad Street. The center is open Monday through Saturday from 9:00 A.M. to 5:00 P.M.; Sunday 1:00 to 5:00 P.M.; closed at 4:00 P.M. from October to April. Tour tickets are $5.00 for adults, less for children, with a maximum family rate of $12. Phone (919) 482–2637.

While you are in Edenton, you can stay at one of the most agreeable inns in the state, **The Lords Proprietors' Inn,** 300 North Broad Street. The inn comprises three separate restored buildings in the historic district. They are set around manicured gardens and a brick patio. Together, these buildings have a total of twenty guest rooms, three parlors, and a library. One of the buildings, the Pack House, used to be a tobacco barn. It was cut in half and moved in two pieces. As you would expect with a tobacco barn, the spaces are huge and the ceilings seem as high as the sky. Guest rooms front on a balcony running around the inside of the building, overlooking common rooms. The old-time feel is accentuated by antiques and chintz upholstery. Breakfast and dinner are served in another building, the Whedbee House, set at the center of the complex. Dinner is served only to guests. The entrees are definitely more contemporary than Old South (a roast pork with porcini mushroom sauce, for instance), but the ingredients, especially game and fish, have always been the main foods of the region. Rates begin at about $120 per room. Inquire about single rates. Phone (919) 482–3641.

Edenton is near two of the most instructive plantations open for tours in the South—**Hope Plantation** and **Somerset Place.** Part of the beauty of these places is that they go beyond the standard Civil War and political themes to show you what daily life was like in the region.

Hope Plantation is about 20 miles west of Edenton, in the little community of Windsor, on State Highway 308, then 4 miles west of the highway bypass. This is a project in process, so when you visit you may find more than is mentioned here. The plantation re-creates rural domestic life in northeastern North Carolina from about 1763. Governor David Stone, who later served as a U.S. senator, owned the plantation, which at one time encompassed more than 5,000 acres, planted in wheat and corn. The plantation was self-sufficient, with mills, woodworking and ironworking shops, and everything else necessary to sustain homestead life.

There are two homes on the Hope Plantation, one built about 1763, the other in about 1803. They have overtones of every kind of architecture from Medieval English through Neoclassical. Touring these buildings, furnished as they might have been during their years as homes, you come to understand how the needs and knowledge of North Carolinians living here must have changed as time passed. When this project is complete, you will find research-based examples of a kitchen reconstructed on its original foundation, outbuildings, and historically authentic gardens. The plantation is open March through December, Monday through Saturday 10:00 A.M. to 4:00 P.M.; Sunday 2:00 to 5:00 P.M. Admission is about $6.50 for adults, less for students. Phone (919) 794–3140.

The other plantation, **Somerset Place,** nearby in Creswell, on Lake Phelps, is historically fascinating, because of the remarkably complete records kept by the family that owned it, the Collinses. Josiah Collins was a merchant who came to Edenton from England in 1774. He joined other investors to form the Lake Company. They had slaves dig a 6-mile-long canal joining Lake Phelps to the Scuppernong River. The family records kept track of all the more than 300 slaves who worked on the plantation by 1860. These records detail the births, deaths, and marriages of the slaves, as well as the particular skills and duties of each one; for instance, because of these records, we know that the slave Luke Davis cleaned carpets, another was good at woodworking, and so on. There is even more information available from the records of the physician Dr. John Kooner, who stayed at the plantation several weeks at a time to treat the Collins family and the slave population. Kooner described a dance from Africa that the slaves performed every Christmas, in which they began at the great house and gradually worked their way in a sort of conga line along the plantation paths, ending up at the slaves' quarters.

The Greek Revival–style house, with fourteen rooms, was built in the 1830s. A tour includes the house, gardens, and restored outbuildings. Guides tell how, during the good years, grist mills and sawmills turned out rice and lumber, which were shipped down the canal to the river. But this is a real-life story, not a fairy tale, and people didn't always live happily ever after. The water required to flood the rice fields, for example, attracted mosquitoes, and the mosquitoes infected the slaves with malaria. Josiah Collins changed the crops to corn and wheat, which required less moisture, and eventually bought out his partners. When he died his son, also named Josiah, took over the property and turned it into a thriving business. In North Carolina, where few people owned any slaves at all, at one time Collins had more than 300. The family also had its share of tragedy: Two of Collins's sons and two slave boys drowned playing in the canal. The Civil War ruined the plantation, and the remaining Collins family moved away. The state runs the site today.

As research continues, more true stories come to light; your tour here won't be a canned spiel. Somerset is open April through October, Monday through Saturday 9:00 A.M. to 5:00 P.M.; Sunday 1:00 to 5:00 P.M. During the winter months the plantation is closed Monday, open shorter hours the rest of the time. Admission is free. Phone (919) 797–4560. To get to the plantation, follow the sign at Creswell marking the turn.

Roanoke Island is part of the region known as the **Outer Banks,** where Sir Walter Raleigh tried, with a group of English men, to establish the first English colony in America in 1584. Because things did not go well, those who didn't die soon went back to England. Raleigh tried again in 1587. This time he included women and children in the group, with John White as leader. Then Sir Walter sailed off on a supply trip, which took three years, and in that time the colony disappeared without a trace, putting the "Lost Colony" forever into American lore. (There is some current speculation that the Lumbee Indians in the Pembroke area of North Carolina may be descended from that early colony.)

Coming Home

One of the difficulties for many black people tracing their family trees in America is that records for slaves were seldom kept as faithfully as for those on the Collins Plantation. Dorothy Spruill Redford, a descendant of the original Somerset slave families, put in years of painstaking research, beginning with the Somerset records, to identify and locate the descendants of other Somerset families. She got in touch with all she could find to arrange a massive gathering at the plantation. She tells the story of the reunion and includes plantation history in her book *Somerset Homecoming: Recovering a Lost Heritage* (Doubleday, 1988).

These events happened well before the antebellum years but are so much a part of the continuum from early settlement through the Civil War that you need to see the sites as part of understanding the forces that shaped the Old South. **Fort Raleigh National Historic Site,** about 3 miles north of Manteo on the island, is a restored fort commemorating the colony and noting the birth of Virginia Dare, the first English child born in America. The **Visitor Center** offers interpretive programs and displays. It is open Monday through Saturday 9:00 A.M. to 8:00 P.M.; Sunday 9:00 A.M. to 6:00 P.M. After Labor Day the hours are 9:00 A.M. to 5:00 P.M. daily. Closed Christmas. Admission is free. Phone (919) 473–5772.

Another memorial, **Elizabethan Gardens,** re-creates sixteenth-century, British-style formal gardens, using plants that thrive in this part of North Carolina. Something is blooming almost all year, beginning with the spring bulbs, azaleas, rhododendrons, and dogwoods, next moving into the bright summer annuals, then to fall mums, and, finally, to camellias through the winter. The complex includes a sunken garden, terraces, garden ornaments, a rose garden, and an ancient live oak tree. You'll see here many of the gardening conventions brought over with the British, that even now influence the gardens for which the South is famous. The gardens are open all year 9:00 A.M. to dusk. A small admission fee is charged; children under twelve are admitted free if accompanied by an adult. Phone (919) 473–3234.

Across the bridge from the Manteo waterfront, the **Elizabeth II State Historic Site** provides a different glimpse of the British influence. The museum exhibits show the nature of life in the sixteenth century. A reproduction of a sailing vessel like the one that brought the first colonists to Roanoke is the centerpiece of the site. A twenty-minute multimedia presentation shows what it would have been like to live on such a ship for the duration of the voyage. The reasons for old Southern pride in owning imported English antiques become clear: They were hard and costly to bring in. The site is open November 1 through October 31, Tuesday through Sunday 10:00 A.M. to 4:00 P.M.; the last tour begins at 3:00 P.M. From April through October the site is open daily 10:00 A.M. to 6:00 P.M., with the last tour beginning at 5:00 P.M. Admission is $3.00. Phone (919) 473–1144.

If you spend the night on the island, you might stay at **Tranquil House Inn,** on the waterfront. The building is new but was built in the style of the inns that were typical in this area during the 1800s. These were places to which those who could afford it retreated from the summer heat inland. Slips for sailboats in Shallowbag Bay come up to the rear of the inn. From the dining room or second-floor veranda, you look out over the bay as the earlier Southerners might have done. Inside, oriental rugs, antiques, and cypress woodwork blend the old and the new comfortably. The inn has a popular restaurant, **The 1587 Restaurant,** where the cuisine is clearly contemporary, but the ingredients—crab, duck, fish, and shrimp— are those that the people of Roanoke Island have been pulling from the area waters for centuries.

Another eating place on the island, a few miles away at **Wanchese,** gives you a sense of the simpler lives of those who earned their livings fishing. Wanchese was named for an Indian who lived on the island and then sailed off to England. Most of the people in this community still like to imagine that life has changed relatively little over the years here. **Fisherman's Wharf Restaurant** is a large, simple restaurant on the wharf where you can order seafood recently brought in on the very ships you see out the windows. The restaurant closes during the winter months, usually opening after Easter. Food is served Monday through Saturday noon to 9:00 P.M. Phone (919) 473–5205.

Much of the rest of these Outer Banks islands has become standard resort territory, though some notable historic sites are scattered about. The Wright brothers flew the first airplane at Kill Devil Hills in 1903, well after the Dixie days. And the Cape Hatteras Lighthouse, the tallest lighthouse in

America, built in 1869, still stands despite coastal erosion and violent storms. In fact, the area is probably better known for its heavy storms and dangerous waters than for its Southern romance. The shifting islands and difficult weather have prevented these areas from developing as seaports. As a result, what hasn't become resort territory tends to be undeveloped. You can still find great stretches of rough but unspoiled beach along the islands and peninsulas.

An exception to these generalizations is **Ocracoke Island,** which harbors a fishing village of the same name. Visually, Ocracoke epitomizes an old Southern island town, with weathered houses, unpaved streets, and live oaks festooned in Spanish moss. Blackbeard the pirate spent a lot of time here. He is supposed to have buried his treasure here. He also lost his head here, but for reasons we'd probably have trouble understanding today, it got carried off to (and, presumably, eventually buried in) Bath. Ocracoke Island is the kind of place about which people like to say "time stands still," partly because of the slow pace of life on the island and partly because its language and traditions go on here much as they have for centuries, due to the island's isolation from the mainland. Indeed, some of the old people still speak in the cadences and vernacular of Old English.

Even the animal life goes way back. The island is famous for its pony pens, a protected area for the descendants of Spanish mustangs.

One of the most interesting places to stay on the island is **Oscar's House,** a small bed-and-breakfast inn named for the lighthouse keeper who once lived in it. It is furnished in comfortable, sturdy antiques—not Victorian torture chairs—that let you relax easily. The innkeeper, Ann Ehringhaus, is also a photographer. Her book *Ocracoke Portrait,* a collection of her photographs with quotations from the people who live on the island, portray a kind of Southern calm unlike anything you'll find elsewhere in the South. The inn is open April through October. Phone (919) 928–1311.

How you get to any of the Outer Banks islands depends on where you are when you decide to cross over. Ferries run from several spots, and bridges span the water in other places. Sometimes the bridges are affected by storms. For full information about ferry schedules and bridges, contact the **Ocracoke Visitor Center** at (919) 928–4531 or the **Outer Banks Chamber of Commerce** at (919) 441–8144.

You'll need a ferry to see another place that is most easily reached from Ocracoke. **Portsmouth Island,** uninhabited now, once was home to about 600 people, in **Portsmouth Village.** Today most of the island is in

Portsmouth Village, on Portsmouth Island, is deserted now because a hurricane in 1846 changed shipping patterns and destroyed the island's economic base. The last two women to live on the island left in 1971.

its natural state. It appeals mainly to rugged outdoors types with four-wheel-drive vehicles who look forward to a week fishing for bluefish and spending evenings in male camaraderie. But everyone can agree that Portsmouth Village is special. Most of the old buildings are still standing, maintained, but not in any way "improved," by the U.S. Park Service. The weathered old Portsmouth Village Methodist Church is open for visitors. Few people visit, but men in fishing clothes sometimes sit quietly on the benches inside. The story of the village is that the bad weather for which this whole northern part of the Outer Banks is notorious, battered the island. A particularly nasty hurricane in 1846 actually changed shipping patterns by opening the Hatteras and Oregon inlets, drawing shipping traffic away from Portsmouth. Without an economic base, the population of Portsmouth Village simply dwindled. The last two women on the island moved off in 1971. It is hard to comprehend how much changing weather patterns have affected development along the coast and on the islands until you see this village. A variety of ferry services can get you to the island, but not always to the village. Services vary with the weather and time of year. For the best advice on how to get there, phone the **Visitor Center** on Harker's Island. The rangers at the visitor center are professional, knowledgeable, and helpful. Phone (919) 728–2250.

THE SOUTHERN COAST AND ISLANDS

Farther south along the North Carolina coast, at the southern end of the Outer Banks, the fishing village of **Beaufort** remains from the days of its early settlement by French Huguenots. This town's port was involved in the American Revolution and the War of 1812. Yankee troops (including General Ambrose Everett Burnside, the guy who made sideburns famous) occupied the town in 1862, shortly after the Civil War began, and remained until the end of the war. And then, either punishing the town further or paying it the ultimate compliment, depending on how you look at it, a lot of those Yankee soldiers stayed on; some brought their wives here to continue living in Beaufort.

The downtown area is a National Historic Landmark, with several of its restored buildings open to the public. This is a good place to see how life in a small Southern fishing village differed from North Carolina plantation life. The best way to learn area history and get inside some of the better buildings is by taking one of the **Beaufort Historic Site Tours.** They leave from the welcome center next to the **1825 Josiah Bell House,** on Turner Street. The tours take something over an hour and include the county courthouse, the county jail, a fisherman's home, and an apothecary shop, with its attendant bottles and bizarre-looking medical instruments of the time. The center is open Monday through Saturday 9:30 A.M. to 4:30 P.M.; tours begin at 10:00 A.M. and end at 3:00 P.M. Admission is $5.00 for adults, less for children. Children under six are admitted free. Phone (919) 728–5225.

From April through October on Monday, Wednesday, and Saturday, a narrated tour aboard an English double-decker bus covers the downtown district, going past a house where Blackbeard and his pirates presumably holed up in the late 1600s. The cost is $5.00 per seat. On Tuesday and Thursday you can take a guided walking tour focusing on architecture, including buildings dating from the early eighteenth to the late nineteenth centuries. Taking about an hour, this tour covers a few square blocks of the two-acre site. Call the welcome center for details of these special tours. In the **Rustell House,** built in 1732, some one hundred local and regional artists offer their work, including many local scenes and seascapes, for sale.

Learn more about early fishing along these shores at the **North Carolina Maritime Museum,** 315 Front Street. If you are interested in natural history, it would be worthwhile to call ahead to ask for a schedule of field trips. They are offered year-round to people wanting to explore the salt marshes and tidal flats. This is also wonderful territory for birdwatching, for looking for fossils, and for finding wildflowers. In the museum, you can study fish in aquariums, inspect fossils from the region, enjoy a model-ship collection, and view a collection of more than 5,000 seashells. The museum is open Monday through Friday 9:00 A.M. to 5:00 P.M.; Saturday 10:00 A.M. to 5:00 P.M.; Sunday 2:00 to 5:00 P.M. Phone (919) 728–7317.

An agreeable place to spend the night in Old South fishing-village style is **Langdon House,** 123 Craven Street. The home was built in 1732. It is the oldest building in Beaufort to be operated as a bed and breakfast. The home has four guest rooms with private baths, and there is lots of room for watching the stars from first- and second-floor verandas. Jimm Prest, the owner and restorer of the building, has furnished it with antiques, paintings, and even musical instruments donated by earlier residents in the interests of authentic restoration. Jimm serves a gourmet breakfast seasoned with local lore. The place is known for Jimm's gourmet cooking, for his special attention to guests, for his knowledge of local history, and for the comfort of the rooms. Rates begin at about $100 per room. Phone (919) 728–5499.

No matter how well you sleep here, the people in the **Old Burying Ground** on Ann Street are probably sleeping better. The stones in this cemetery date back to the very early 1700s. (The numbers are difficult to read, causing some disagreement about exact dates.) The cemetery was deeded to the town of Beaufort in 1731, but it had been used as a burying ground for the local Anglican Church long before graves were even dated.

It tells you something about the religious attitudes of the early Southerners in Beaufort that the older graves face east, so that the dead will be looking in the right direction when they rise to the sun on Judgment Morning. Researchers also know that in this graveyard, a Revolutionary

War soldier is buried standing up, with his boots on. He was a British soldier who wanted to be buried saluting his king and who swore that he would never lie down on foreign soil. From the War of 1812, a sailor off the ship *Snapdragon* is buried on top of the ground, with a cannon from the ship mounted on top of the grave.

And a little girl is buried in a keg of rum. The story is that her father took her off to England on a ship only after promising her mother to bring her back. The child died aboard ship. This rummy embalming was the only way the father could keep his promise.

How do researchers learn this stuff? Well, partly through archaeological research. Then there's that wild coastal weather, with hurricanes and flooding moving things around, uncovering what once was buried. The Beaufort Historical Association sometimes conducts tours of the graveyard, but you may pick up a tour brochure at the visitors' center and walk through the burying grounds yourself anytime.

Farther south, on U.S. 17, the town of **New Bern** epitomizes the open friendliness of the Old South. According to the people at the North Carolina Travel and Tourism Division, New Bern has more than 150 landmarks listed in the National Register of Historic Places. To plan any serious touring, stop on Middle Street for maps and brochures at the **New Bern Area Chamber of Commerce,** in Eby Maxwell House near the Trent River, about 2 blocks from State Highway 70. Signs direct you from all major entrances. Open Monday through Friday 9:00 A.M. to 5:00 P.M. Phone (919) 636–3111.

You might prefer to stop at the **Tryon Palace Restorations and Gardens Complex** to pick up tour maps and cassettes guiding you to the town's major sites. The palace and gardens themselves are a rewarding destination. The Georgian buildings were built in the late 1700s as a meeting place for the colonial assembly and a home for governor William Tryon. An independent state government was housed here next. In colonial times people who saw it considered Tryon Palace the most beautiful building in America. Appropriately ornate period antiques and art furnish the restorations, and the gardens are laid out geometrically, as formal gardens of the eighteenth century usually were. Guides in costume lead you through the palace, showing you demonstrations of cooking, weaving, and other activities of the time. The guides can tell you about the buildings and the people who lived in them. At this same site, **John Wright Stanly House,** a townhouse built in 1783 for a Revolutionary War Patriot, features American antiques. The **Dixon Stevenson House,** built in about 1828, has fine antiques from the Empire and Federal Periods. The Tryon Palace complex is open Monday through Saturday 9:30 A.M. to 4:00 P.M.; Sunday 1:30 to 4:00 P.M. Closed major holidays. Admission is about $8.00 for adults, half that for students with ID. Tickets for viewing both houses and gardens are priced the same. Phone (919) 638–1560.

Of the several bed-and-breakfast accommodations in New Bern, **Harmony House Inn,** 215 Pollock Street, is most likely to give you a view of the quirky side of old Southern families. This is not to say that the owners, Ed and Sookie Kirkpatrick, are quirky. They are hospitable, competent innkeepers. And they'll tell you about the history of the house; this is where quirky comes in. The Greek Revival house was built in about 1850. As the owner's six children were born, he built additions to the house to accommodate them all. As grown-ups, two of the sons wanted to live in the house with their own families. To settle the issue, they sawed the house in half and moved one half of it 9 feet away. This allowed the addition of a hallway, front door, staircase, and sitting room to the moved half. Each family lived in one half of the house, separate but under the same roof, for about twenty years.

Now, all one house again, Harmony House Inn has nine guest rooms and a suite—and two halls, two sitting rooms, and two front doors, side by side. The result is wonderfully spacious and light. The parlor is furnished with antiques and memorabilia, including a pump organ in perfect working condition. Rates, including a full breakfast, begin at about $85 per night for doubles, less for singles. Phone (919) 636–3810 or (800) 636–3113.

Just a couple of doors down the street, at 216 Pollock, **Henderson House,** a restaurant that has been popular in New Bern for more than twenty years, serves upscale lunches and dinners with a fine Southern flair. The house was built about 1809 and has Greek Revival–style woodwork on the first floor, in line with the early Southern tradition of making the public rooms elaborate and allowing the private, upstairs rooms to be more simple. The menu includes fine seafood dishes, including broiled crabmeat, and a gourmet version of Southern peanut soup. All spirits are served. You can pick up a brochure giving the history of the house going back to when the lot it is built on was purchased in 1749. Lunch is served from 11:00 A.M.; dinner begins at 6:00 P.M. Phone (919) 673–4784.

Harmony House and Henderson House are in a neighborhood where people take a lively interest in restoration and preservation. A simple walk around a block or two will give you a chance to see lots of fine old homes.

It is not uncommon for visitors walking these streets to strike up conversations with the owners of the buildings, especially during the evening porch-sitting season. Sometimes owners invite visitors in to look around; sometimes visitors end up sharing tea or cocktails on the porch. That easy hospitality is New Bern's style.

Living Through the Occupation

Union forces took New Bern on March 14, 1862. It wasn't an even battle—there were only about 800 Rebel troops against 11,000 Union men. The townspeople were so scared that some of them took off without even removing food cooking on the stove. After their victory the Yankee troops took over the town. They pitched tent camps on lawns and established headquarters in homes (including the Isaac Taylor House, which still stands at 228 Craven Street). They used the New Bern Academy, the Masonic Building, and Stanly Hospital as their hospitals. They turned the Jones House, on Eden Street, into a jail for Confederate prisoners of war.

As time passed the Yankees established their routines, and the locals set up their own communication and transportation networks. The newspaper continued to print. Everybody had enough to eat. Many slaves escaped into the city because it was federally held territory—getting into it automatically made them free. Although the city suffered repeated looting during the Civil War, it was never burned. Many old buildings still stand. The site of the 1862 battle is somewhat intact, with earthworks and a petrified tree still full of old bullets. In Cedar Grove Cemetery, a Confederate memorial, erected in 1878 by the Ladies Memorial Association of New Bern, stands on a brick vault. It contains the remains of about seventy Confederate soldiers.

Bruce Godfrey told the full story in the March 1995 edition of *New Bern Magazine*. Bonnie Hobbs wrote about the battle and what remains of the site in the *Sun Journal* newspaper. And New Bern historian John Leys prepared a brochure about the battle strategy and occupation. For more details, contact Leys at (919) 637–9400. For more details about seeing the battle site, phone Will Georges at the New Bern Civil War Museum, (919) 633–2818.

Two other attractions give a taste of what it would have been like to live here during the antebellum and war years. The **New Bern Civil War Museum,** 301 Metcalf Street, has a fine collection of Civil War artifacts, including a chair that General Ulysses S. Grant used for sitting in the field, Union and Confederate Army uniforms, items from the troops battle-camps, and, of course, weapons. The museum is open Tuesday through Sunday 10:00 A.M. to 4:00 P.M. Closed holidays. Admission is about $2.50 for adults, less for senior citizens and children. Phone (919) 633–2818.

At 411 Hancock Street, the **Fireman's Museum** displays a collection of equipment belonging to the local fire company, which was North Carolina's first, founded in about 1845. There are also some items from the Button Company, a rival volunteer company. Early pump wagons and steamers and lots of photographs demonstrate that even in the days of horse-drawn vehicles, volunteer firemen helped preserve our homes and businesses. The museum is open Tuesday through Saturday 9:30 A.M. to noon and 1:00 to 5:00 P.M.; Sunday 1:00 to 5:00 P.M. Admission is about $2.00 for adults, half that for children. Phone (919) 636–4087.

Still moving south along the coast of North Carolina, you will come to **Wilmington,** settled before the American Revolution and even now a thriving deep-port city on the Cape Fear River. Wilmington was the last Atlantic port open to Civil War blockade-runners. Because the area boasts a lot of history, residents have worked hard to preserve important sites. The **Historic Wilmington District** includes a variety of homes, businesses, churches, and gardens.

The **Burgwin-Wright House and Garden,** at the corner of Third and Market Streets, dates back to the American Revolution, when Lord Cornwallis headquartered in it. It was built in 1770 on the foundation of the old Wilmington City Jail, with part of the old jail walls forming the foundation of the house. A separate cookhouse and the gardens are included in the tour. The Colonial Dames and the State of North Carolina own and operate this project. The house is open Saturday through Tuesday 10:00 A.M. to 4:00 P.M.; Saturday 10 A.M. to 3:00 P.M. Admission is about $3.00 for adults, $1.00 for children. Phone (910) 762–0492.

Nearby, at 126 South Third Street, the **Zebulon Latimer House,** a four-story, colonial gentleman's townhouse dating from 1852, is remarkable for having been owned by the same family until the Historical Society (which is housed there now) took it over in the 1960s. Well over half the furnishings in the house today belonged to the original family. Three of the four floors in the building are open to the public, giving you a chance to see every aspect of daily life, from breakfast downstairs to day's end in the bedrooms. The house is open, with guided tours, Tuesday through Saturday 10:00 A.M. to 4:00 P.M. Admission is about $3.00 for adults, $1.00 for children. Phone (910) 762–0492.

An appealing way to learn about the area is through the **Wilmington Adventure Tours,** offered by Bob Jenkins. Jenkins calls his tours a "casual stroll," but he offers lots of information as you move along the original survey of the 1734 city. Tours begin at the foot of Market Street, on the Cape Fear River. Tickets are about $10.00 for adults, half that for children. Phone (910) 763–1785.

Should walking seem too strenuous, try a **Springbrook Farms** carriage or trolley tour. Both leave from the corner of Water and Market Streets. Hours and days of operation vary with the season, however, and costs vary with the kind of tour that you book, so be sure to call ahead for specifics (910–251–8889).

Another option is a water tour. **Captain J. N. Maffitt River Cruises** leave from Riverfront Park, at the corner of Market and Water Streets. Narrations cover the history of Wilmington and the waterfront. Tickets are about $9.00 for adults, $4.00 for children. Hours and days of operation vary with the seasons. Phone (910) 343–1611 or (800) 676–0162.

Cape Fear Museum, 814 Market Street, tells the story of the area mainly from a nautical perspective. One of the most popular exhibits is a large, glassed-in scale model of the Wilmington waterfront district in 1863. Another popular exhibit, "Sea-Skiff," gives you an idea of the continuing importance of boats in Wilmington. The exhibit tells the story of a cabinet maker named Simmons who, without diagrams or earlier boat-crafting experience, built such a fine a vessel that his reputation as a boatbuilder took hold and swelled. While he lived and worked in this century, the value that people placed on his skills was a holdover from the early years on the water. The museum also features a diorama in which the Battle of Fort Fisher is re-created, complete with lights and sound. The museum is open Tuesday through Saturday 9:00 A.M. to 5:00 P.M.; Sunday 2:00 to 5:00 P.M. Closed holidays. Admission is about $2.00 adults, half that for children and senior citizens. Phone (910) 341–4350.

A good place to stay in Wilmington for a dose of real Southern hospitality is **Catherine's Inn.** This Italianate house, on the waterfront, was built in 1883. That's a little late to qualify as an antebellum mansion, but when it comes to old-style hospitality, Catherine Ackiss, the innkeeper, could have taught even Scarlett a few things. As she tells the story, Catherine had a passion to be a hostess and she looked around Wilmington until she found a place suitable to operate as an inn. Her first inn was on Orange Street, near the center of the historic district. When she outgrew this site, she moved to her current location, 410 South Front Street. She filled the house with family antiques, including many pieces that she refinished herself, and put into practice the niceties that she had come to enjoy as a traveler herself. For instance, she leaves coffee outside the guest rooms early in the morning for those who rise well before breakfast. Breakfast itself is a time of excellent homemade food and laughing conversations. At other times, on an upstairs screened veranda, you may help yourself to wine, beer, and soft drinks kept in a refrigerator for guests. From here you can watch the sun set over a 300-foot lawn overlooking a sunken garden and the Cape Fear River. Catherine's rates begin at about $65 per room, including a full breakfast. Phone (910) 251–0863 or (800) 476–0723.

About 20 miles south of Wilmington is an attraction that demonstrates the continuity of our history in an unusually graphic way. **Brunswick Town** has two important sites. The first is the excavated remains of colonial Brunswick Town. This was a busy seaport in the 1700s from which lumber and naval supplies were exported. It is also where colonists defied the British in rebelling against the Stamp Act in 1765. The British burned the town in 1776, after which it was not rebuilt. But in 1862 the Confederate Army built Fort Anderson to defend the Port of Wilmington against Union troops. The Confederates built the fort on top of the Brunswick Town site, but they didn't use it for very long—they left in February 1865, just a month after the Yankees took Wilmington.

When you visit here today you see both the ruins of the colonial town and the earthen mounds of the Confederate Fort Anderson, with interpretive exhibits strategically placed throughout. You will learn more if you stop first at the visitors' center to look at maps and exhibits and watch the fourteen-minute slide show about the site's history. The walking tour, which includes the ruins of St. Philips Anglican Church, one of the oldest churches in the state, will take at least another hour and a half. The brick walls of the church still stand, showing the placement of doors and windows. The roof is gone, as is the floor, so that standing inside gives you an eerie feeling as you put your feet on the ground and look up directly at treetops and sky. To get to Brunswick Town, take U.S. Highway 17 south to State Highway 133 and follow the signs. Admission is free. The site is open April through October, Monday through Saturday 9:00 A.M. to 5:00 P.M.; Sunday 1:00 to 5:00 P.M. During the fall and winter months, hours are shorter and the site is closed Monday. Phone (910) 371–6613.

Also on State Highway 133, **Orton Plantation,** originally an eighteenth-century rice plantation, welcomes visitors to its gardens. The mansion, built in 1735 and considered an excellent example of antebellum architecture, is still used as a residence and is not open to the public, although you are welcome to study the building from the outside. This mansion survived the Civil War because it was used as a hospital for Union soldiers. The gardens, covering about twenty-five acres, are loveliest in early spring, March and April, when azaleas, dogwoods, fruit trees, and camellias are all blooming. During the summer months, though, daylilies, gardenias, annuals, and crape myrtles also put on a fine show. The gardens include formal and informal plantings, some statuary, a fountain, and, near the entrance, a small white chapel. Also, the grounds are dotted with some very old examples of that most Southern of trees, the live oak. The gardens are open March through November, every day from 8:00 A.M. They close at 6:00 P.M. in the spring and summer, and at 5:00 P.M. in the fall and winter months. Admission is about $8.00 for adults, with discounts for senior citizens and children. Phone (910) 371–6851.

Back closer to Wilmington, visit **Fort Fisher State Historic Site,** 3 miles south of Kure Beach, on State Highway 421, to see where the earlier battle that led to the abandonment of Fort Anderson took place. The fort sustained heavy naval attack during the Civil War, and for a time the 25-foot earthen fortifications kept the Cape Fear River and the Port of Wilmington protected from Union forces. Some of the fortifications still stand, leaving you to marvel at the extraordinary amount of human labor that must have been required to build them in those days before heavy equipment did the hauling. You can learn more by studying the reconstruction of gun placement and walking the history trail. Inside, the museum exhibits include Civil War artifacts and a slide show detailing the fort's story. Fort Fisher is open April through October, Monday through Saturday 9:00 A.M. to 5:00 P.M.; Sunday 1:00 to 5:00 P.M. Hours are shorter and the site is closed Monday during the other months. Admission is free, but donations are appreciated. Phone (910) 458–5538.

Finally, if you travel north rather than south on U.S. Highway 17, you will come to **Poplar Grove Plantation,** a good place to learn about the day-to-day routines of a North Carolina plantation. Before the Civil War the plantation operated as a self-supporting agricultural community, with more than sixty slaves. The manor house burned down in 1849 and was rebuilt the following year. This three-story, Greek Revival–style building is the house you tour when you visit today.

Guides in antebellum costume lead you through the manor and out-buildings. In the manor, bedrooms occupy the top floor; a parlor, dining room, and library fill the main floor; and displays of handmade textiles, quilts, and coverlets take up part of the lower floor. In the textile area, such old pieces of equipment as looms, spinning wheels, and an early sewing machine are displayed. In another area, agricultural displays emphasize the production of peanuts, the crop that made the plantation profitable again after the devastation of the Civil War. Among the outbuildings are a tenant house, smokehouse, herb cellar, kitchen, and blacksmith shop, as well as some rough tenant houses. In the cultural arts center, craftspeople demonstrate the activities that kept the plantation going. A nice general store offers souvenirs and craft items, such as rugs and baskets, made on the property. The Poplar Grove grounds have lots of open spaces, with some farm animals and, for cooling shade, live oaks and sycamores.

The plantation's restaurant, housed in a new building put up especially for the purpose, serves basic Southern cooking for lunch and dinner, with an emphasis on locally grown fresh fruits and vegetables. You may see the people who work in the restaurant arrive with produce from their own gardens to prepare in the restaurant kitchen. Vegetables have always been the backbone of Southern cooking, during good times and bad, so you'll be sampling authentic Southern food when you eat here. Phone (910) 686–9503.

The plantation is open Monday through Saturday 9:00 A.M. to 5:00 P.M., Sunday noon to 5:00 P.M. Closed from December 24 through January and Thanksgiving Day. Admission is $6.00 for adults, with discounts for senior citizens and children. Phone (910) 686–4868.

THE PIEDMONT

The junior high school student who wrote, "Everything that isn't a mountain or a beach in North Carolina is the Piedmont," had it just about right. The Piedmont stretches from the coastal plain on the east through the foothills of the Appalachian Mountains. This agreeable area makes up about two fifths of the state. The topography is primarily rolling hills and red clay. Though difficult to manage, this sticky clay tends to be fertile and has contributed to the state's economy in at least three ways: It has supported the growth of tobacco and cotton and the production of pottery. Few big plantations existed here in the antebellum years, because the hilly land seemed to lend itself more to small family farms than to sprawling properties large enough to support slave populations. Moreover, you would not have found important river trade in this region, because the tributaries ran narrow and swift, not at all appropriate for moving large shipments of goods and materials. The weather in the region tends to be temperate, warmer than the mountains by about ten degrees Fahrenheit, and cooler than the coast by about the same amount.

Raleigh is the capital of the state and was planned as such from its founding in 1792, even though Edenton had been the capital of the province and New Bern the capital of the colony. From 1794 on, Raleigh was the capital city. This area is growing so fast today that it is hard to tell where Raleigh stops and **Durham,** 23 miles away, begins. Even before the populations of the two areas began moving together, the important events of the antebellum years were connecting both communities. Raleigh and Durham form two sides of what is known now as "The Triangle." **Chapel Hill** is the third side.

In Raleigh, the cross-shaped **State Capitol Building,** with its copper dome, has been standing on Capitol Square since 1840. The body of the Confederate president, Jefferson Davis, lay in state in the rotunda in 1893. Obviously, you can look at the exterior of the building any time; for a guided tour, though, you need a reservation. Phone (919) 733–4994. The tours are free.

Although General William Tecumseh Sherman came to this area with his troops, the government buildings were spared, probably because many people in this part of the state had strong ties with Northern manufacturers, who sympathized little with Confederate plantation owners and slaveholders. The mayor of Raleigh met Sherman outside the city to surrender, probably preventing the destruction by marauding Yankees that befell so many other Southern cities.

You will gain a sense of the continuity of history when you visit the **Oakwood Historic District,** at North Person Street between Jones and Boundary. The district was started when Colonel Heck, a retired Confederate officer, built a couple of homes. The community quickly gained in popularity, and today more than 400 Victorian homes remain, many of which have been restored. It is a rare and excellent example of an unspoiled Victorian neighborhood, still reflecting the taste and values of the earlier years. You can pick up a free walking-tour map, with descriptions of some of the buildings and history of the area, at the **Capital Area Visitors Center,** 301 North Blount Street. The center is open Monday through Friday 8:00 A.M. to 5:00 P.M.; Saturday 9:00 A.M. to 5:00 P.M.; Sunday 1:00 to 5:00 P.M. Closed Thanksgiving, Christmas, and New Year's Day. Phone (919) 733–3456.

You can spend the night in the neighborhood at **Oakwood Inn,** 411 North Bloodworth Street. This six-guest room bed and breakfast, in a home built about 1871, is furnished throughout with Victorian antiques, although the guest rooms are fully contemporary, with private baths and telephones. This inn is popular for small gatherings when people want to observe a special occasion in a romantic Southern atmosphere. The proprietors, Jim and Vera Cox, know a lot about the history of the area and can offer knowledgeable suggestions about things to see and places to visit. They offer a full gourmet breakfast and, with advanced notice, will accommodate special requests and dietary needs. Rates range from about $65 to $110 per room. Phone (919) 832–9712 or (800) 267–9712.

Going north on Person Street to 1 Mimosa Street brings you to the **Mordecai Historic Park.** On its grounds is a plantation home, built in 1785, that today is still furnished with the original furnishings of the Mordecai family. Some other important buildings have been moved into the park. The 12-by-18-foot house in which President Andrew Johnson was born has been restored and furnished as it might have been then. There are also a building that may have been a post office in the middle of the 1800s and a chapel from 1847. Perhaps most interesting of all, the **Ellen Mordecai Garden** has been created based on notes from her diaries of the 1830s.

In the spirit of mutual cooperation by which the South has survived, the gardens are maintained now by the Mordecai Gardeners, a group of volunteers from the community. The gardens are at their peak in April and May. The park is open weekdays noon to 4:00 P.M.; weekends 1:00 to 4:00 P.M. Admission is about $3.00 for adults, $2.50 for senior citizens, and $1.00 for children. Hours of operation may change, so it is a good idea to call ahead. Phone (919) 834–4844.

One other home, **Joel Lane House,** 728 West Hargett Street, is a must-see for people interested in old architecture. Possibly the oldest home in Raleigh, it was built in the 1760s, a one-and-a-half-story, white frame building. It has been restored and furnished with antiques of the eighteenth century. The house is open from early March to mid-December, Tuesday, Thursday, and Saturday 10:00 A.M. to 2:00 P.M. Admission is free. Phone (919) 833–3431.

Meanwhile, less than 25 miles away, near Durham, the Civil War theme emerges again. At **Bennett Place,** 4409 Bennett Memorial Road, a simple farmhouse marks the spot where Generals Albert Sidney Johnston and William Tecumseh Sherman negotiated the terms of a Confederate surrender. This is recorded as the site of the largest troop surrender of the Civil War. The surrender ended the war in the Carolinas, Georgia, and Florida, mustering out nearly 90,000 troops. Historians say that the surrender spared North Carolina the destruction experienced in some of the other Southern states. Visitors can tour a restored house; the original burned in 1921. Exhibits in the house include Civil War weapons, uniforms, and photographs, and an audiovisual presentation is available. Bennett Place is open April through October, Monday through Saturday 9:00 A.M. to 5:00 P.M.; Sunday 1:00 to 5:00 P.M. It keeps shorter hours and is closed Monday during fall and winter months. Admission is free. Phone (919) 383–4345. To get to Bennett Place, take exit 172 south or 170 north off I–85 onto U.S. Highway 70.

During the meetings to arrange the troop surrender, a new element came upon the scene: brightleaf tobacco. The local name for brightleaf is Carolina Bright. Neither the Confederate nor the Union men (except for locals) had tried it before, and when they did, they thought it was the best tobacco they had ever had. They wanted more. And so the Durham region became a tobacco center. The **Duke Homestead State Historic Site and Tobacco Museum,** 2828 Duke Homestead Road, on what used to be the Duke family farm, explains the region's historical tobacco mystique and money. The museum comprises the old family house built in 1852, two old tobacco factories, a curing barn, and a packhouse. Exhibits show you everything from how tobacco is planted to its curing. A movie explains the history and economic significance of tobacco in the area.

The site and museum are open April through October, Monday through Saturday 9:00 A.M. to 5:00 P.M. They keep shorter hours and are closed Monday during November through March. Admission is free. Phone (919) 477–5498. To get to the tobacco museum, take the Guess Road exit off I–85.

In Durham, you can spend the night in **Arrowhead Inn,** 106 Mason

Road, a bed and breakfast. The house was built in about 1775 and belonged to the Lipscome family, which had a plantation and slaves here for more than one hundred years. There are five guest rooms in the house, two in a carriage house, and a suite in the Land Grant Cabin, all on four acres, with 150-year-old magnolias and a great number of birds. The rooms are decorated to evoke the feel of Southern romance. Rates, including a full breakfast and afternoon tea, begin at about $75 per room. Phone (919) 477–8430.

While you are in this part of the state, you might want to drive north on state Highway 86 to **Hillsborough,** a little town of about 5,000 people that is rich in history. Hillsborough was a center of politics in colonial and revolutionary times; the state convention to ratify the federal Constitution met in Hillsborough in 1788. General Johnston headquartered here. All these eras are reflected in the colonial, antebellum, and Victorian architecture of the town. People live in the houses—they are not tour buildings—but you can still study the exteriors. The **Orange County Historical Museum** will give you a map for a walking tour prepared by the Historical Society. For further details, phone (919) 732–8648 before noon.

Driving about 80 miles west of Durham on I–40 brings you to Winston-Salem, another tobacco town. There, near the intersection of I–50 and U.S. Highway 52, you will find **Old Salem.** People sometimes liken Old Salem to Colonial Williamsburg, but if anything, it is even more interesting. The town was founded in 1766 by Moravians, a utopian religious community. The church elders planned the community around an open square, with separate homes for the single brothers and sisters, a tavern, a store, and, just off the square, a school and a variety of businesses and shops. The Moravians were good workers and good businesspeople; the community thrived until about the mid-1800s, when larger business concerns and the development of the city of Winston eroded Old Salem's appeal.

But during the good years in Old Salem, the Moravians lived here, geographically and temporally part of the antebellum South. The modest long skirts, aprons, and head coverings of the Moravian women contrasted with the petticoats, pinched waists, and frilled bonnets of plantation mistresses. The Moravians believed that they should accept people of all races as God's children; elsewhere in the South, slavery was accepted by many people as the natural order of things. The Moravians valued craftsmanship and used a guild system to train young apprentices to produce high-quality goods; on the plantations, young men were encouraged to learn about shipping, trade, and property management.

Neither way of life survived unchanged in the South. A shifting economy and a growing city population changed Old Salem, and the Civil War changed the nature of plantations forever. Considering the tour plantation homes and Old Salem in juxtaposition will reveal fascinating details about the very different ways of life that existed at the same time in the Old South.

Begin a tour of the Old Salem restoration at the **Old Salem Visitor Center,** where a slide show will orient you to the rest of the town. The center is open Monday through Saturday 9:30 A.M. to 4:30 P.M.; Sunday 1:30 to 4:30 P.M. Phone (919) 748–8585. You can stroll the village streets for free, but you must buy tickets to tour the approximately dozen buildings that are open to the public. Tickets for all Old Salem tour buildings are sold here. Admission for adults is about $12, half that for children, with discounts for families.

Each building shows signs of some impressive work by the staff, who try to piece together the day-to-day lives of the Moravians as accurately as possible. The staff study old diaries, letters, and journals to prepare research papers so that they will all understand how life went on. Some of the buildings are private homes, not open to the public. The mixture of restored tour buildings and restored buildings for private living keeps a feeling of life and activity in the area.

The tour buildings include the Single Brothers' House (built in 1769), the Vierling House (1802), the Boy's School (1794), the Miksch Tobacco Shop (1771), and the Winkler Bakery (1800). You can buy Moravian baked goods, including delicious, paper-thin ginger cookies, in the bakery. Inside the Single Brothers' House, shops representing various crafts (tin shop, gun shop, weaver's room, cooper's shop, and so on) feature demonstrations of craftspeople's work. The goods that came out of these shops in earlier times contributed significantly to Salem's booming economy. Other demonstrations include cooking over an old fireplace and ironing with flatirons.

You can pick up reproductions of some of the Moravian crafts as well as books about the Moravian community at two gift shops, one in the 1775 T. Bagge Community Store, the other in the 1810 Inspector's House, both restored buildings.

Along with work and food, church was a central part of life to Moravians. The Home Moravian Church looks from the outside about the same as it did when built in 1880. It is still used by a Moravian congregation. Another fascinating building is the Salem Tavern Museum (1784), a brick building that once provided lodging, food, and spirits for travelers. George Washington slept here! Sorry about that, but he did.

Old Salem was a celibate community of Moravians founded in 1766. Their modest lives contrasted vividly with life on the extravagant plantations of the deep South. Here costumed interpreters hang freshly scoured wool behind Vierling House in preparation for spinning and weaving.

At **Salem Tavern,** 736 South Main Street, built in 1816, costumed staff serve Moravian-style food by candlelight. Some food, especially game and gingerbread, is prepared from classic old recipes, although those of timid palate can always order reliable beef and chop entrees. The Moravians were not teetotalers; all spirits are served in the dining rooms. The dining rooms are open for lunch, Sunday through Friday 11:30 A.M. to 2:00 P.M.; for dinner, Monday through Thursday, 5:30 to 9:00 P.M. and Friday and Saturday 5:30 to 9:30 P.M. Phone (919) 748–8585.

Old Salem also operates the **Museum of Early Southern Decorative Arts,** where exhibits and literature give you a closer look at the regional decorative arts of the Old South. Exhibits include textiles, paintings, furniture, ceramics, and silver. Printed material in the library even includes some original manuscripts of early Southern cookbooks. Some of the displays are of rooms from homes. The museum, begun in 1965, encompasses nineteen rooms, with six different galleries. Exhibits cover the years from about 1690 to 1820. The museum is open Monday through Saturday 10:30 A.M. to 5:00 P.M.; Sunday 1:30 to 5:00 P.M. Tickets are sold in the Old Salem Visitor Center. Admission is about $6.00 for adults, $3.00 for children, with discounts for combination tickets and families.

The town of **Salisbury,** about 40 miles south of Winston-Salem, just off I–85, packs a lot of history into a small area. It dates back to 1753, when the area was settled by the Scotch-Irish and Germans. From the interstate, head away from the strip city area into town on Innes Avenue, or take U.S. Highway 70 directly into the 30-block National Historic District, which includes a substantial number of commercial and residential buildings dating from the 1820s. Stop at the **Rowan County Visitor Information Center,** in the restored Railroad Depot at 215 Depot Street, for a map and brochure for a self-guided tour of the historic district. The center is open Monday through Friday 9:00 A.M. to 5:00 P.M.; Saturday 10:00 A.M. to 4:00 P.M.; Sunday 1:00 to 4:00 P.M. Closed Easter, Thanksgiving, Christmas, and New Year's Day. Phone (704) 638–3100.

One of the interesting homes in the district is the **Dr. Josephus Hall House,** 226 South Jackson Street. This 1820 Federal-style house, surrounded by old oaks, was Dr. Hall's home when he was chief surgeon at the Salisbury Confederate Prison. Additions with Greek Revival and Victorian features were made later. Inside, you will see painted ceilings, original fixtures, and a collection of mid-Victorian antiques that were actually used by the Halls. Costumed guides tell you the story of the house and family. The house museum is open Saturday and Sunday 2:00 to 5:00 P.M. Admission is about $3.00 for adults, $1.00 less for children.

A few doors down, **The Rowan Museum/Utzman-Chambers House,** 116 Jackson Street, an 1819 Federal townhouse, gives you an idea of how affluent people of the early 1800s lived. The house has a curved staircase and notable interior moldings. It features period furnishings, Civil War artifacts, and tools used in the 1800s. Some of the furniture was made by Rowan County craftspeople. The original flag from the Salisbury Confederate Prison is displayed. The toy room has some good-quality dolls and displays of miniature dishes. In a clothing display, costumes, including dresses, two wedding dresses, and men's clothing of the 1800s, are shown on life-size forms. Outside the house is a nineteenth-century formal garden. Open Tuesday through Sunday 2:00 to 5:00 P.M. Admission is about $3.00 for adults, $1.50 for children. Phone (704) 633–5946.

If the Civil War items pique your interest, visit the **Salisbury National Cemetery,** where more than 5,000 Union soldiers who died at the Salisbury Confederate Prison are buried. You can pick up a pamphlet for a walking tour at the office on the grounds, 202 Government Road. The office is open Monday through Friday 8:00 A.M. to 4:30 P.M. The grounds are always open. Phone (704) 636–2661.

Well before the Civil War, commerce flourished in Salisbury because of its location, where two major travel routes came together. Exhibits detail the development of transportation in North Carolina at the **North Carolina Transportation Museum and Historic Spencer Shops,** 411 South Salisbury Avenue. The site, at the halfway point between Atlanta and Washington, D.C., was once Southern Railway's largest steam-locomotive servicing facility. The transportation display ranges from dugout canoes to vintage automobiles and airplanes. Sometimes you can ride a train around the area. Admission is free. Open Monday through Saturday 9:00 A.M. to 5:00 P.M.; Sunday 1:00 to 5:00 P.M. November to March, the hours are shorter, and the site is closed Monday. Phone (704) 636–2889.

Rowan Oak House, 208 South Fulton Street, offers bed-and-breakfast accommodations in a fine old Victorian house that still has the original fixtures and wallpaper. Intricately carved woodwork, an elaborately carved staircase, and stained and leaded-glass windows evoke thoughts of an earlier, romantic era. The furnishings are period antiques and reproductions, with a collection of artifacts belonging to the home's original builder. The house is in a neighborhood with a number of other impressive Victorian homes in various stages of rescue and restoration. Rates begin at about $85 per room. Phone (704) 633–2086 or (800) 786–0437.

The **History/Genealogy Room at Rowan Public Library,** 201 West Fisher Street, provides resources for family historians whose ancestors came from the original Thirteen Colonies. The collection focuses on North Carolina, but it holds documents from bordering states as well. You are welcome to research your own family tree. The library is open Monday through Thursday 9:00 A.M. to 9:00 P.M.; Friday and Saturday 9:00 A.M. to 5:00 P.M.; Sunday 1:00 to 5:00 P.M. Closed Sunday during fall and winter months. Phone (704) 638–3021.

Study African-American heritage at **W. J. Walls Heritage Hall,** on the campus of Livingstone College, 701 Monroe Street. The hall contains an extensive collection of African, African-American, and African-American Episcopal Zion Church artifacts, books, and records. The materials are on exhibit and available for research. The hall is open September through June, Monday through Friday 9:00 A.M. to 4:30 P.M. It is open other months, except July, by appointment. Admission is free, but donations are accepted. Phone (704) 633–5664.

If you drive south on U.S. Highway 52 from Salisbury, you will come to the village of **Gold Hill.** Gold was discovered here in 1824. Gold Hill was a rowdy mining town for a long time. Then, as the mining business dwindled, things settled down. But the people, many of whom have lived their entire lives here, have been restoring the buildings and improving **Gold Hill Mines Historic Park,** the site of three gold mines. In the park, you can peer into a small jailhouse, wander through Mauney's 1840 Store and Museum, and picnic or relax while the kids play in the playground. A local contractor has established a small working mine in the park to demonstrate old-fashioned mining techniques. As you walk around the grounds, you may pick up small pieces of stone containing flecks of real gold.

The park is open daily until dark. The store and museum are open Thursday and Friday noon to 5:00 P.M.; Saturday 11:00 A.M. to 5:00 P.M.; Sunday 1:00 to 6:00 P.M. Admission is free. Phone (704) 279–5674. If you plan a spring visit to the area, call to find out the exact date of the Old Miners' Jubilee, held each May. This is a town-wide celebration, with food, country music, mock trials of local officials who wait in the jail, and a general small-town, good-time spirit—much like the town must have celebrated in the antebellum era.

Another interesting little jaunt from Salisbury is **Kerr Mill,** in **Sloan Park** at **Mount Ulla.** The mill was built in 1823. It provided cornmeal for people in the western part of the county. Although the milling equipment and artifacts exhibited today date back to the early 1800s, the mill still operates to produce fresh cornmeal, which you can buy. For information about bluegrass and country music festivals, with homemade ice cream and games in the Southern rural tradition, phone (704) 637–7776. In addition to the mill, Sloan Park has picnic and playground facilities. The park is open daily 9:00 A.M. to 5:00 P.M. In summer hours are extended to 9:00 P.M. The mill is open 1:00 to 5:00 P.M. on weekends, but sometimes you can find someone on the property to let you in earlier. Also, you can call to request admission at other times. Closed Thanksgiving and Christmas. Admission is free. Sloan Road turns off State Highway 180, which leaves U.S. Highway 70 about halfway between Salisbury and Statesville.

If you continue south to **Charlotte,** you will find **Historic Latta Place,** in **Latta Plantation Park.** The park is a nature preserve on Mountain Island Lake. Historic Latta Place is the restored 1800 Catawba River plantation home of an area merchant. Touring the home will give you an idea of how well-to-do North Carolina pioneers lived before the war. The Federal-style home was unusual for the times, because it was built of clapboard rather than the more common logs or stone. The house is furnished appropriately for the period. The tour includes both floors of the main house, where there is some intricate woodwork, plus the separate kitchen, smokehouse, and wash house. Latta is open March through December, Tuesday through Friday 9:00 A.M. to 5:00 P.M.; Sunday 1:00 to 5:00 P.M. Admission is about $2.00, less for senior citizens and children. Phone (704) 875–2312. To get to Latta Place, exit I–85 to go west on State Highway 73, north of Charlotte. The park is about 6 miles from the little community of Huntersville.

THE MOUNTAINS

Driving through the North Carolina mountains, you won't come across anything like what you might think of as an "Old South experience." Indeed, except around such population centers as Asheville and tourist areas like Highlands, Boone, and Blowing Rock, you will travel on narrow, twisting roads for long stretches of time without seeing much sign of people at all. It is easy to understand how people who lived in one little mountain village would seldom have traveled elsewhere, because the mountains made traveling even short distances arduous. But while you should not come into this part of the state looking specifically for the Old South, you will find some instructive places to visit if you are already nearby.

In **Hendersonville,** a resort during the days when people from the hot low country came to spend the summer, two early boarding house–style lodgings, established shortly before the turn of the century, continue today as bed-and-breakfast inns. **Claddagh Inn** and **The Waverly Inn** sit more or less side by side on North Main Street. At one point Claddagh Inn was called The Charleston Boarding House, reflecting the large number of people from Charleston, South Carolina, who summered here to escape the heat and humidity. Each inn has three stories, fourteen rooms, spacious common areas, and large porches where early guests would have sat to enjoy the cooler mountain air. Air-conditioning has not diminished the value of such porches; rocking and chatting there while watching the activities on Main Street is as much an occupation for guests as ever. Rates for Claddagh (704–697–7778) and The Waverly (704–693–9193) begin at about $70 per room, depending on the season. To get to Hendersonville, take the State Highway 64 exit from I–26.

While you are in the North Carolina mountains, plan to spend some time on the **Blue Ridge Parkway.** This 470-mile stretch running from the Great Smoky Mountains National Park to Shenandoah National Park in Virginia is part of the National Park System. It is designed for leisurely sightseeing: The speed limit is 45 miles per hour. The vistas range from ridge after ridge of mountains to rolling farmland. And although the area's first appeal is its unspoiled nature, you will also see old highland farms and some important old buildings. Some of what you see, such as the Civilian Conservation Corps shelters at Craggy Gardens (milepost 364.5), built for the U.S. Forest Service in the late 1930s, are relatively young, but other sites date back farther. At the **Moses H. Cone Memorial Park** (milepost 294.0), a manor house, built in the late 1800s, now serves as a visitors' center and shop for the Southern Highland Handicraft Guild. Moses H. Cone made his fortune in textiles, mainly with denim. He came from New York, a good example of the ongoing relationships between Northern and Southern business interests that developed before the Civil War and continued afterward in spite of it.

At milepost 276.3, near Boone, the **Civil War Earthworks at Deep Gap** marks the spot where Union forces built defenses in the mountain gap to protect the forward march of Major General George Stoneman, on his way from Tennessee to raid Salisbury in 1865.

The **Jesse Brown Farmstead** (milepost 272.5) has a log cabin built sometime before 1840. Easy to see from the highway, the house was moved into its current position by the National Park Service. It had been moved twice before by the people who lived in it, well before the days when heavy equipment was available to simplify the task. Ian J. W. Firth, who wrote profiles of many important sites along the Blue Ridge Parkway, observed in a parkway research paper that the house serves as a reminder that taking log buildings apart and moving them was an almost routine part of mountain life: "It was made possible by the type of construction, and desirable by the frugal nature of mountain life." It is a vivid contrast to the plush plantation life of parts of the Deep South.

According to Firth, **The Johnson Farm,** at Peaks of Otter (milepost 85.2), is the "most complete and authentic mountain farmstead now being preserved along the Parkway." The first Johnson was John, who bought land here in 1852. The John Johnsons had thirteen children. The house was variously enlarged and modernized over time and remained in the Johnson family until it was acquired by the National Park Service in 1941.

One easy access route to the parkway is at **Asheville,** from where you might also make a short side trip into Weaverville, off Highway 19/23, to see the **Zebulon B. Vance Birthplace State Historic Site.** This is a reconstructed log house in which Vance, the governor of North Carolina during the Civil War, was born. The two-story house is built of pine logs and furnished with some furniture from the original 1790 house. The outbuildings are made of log, too—the slave house, springhouse, corncrib, smokehouse, tool house, and loom house. Exhibits in the visitors' center/museum illustrate the life of mountain homesteaders at the time. The site is open April through October, Monday through Saturday 9:00 A.M. to 5:00 P.M.; Sunday 1:00 to 5:00 P.M. It keeps shorter hours in the fall and winter months. Donations are accepted. Phone (704) 645–6706.

Another good access route to the parkway is farther east, at **Blowing Rock.** You will find more information about mountain life here. **The Appalachian Heritage Museum,** in a house built in the 1800s, displays antiques and tools of the era and often presents demonstrations of mountain craftsmaking. The museum is open from Memorial Day to Labor Day, daily 9:00 A.M. to 6:00 P.M. It closes one hour earlier in the fall and winter. Admission is about $3.00 for adults, less for children. Phone (704) 262–0399 or (800) 438–7500. To get to the museum, drive 2 miles north of Blowing Rock on State Highway 312.

South Carolina

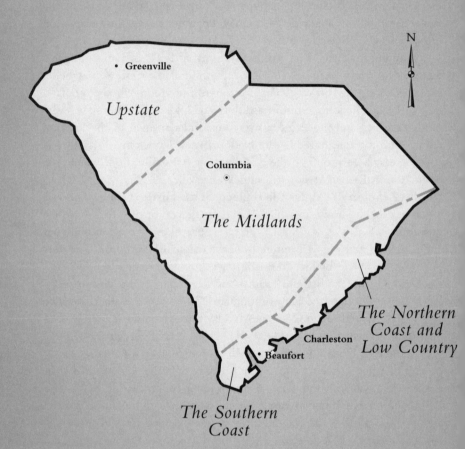

South Carolina

 SOUTH CAROLINA OBVIOUSLY ISN'T OUR MOST SOUTHERLY state, but it may be the most *Southern* in its fidelity to preserving the historic sites of the Old South and practicing the traditional customs of Old Dixie. The state figured significantly in the American Revolution. And South Carolina was the first state to secede from the Union. South Carolinians believed that the Civil War was as much a war for freedom as the Revolutionary War. During the prosperous, cotton-producing years before the Civil War, the state became a social and mercantile center. Falling cotton prices, the Civil War, Reconstruction, and periodic natural disasters brought economic problems from which the state seems only now to be recovering.

But even through the worst situations, South Carolinians have always revered their history. They revere their ancestors; they talk like them, too. You can hear as many as seven distinctly different regional accents when you travel from the up country, through the midlands, and down into the low country and coastal plain. It won't take you long to notice that South Carolinians say "Yes, ma'am," and "No, sir," and "Y'all come back" with a level of politeness that startles visitors not used to such ritualistic courtesy. You will discover that this routine politeness does a lot more to oil the wheels of society and commerce than does the routine rudeness you encounter in some other places. For travelers, this courtesy becomes of-a-piece with Southern hospitality.

THE NORTHERN COAST
AND LOW COUNTRY

The largest and best-known coastal city of South Carolina is **Charleston.** Southern hospitality could have been invented by this town. This is where the English first settled successfully in South Carolina. They established Charles Towne at Albemarle Point on the Ashley River in 1670.

This site, now known as **Charles Towne Landing Nature Preserve and Historic Site,** is at 1500 Old Towne Road. You can see here what the colony's early years would have been like. This period predates the glory days of Charleston's antebellum period, but seeing it helps you understand how the area developed. The boundaries of the colony have been uncovered so you can actually see the lines of the original fortified town. You can also climb aboard the full-scale replica of the seventeenth-century trading ship *Adventure,* the kind of ship that moved goods across the Atlantic. In the Settler's Life area of the park, there are demonstration gardens of the vegetables and cash crops that eventually led to Charleston's wealth and reputation for splendid food. The site is across the Ashley River just northwest of the city on State Highway 171, between I-26 and U.S. 17. It is open daily from 9:00 A.M. to 5:00 P.M.; Memorial Day through Labor Day 9:00 A.M. to 6:00 P.M. Closed Christmas Eve and Christmas Day. Admission is about $5.00 for adults, half that for children and senior citizens. Phone (803) 556-4450.

Just ten years after this settlement was established, it moved to the end of the peninsula, bounded on the west by the Cooper River and on the east by the Ashley, where it thrives today as Charleston. Some local people insist that at the end of the peninsula, the Ashley and Cooper Rivers join to form the Atlantic Ocean. Standing here, in **White Point Gardens,** a park area on the waterfront, watching the waters, usually dotted with sailboats moving oceanward, the idea seems reasonable.

The rowdiness of the early port town, combined with the later affluence that indigo, rice, and the slave trade brought to the area, inspired the love of parties, fun, good food, and ample drink that flourished during the antebellum years and that characterize Charleston to this day. During those early years, the European culture left its mark, too, in the fondness for the arts and music that Charlestonians still display. Nor can you underestimate the influence of the many people brought from Africa. Most were bought

The African-American women of the Charleston area weave sweetgrass baskets exactly as their African ancestors did centuries ago.

and sold as slaves, but the strength of their presence, even in this way, shaped the cooking and crafts of the area. Low-country cooking carries strong African overtones, and the sweetgrass baskets sold at market in Charleston are made exactly as they were centuries ago by African women.

All this means that when you visit Charleston, you can expect a great party: good food and spirits, easy access to important historic sites, interesting shopping, gracious lodgings, and, of course, a hospitable welcome.

Let's start with the welcome. The **Charleston Visitors Reception and Transportation Center,** 375 Meeting Street, is housed in the renovated Railroad Freight Depot, built in 1856. It has everything you need to get oriented, make plans, and decide about transportation before you begin exploring the city.

Be sure to study the model of the peninsula on the floor at the front of the building after you come through the entry hall. The scale model shows the Ashley and Cooper Rivers and the layout of the city, complete with buildings and streets. Large maps on the walls show you where everything in Charleston is in relationship to the water. This helps a lot in keeping you from getting lost as you negotiate the narrow, one-way streets.

Video stations marked "How to Visit Charleston" let you call up tourist information on television screens that you activate by touch. On telephones next to them, you can get additional information about your specific questions.

Toward the center of the building, people at a service desk answer questions, sell books and tickets to current events, and dispense maps. You can pick up free brochures about restaurants, lodging, attractions, and tours from display units along the walls.

The center is open daily most months, 8:30 A.M. to 5:30 P.M.; November, December, and February, daily 8:30 A.M. to 5:00 P.M. Closed Thanksgiving, Christmas, and New Year's Day.

Before you leave this area, take a few minutes to go across the street to the **Charleston Museum,** 360 Meeting Street, even if you're not interested in spending much time in museums. This one opened in 1773; it is the oldest museum in the country. It owns and operates important tour houses in Charleston and has a variety of displays on history, ornithology, archaeology, and the decorative arts. Children's touch exhibits emphasize the low country. But for now, you don't even have to go in to see a unique Dixie exhibit. In front of the museum sits a replica of the Confederate submarine *Hunley,* which in 1864 sank the Union *Housatonic* in Charleston Harbor. The *Hunley* was the first submarine to sink an enemy vessel, though it wasn't much of a victory, because everyone on board the submarine was killed. Not only that, but everyone aboard an earlier test submarine had been killed just trying to make the thing work. When you inspect the *Hunley* replica, you will be amazed that any sailor, on either side, could be persuaded to go below the surface of the water in anything so small.

To enter the museum, you'll need a ticket, which will cost about $6.00 for adults, a couple of dollars less for children. The museum is open Monday through Saturday, 9:00 A.M. to 5:00 P.M. Or you can buy a ticket that gives admission not only to the museum but also to two historic tour homes owned by the museum: the **Heyward-Washington House,** and the **Joseph Manigault House** (see pages 222–23). The combination ticket costs about $15 for adults, several dollars less for children; you can also skip the museum and just tour the two homes for $10. Since you don't know yet how tired you're going to get or how many homes you'll actually want to tour, you may decide just to wait and buy on-site tickets at the houses you choose to tour. The museum phone is (803) 722–2996.

Wherever you want to go next, you will be surprised at how easy it is to get far from the Visitors Center without driving. Charleston's old, narrow cobblestone streets make for picturesque sightseeing and fascinating walking, but driving and trying to park in them takes the fun out of the city. It works much better to use the parking at the Visitors Center or at your lodging, relying mainly on public transportation and your own feet. You can pick up shuttles for the **Downtown Area Shuttle (DASH)** at the Visitors Center and around the city. Shuttles come along every fifteen minutes and loop through major tourist areas, beginning and ending at the terminal. As you ride, you can identify areas that you would like to see more closely on foot. Daylong passes for DASH are only $1.00.

Another good way to get oriented before you begin serious exploring is by taking a narrated tour. Tour companies offer a variety of possibilities— carriage tours, walking tours, limousine and bus tours, and boat tours. Approved guides are licensed by the city to make sure that you get accurate information. The touring business is closely controlled in Charleston, partly to protect the old streets from too much traffic and congestion; so when you arrange for a tour, find out exactly where you will be going before you pay for a ticket, as not all tours are allowed in all parts of the city. Many tours will pick you up at your door if you are staying on the peninsula. Carriage tours usually start at the Market. Don't worry about finding them because guides and salespeople, often in costumes, stand on the corners looking for business. In busy times, though, a reservation is a good idea.

The Charleston Carriage Company offers hour-long, horse-drawn tours of the historic district. Phone (803) 577–0042. Guides for the **Old South Carriage Company** wear Confederate uniforms. Phone (803) 723–9712. Both companies operate from 9 A.M. to dusk, every day but Christmas. Tickets cost between $12 and $14 for adults, a few dollars less for senior citizens and children.

The tour you choose may depend on the time of year. A carriage tour can be fun in the crisp days of late fall but pure misery in the heat and humidity of summer, when an air-conditioned limousine will seem very appealing.

The **Adventure Sightseeing Tours** company, owned by a Charleston family, is often recommended by the staff people of area inns. The company offers a variety of limousine and walking tours. For lively narration with local lore and gossip to lighten the history, try to get onto a motorized tour guided by Claire Johnston. Call the company from 7:30 A.M. to 10:00 P.M. daily for reservations and information. Tickets for adults cost from about $12 to $19, depending on the length of the tour. Tickets for children are usually a few dollars less.

If you dress comfortably, a walking tour can be fun any time of year. Pick up walking-tour brochures at the Visitors Center or hire a guide. Self-guided tours work well for general orientation. If you want to pursue a particular interest, though, a guided tour may be more instructive and get you into some places not otherwise accessible. For instance, **Architectural Walking Tours of Charleston** offers one tour that focuses on the Georgian architecture inside the original walled city. Another emphasizes Greek Revival and Victorian structures. These tours include some private homes and gardens as well as public buildings. Tickets cost about $12.50 for adults. Phone (803) 893–2327.

Since you can get to **Fort Sumter,** where the first shot of the Civil War was fired, only by boat, you may want to book a boat tour, too. Tours by the company **Fort Sumter Tours, Inc.,** leave from the city marina and from Patriots Point Naval and Maritime Museum in Mount Pleasant. Fort Sumter is a national monument administered by the National Park Service, with rangers on site to answer your questions. This manmade island took thirty-one years to build; finally it was finished on December 26, 1860. Union soldiers from Fort Moultrie came here first. Then, when South Carolina seceded from the Union, the South demanded that Union soldiers leave the fort. Of course, they refused—everybody has to play, or you can't have a war. The South Carolina troops fired on the fort on April 12, 1861—the famous "first shot of the Civil War"—and continued their bombardment for two days. When the Confederate troops evacuated the fort five years later, only rubble remained. Now a museum tells the story.

Should you prefer to ignore the "War for Independence," or "War of Northern Aggression," or "Recent Unpleasantness," as Southerners have variously called the Civil War, choose between sightseeing and evening dinner cruises in these same waters; on these tours, less emphasis is placed on the historic significance of the area. Tickets for sightseeing cruises cost about $9.00 for adults, half that for children. Phone (803) 722–1691. The dinner and dancing cruises last three hours, and while they don't serve distinctly Southern food, the party spirit is certainly right. These cruises cost about what dinner in a good-quality restaurant would cost. Phone (803) 722–2628 for more details and reservations.

Not that you have to get onto a boat to have a good meal. Charleston has wonderful restaurants. In recent years the offerings have become increasingly eclectic. Indian, Chinese, Japanese, Mexican, Italian, even Australian—the city's got them all. But the traditional cuisine of the region is low-country cooking, based on the crops and seafood indigenous to the area. The basic low-country delicacies were created in earlier times by the black people cooking in the kitchens of plantations and Charleston city mansions. Low-country cooking means fresh seafood, especially shrimp, crab, and oysters; rice; okra; sweet potatoes; and, of course, biscuits. She-crab soup may be the most famous, and delicious, low-country specialty, with sautéed shrimp and grits running a close second. Of the many restaurants in Charleston, Poogan's Porch, 82 Queen, and Colony House reliably offer specialties that legitimately can be called low country. There are others as well, but these three remain consistent year after year.

Poogan's Porch, 68 Queen Street, is now in its second home. The original building, at 78 Queen—where a pooch named Poogan slept on the porch—burned in 1972, but the ambience and the food haven't changed in the new location. The menu always includes gumbos and jambalayas, dishes with crab meat, and Carolina quail. (Southerners have always enjoyed all kinds of game. During some hard years, wild game was the main source of meat.) Poogan's is open every day for lunch and dinner. Phone (803) 577–2337.

At **82 Queen,** located, logically enough, at 82 Queen Street, the upscale menu includes fresh seafood and emphasizes the low-country vegetables and seasonings. Sample the barbecued shrimp with grits; pork loin roasted with rosemary and garlic, served with bourbon-glazed pears; and Daufuskie crab cakes. The restaurant has an extensive wine list. Open daily for lunch and dinner. Call (803) 723–7591.

Colony House, 35 Piroleau Street, at Waterfront Park, claims to be Charleston's oldest restaurant. It specializes in low-country cooking, too. Expect the menu to include she-crab soup, black bean soup, pulled pork on corn cakes, and the most astonishing crab cakes you ever tasted, made about the size of saucers, made mostly of crab with little breading. They are pan sautéed, not deep fried. Open for lunch and dinner every day, and Sunday brunch. Phone (803) 723–3424.

Although black people, slave and free, have played a tremendous role in everything about Charleston, from its cooking and woodworking to its crafts and agriculture, it has been difficult until recently to learn systematically about these contributions. Today **Sights and Insights Tours— Black History Tours of Charleston** offers one- and two-hour tours in air-conditioned buses and vans that show you historic sites and narrate the history from a black perspective. The sites include the **Emanuel A. M. E. Church,** slave and servants' quarters, the site of the work house, and black neighborhoods. The narration covers slavery and free blacks, rebellions and uprisings, the Civil War, and black slave masters, as well as Charleston's sea islands, the home of Gullah culture. Rates are about $10 for one-hour tours, $15 for two-hour tours. Group rates are available. Walking tours are also available but must be arranged individually. To schedule any tour, call Al Miller, licensed tour guide, at (803) 762–0051, or write Sites and Insights Tours, P.O. Box 21346, Charleston, SC 29413.

Your first visit to Charleston must include some time at the **Market.** This open-air, roofed marketplace between Church and East Bay Streets rents stalls to local craftspeople and vendors of all kinds, who sell everything from jewelry and clothing to sweetgrass baskets and knives. Much of what the vendors sell is standard tourist fare; some is better than that. But the riot of color and press of people give you a sense of what market days might have been like in old Charleston. This was never a slave market; in fact, one of its original rules in antebellum days was that slaves could never be traded there. The Market sold fresh produce, fish, and meat.

The Old Slave Mart, at 6 Chalmers Street, was one of the slave-trading sites. In recent years a museum of African-American art and history was housed here, but at present the building is closed. You can still get an idea of what it was like, however, by walking about the building. Slave auctions were held also in streets like Vendu Range, though when you visit there now, you will see no signs of such activity.

While you are in Charleston, be sure to see the **Heyward-Washington House** and the **Joseph Manigault House,** as examples of Charleston's fine old homes. The Heyward-Washington House, 87 Church Street (803–722–0354), built in 1772, was home to Thomas Heyward, Jr., one of the signers of the Declaration of Independence. The house has an outstanding collection of Charleston-made furniture. This is the only place in Charleston where you can tour a kitchen house—the building behind the main house in which meals were prepared.

A Ticket to Freedom

In early days lotteries were frequently used to raise funds for charities and public works in Charleston. In 1800 a slave called Denmark bought a chance in the East Bay Lottery. Slaves were forbidden to learn to read or write, but Denmark had beaten the system; now in his early thirties, he could read, write, and speak several languages. Folklore has it that he came from the Caribbean island of St. Thomas (then in the Danish West Indies, but today one of the U.S. Virgin Islands). He won $1,500 in the lottery and used $600 of it to buy his freedom. A skilled craftsman, he set himself up in business as a carpenter and prospered enough to purchase several thousand dollars' worth of property, including a home at 20 Bull Street. He was an active participant in the African Church of Charleston, founded in 1818. Today his name is one of the best known in the city.

In the Joseph Manigault House, 350 Meeting Street (803–723–2926), you can see how a wealthy merchant lived and entertained. Joseph's brother Gabriel, an architect, designed the house. A Federal-style structure, it was built in 1803 and has changed little over the years. Its unsupported circular stairway commands your attention, making it easy to imagine hoop-skirted women with nipped-in waists sweeping down into the party below. The downstairs rooms are much more elaborate than those upstairs, suggesting that Manigault cared more about the image he presented in entertaining than he did about the quarters in which he lived the rest of the time. The house has what preservationists say is the first powder room built in the city.

Tickets for the tour homes are available at the sites and at the Charleston Museum (see page 218). The homes are open the same days and times as the museum.

While you are in this general area, you might walk up East Bay Street the 4 or 5 blocks it takes to get to Charleston's only Civil War restaurant, **Moultrie Tavern 1862 Museum,** 18 Vendue Range. It is close to the water and has a distinctly old-tavern feel, with dim lighting, a visible bar, wood floors, and a private collection of eighteenth- and nineteenth-century artifacts, mostly relating to the Confederacy, displayed throughout the dining area. The menu features such old Southern favorites as game pie, chicken pie, stews, roasted meats, and gumbos. The food reflects the early Charleston use of game, seafood, and local produce. They serve an unusual bean soup here, almost creamy in color, slightly sweet and slightly smoky to taste, for which the recipe is the chef's secret. One waiter says it "has something to do with molasses." The tavern also offers mint juleps, but if a drink consisting mainly of bourbon seems a bit risky before you go back out for more walking, have wine or a beer or the South's ubiquitous comestible, iced tea. The tavern is open daily from 11:30 A.M. to 4:30 P.M. for lunch and from 5:30 to 10:00 P.M. for dinner.

To see a side of Charleston social life that was decidedly more formal than taverns, yet obviously plenty rowdy in its own way, visit the John Rutledge House, 116 Broad Street. John Rutledge was one of the signers of the Constitution. He built the home in 1763 and lived in it until 1800. Set back from the street about 6 feet, according to the custom of the time, the house had a narrow driveway, wide enough for a carriage, with gardens and a slave house in back. The gardens extended all the way to Queen Street. This house was built mainly for entertaining. It has a huge dining room on the first floor. Upstairs, a drawing room and library could be opened to serve as a ballroom or a meeting spot for important politicians. There were only two bedrooms for the family in the rear of the house. One of the most important rooms in the house was the wine cellar, which measured 30 by 20 feet and held 220 gallons of Madeira as well as port, schnapps, sauterne, porter and ale, French brandy, West Indian rum, and Irish whiskey.

The wine cellar is no longer so generously stocked, but the building has been restored and furnished with antiques and historically accurate reproductions of the period. The John Rutledge House is now a bed-and-breakfast inn. You can tour for free or stay in a bed-and-breakfast arrangement in one of the rooms. In the evening wine and sherry are served in the ballroom where patriots, statesmen, and presidents met to shape the course of South Carolina and the nation. If you stay here, you can leave your car in the parking lot where some of the gardens used to be. The antebellum residential area known as "South of Broad" begins just across from the inn; you can walk through the area on your way to restaurants, shopping, and theaters. Room rates begin at about $115 a night. Phone (803) 723–7999 or (800) 476–9741.

Many of Charleston's lodgings are in restored antebellum mansions. Staying in them gives you a sense of what living in one must have been like, although you can be pretty sure the mattresses are better these days.

The Sun Didn't Even Have to Be Over the Yardarm

Richard Barry, in his book *Mr. Rutledge of South Carolina* (Books for Libraries Press, New York; 1942), says that spirits played a big part in the early life of Charleston—if you were male. According to Barry, "The drinking habits of the day reflected those of London; that is, sobriety in gentlemen was considered unimportant socially, but ladies seldom drank." Henry Laurens, an important public figure and a good friend of Charleston's John Rutledge, limited himself to a single bottle of Madeira a day, which was considered a bit wimpy. By contrast, "Rutledge was a two-bottle man and proud of it," Barry writes. This attitude comes through explicitly in the *Letters of William Gilmore Simms* (Volume V; University of South Carolina Press, 1982), a distinguished historian and literary writer of South Carolina. He wrote to a friend in the spring of 1842, "That noggin last night! Let it be no more called punch, but Judy. Never was a thing more feminine—nay, it was positively old womanish."

In at least one case, breakfast in a Charleston inn recalls the bounty of good times. Guests who can't remember what they had for dinner last night can tell you in detail about every breakfast they have had at **Cannonboro Inn,** 184 Ashley Avenue. A typical breakfast might include bread pudding; a soufflé of eggs, grits, ham, and cheese; biscuits; fruit; juice; and coffee. The Cannonboro also serves afternoon tea in the parlor, with homemade cakes, cookies, and sherry. This inn is in a restored 1850 Charleston single house decorated in pale blues, greens, and mauves. Its high ceilings are brightened by large windows, which are minimally draped to let in as much light as possible. Outside, you can sit in the shade on the first- and second-floor piazzas (porches and balconies to Yankees) or in the tiny formal garden with a fountain and a goldfish pond. Double rooms here start at about $80. Phone (803) 723–8572.

Just down the street at 201 Ashley Avenue, the **Ashley Inn Bed and Breakfast,** a sister inn to the Cannonboro, serves equally sumptuous breakfasts. Expect offerings such as sausage soufflé with zucchini and cheddar biscuits, crunchy French toast with hazelnut peach syrup, and grits casserole with white cream gravy. The same people who concentrate on preparing food at the Cannonboro participate here, too. The Ashley, an 1832 Charleston House furnished with antiques and good reproduction pieces, has 13-foot ceilings, Victorian crown moldings and medallions, and brass chandeliers original to the house. The guest rooms have reproduction rice beds and televisions hidden in built-in armoires. The people who run these inns like to say that staying at the Cannonboro is like visiting your grandmother, while being at the Ashley is like visiting a rich aunt. Double rooms at the Ashley begin at about $80. Phone (803) 723–9080.

So far, your explorations have concentrated mainly on the city of Charleston, a place made wealthy in its boomtimes by merchants and by the planters of indigo, rice, and cotton. To get the feel of another aspect of Dixie, you'll want to visit some of these planters' plantations.

It's Not What You've Got; It's Who Knows You've Got It!

The South Carolina planters emphasized family connections, landed wealth, agreeable manners, sociability, and conspicuous leisure. They influenced Charleston far more than did the people in the governing circles of City Hall. Visitors noticed this; one remarked on "a class of . . . closely associated" wealthy citizens who "think and act precisely as do the nobility in other countries." The importance of family and ancestry to the low-country gentry is dramatized in the antebellum doggerel based on the old family names Porcher, Huger, and Petigru: "I thank thee Lord on bended knee I'm half Porcher and half Huger (pronounced 'You-gee'). . . . For other blessings thank thee too—My grandpa was a Petigru."

— From Walter J. Fraser, Jr., *Charleston! Charleston!: The History of a Southern City* (1989, University of South Carolina Press).

As a vigorous port city, Charleston attracted not only wealth and rowdiness but also religion. Religion has always been important in the South. Of the original Thirteen Colonies, South Carolina, which even today is part of the "Bible Belt," had the broadest laws in support of religious freedom. People of every denomination, from Quaker to Episcopalian to Jewish, formed congregations here. The city is often called "The Holy City" because so many churches—more than 130—have been part of the community.

One way to see some of these historic buildings is to attend services in them. (Review the Saturday listings of services in the *Charleston News and Courier* for schedule details.) But some churches also welcome you for tours at other times. Such tours are usually managed by volunteers. It is important to call ahead if you wish to be sure of getting into a particular church.

St. Michael's Episcopal Church, 80 Meeting Street, is the oldest church building in Charleston. Finished in 1762, the structure survived the Revolutionary War without damage and was hit by only one shell during the Civil War. The white spire of the church gleams over the city by day

Saving the Bells

During the Civil War, the congregation of St. Michael's Episcopal Church painted the church spire black so that it would be inconspicuous and not attract enemy fire. To protect the church bells, they took them out and sent them to Columbia, but General William Tecumseh Sherman surprised the Confederates by burning Columbia, where the bells were damaged. They were sent to England for repair. Hurricane Hugo damaged them again in 1989; they were sent to England a second time to be repaired.

For a full history and color photographs of some of Charleston's most important churches, see the book *The Churches of Charleston and the Lowcountry,* put together by the Preservation Society of Charleston, edited by Mary Moore Jacoby, with an introduction by George C. Rogers, Jr., and photographs by Ron Anton Rocz, (University of South Carolina Press, 1994).

and, lighted, at night. Inside the Georgian-style building, the original pulpit and wooden box pews remain in place. George Washington and, later, Robert E. Lee sat in them. Phone (803) 723–0603.

Although a Jewish presence doesn't fit the stereotypical notion of the South, Charleston had a strong Jewish population from its beginnings as Charles Towne. The first Jews in the community were Orthodox, but the **Kahal Kadosh Beth Elohim,** 90 Hasell Street, phone (803) 723–1090, is considered to be the birthplace of Reform Judaism in the United States. The Greek Revival building that you see today replaced the synagogue that was destroyed by fire in 1838. It is the oldest synagogue in continuous use in the United States. It was also the first synagogue in the country to use organ music in worship.

Although many black people attended the churches of their white masters before the Civil War, the African Methodist Episcopal Church was formed specifically to serve blacks. Known as the Bethel Circuit, three churches held services, led by a free black preacher, the Reverend Morris Brown. He founded the **Emanuel A.M.E. Church,** 110 Calhoun Street, phone (803) 722–2561, from an earlier congregation of the Bethel Circuit. This is the oldest A.M.E. church in the South. By 1818, Brown's church had about 1,000 members. White citizens later burned the church when they learned that insurrection was being planned there, thereby forcing many of the congregation to go back to white churches. In 1834 the state legislature closed all black churches in South Carolina, trying to eliminate sources of rebellion. As a result, blacks went underground in growing numbers to continue to worship in their own churches. The Congregation of Emanuel A.M.E. built a new wooden church after the Civil War, in 1872. The white brick building that you see today was finished in 1891; it replaces the wooden one that was ruined by the earthquake of 1886.

Roman Catholicism first became visible in Charleston when an Italian priest sailed into the harbor toward the end of the 1700s. Old Southern Roman Catholics were refugees from other colonies and the West Indies. Local Protestants didn't trust "Papists"—an attitude that persisted until recently and that exists even now here and there. **St. Mary's Catholic Church,** 89 Hasell Street, phone (803) 722–7696, is the oldest Roman Catholic church in South Carolina. It was started in 1789 in a small wooden building that had earlier been a Methodist church. A brick building replaced it in 1805; it was hit so often by weapon fire during the Civil War it became unusable. The building that stands on the site today wasn't finished until 1901. It is thus the *congregation* that has the long history.

Exploring Charleston proper gives you a strong sense of the mercantile and social life of the city, but just as today we have city folk and country people, so in the Old South there were merchants and shippers and planters. Although planters might have homes in the city, they lived with their families and slaves and socialized mostly on the plantations where they made their money.

A South Carolina plantation was really just a big, self-sufficient farm with many people living and working on the property. The main house was usually elaborate, intended to make a statement about the wealth of its owner, and large enough to accommodate an extended family. Outbuildings on the property included everything from slave cabins to kitchen houses to a blacksmith's shop. Some of these plantations survive today, though they don't usually produce cash crops anymore, (unless you consider tourists a crop). Several large plantations and gardens are open for tours.

At one, **Lowndes Grove Inn,** 266 Margaret Street, you can spend the night. Built in 1786, Lowndes Grove is the only surviving plantation on the Charleston peninsula. The Greek Revival mansion was once part of a 328-acre plantation directly across the Ashley River from Charles Towne Landing. Although the estate is only minutes from modern Charleston, its extensive grounds, the house, and its furnishings make it seem a world apart. The owners have preserved architectural details original to the house. The inside wooden shutters and a front door (made in 1786 of cypress with an iron-and-wood bolt) were defenses against attacks by Indians. The ceilings are 11 feet high.

As an inn, the place offers a music room with a baby grand piano, formal sitting room, solarium, piazza, and grounds and gardens kept much as they would have been during the earlier life of the plantation. The drapes dip in swags across the tops of windows to puddle on the floor. This was a sign of affluence in earlier days; it meant that the owner could afford to buy extra fabric, imported at great cost from Europe, purely for decoration.

The guest rooms, like the rest of the house, are grand in scale and furnished with antiques and reproduction furniture, including four-poster canopy beds. Sherry is served on the piazza overlooking the river in the evening. Weddings are often held here. If you don't like the idea of staying at the plantation when a wedding is going on, be sure to ask about it when you make your reservations. Room rates begin at about $75. Phone (803) 723–3530. To get to Lowndes Grove Inn, take the Rutledge Avenue exit from I–26. Go 1 mile, then turn right on St. Margaret Street. Drive to the end of the street; Lowndes Grove will be on your right.

A more common way to learn about plantations is by taking a tour. A short drive northwest from Charleston on State Highway 61 (Ashley River Road) will bring you to Drayton Hall, Magnolia Plantation and Gardens, and Middleton Place.

Be sure to visit **Drayton Hall** if you are interested in architectural preservation. This is the only pre-Revolutionary War plantation house remaining on the Ashley River. The Georgian-Palladian structure was built between 1738 and 1742 on a gentle hill overlooking the river. The property belonged to the Drayton family for seven generations; now it is owned and operated by the National Trust for Historic Preservation. The house has survived in virtually its original state, with Trust activities working to continue that preservation and accommodate visitors without damaging the building.

The interior has detailed, handcrafted woodwork and plaster ceilings. Some of the original paint remains on the walls. Because the house is not furnished, you can see its architectural details clearly. This may sound spartan, but the effect is just the opposite: As guides explain the features of the house, talk about how the place was used, and describe the preservation process, one is simply awed with the grandeur of the building. If you visit only one plantation in the area and want as authentic a sense as possible of how things used to be, choose Drayton Hall.

Around Christmas, concerts of West African work songs are held in the building. The acoustics of the rooms, without furniture to absorb sound, do fine things to the music. If you plan to be in the area during the holidays, call for specifics. The plantation is open November through February, daily 10:00 A.M. to 3:00 P.M.; March through October, daily 10:00 A.M. to 4:00 P.M. Closed Thanksgiving, Christmas, and New Year's Day. Tickets are about $6.00 for adults, half that for children.

A mile farther down Ashley River Road is **Magnolia Plantation and Gardens,** said to be America's oldest gardens. Fifty acres of formal and informal gardens blaze most of the year with seasonal blooms—900 varieties of camellias, 250 of azaleas, and more than 150,000 new bulbs every year. The plantation's owner, Drayton Hastie, tries to introduce as many new plants to the property every year as possible. The result is color and bloom almost year-round, some in formal and theme gardens, others in casual cottage-style gardens.

Each style has had its period of popularity. Some plantations would tear out everything decorative and start over in order to follow a new fashion. Here, where gardens were always a priority, each new gardening fad was simply fitted onto the property without giving up what had already been done. Today it takes a staff of eighteen gardeners to maintain it all. March, when the weather is still cool, is a peak time for bloom. Interestingly, mosquitoes are not a problem in the swamp, even in summer, although it is not sprayed, but they are a problem in the gardens, which must be sprayed regularly. Small footbridges and boardwalks create walkways into the Audubon Swamp Garden, 60 acres of black water in a natural cypress and tupelo swamp filled with water birds, small animals, and alligators.

You may tour the plantation house to see some Hastie family furniture, silver, and a copy of the Declaration of Independence on silk. The second story of the building remains about the same as it was after the Civil War, giving you an idea of the lean times of Reconstruction. Open daily 8:00 A.M. to 5:00 P.M. Tickets for the gardens are about $8.00, $4.00 more for the house, and $2.00 more for the swamp, with reduced rates for senior citizens and children. Phone (803) 571–1266.

Next, drive 4 miles beyond Magnolia Plantation to **Middleton Place** to see the oldest formal landscaped gardens in America, planned in 1741 along the banks of the Ashley River. It took ten years and a hundred slaves to finish the project. Like Magnolia Gardens, Middleton Place incorporated new planting vogues into the existing designs rather than destroy any of the original formal gardens. The Civil War and the poverty following it, however, took a toll here. Sherman's troops burned the main house. Eventually, the family restored part of the building to live in, but today it is a museum where you can tour rooms furnished in plantation style.

The emphasis here is on things to do and things that used to be done. The stableyard has been restored so that it looks almost new, with well-maintained fences and rings. Craftspeople demonstrate many of the old plantation activities. You can watch spinners and weavers, learn about making candles, see corn ground, even see a cow being milked without machines! This is a good opportunity for children to see the activities and animals of the old plantation life. The grounds are open daily 9:00 A.M. to 5:00 P.M. Admission is about $12 for adults from the middle of March until the middle of June, a little less the rest of the year; children's and senior cit-

The formal gardens at Middleton Place were planned in 1741 to lie along the banks of the Ashley River. It took ten years and a hundred slaves to finish the project.

izens' rates are less. The museum house is open Tuesday through Saturday 10:00 A.M. to 4:30 P.M.; afternoon only Sunday and Monday. Museum tickets are about $5.00.

Different from the preceding three plantations, in that it has tried to remain a crop-producing plantation, is **Boone Hall,** 8 miles north of Charleston on U.S. Highway 17, 1054 Long Point Road. It epitomizes the Charlestonian determination to survive disaster.

The plantation had long since recovered from the Civil War and Reconstruction and was growing pecans and a variety of field crops when Hurricane Hugo swept through the area in 1989, peeling the roofs from all the buildings and destroying most of the grounds. It took thirty workers nearly half a year to get the place together again. When the plantation reopened for visitors, Nancy McRae, the owner, put out a sign inviting

In the Charleston spirit of rising above adversity, Boone Hall and its Avenue of Oaks have survived a series of disasters, from the Civil War to Hurricane Hugo.

A Bane at Boone

If you visit now, you may see evidence of the latest, and most surprising, threat to the Boone Hall grounds: foraging deer. As new construction all around the plantation eats up wooded areas, the deer are looking for new places to live and feed. So far at Boone Hall, the deer have tried wheat, peas, and wildflowers and found them all good. The owners hope their experiments with such nursery stock as shrubs will produce crops the deer don't like.

everyone to come celebrate and listing all who had helped in the reclamation. More than 3,000 people came for lunch and stayed to play games, a survivors' party in the true Charleston spirit.

Farther from Charleston (about an hour north) than the previously described plantations, **Rice Hope Plantation Inn,** in Monck's Corner, gives you another opportunity to stay in a plantation mansion, eat some Southern food, and walk on old plantation grounds.

Rice Hope Plantation was cleared in 1795 by Revolutionary War officer William Read and his wife, Sarah Harleston Read. The formal gardens were created in that era. The plantation houses that used to stand on the site, on a bluff overlooking old rice fields along the Cooper River, are gone. No one is sure exactly what happened to these houses. The current house, comprising 9,000 square feet, was not built until the 1920s. It is built of cypress, with a slate roof. While you do not stay in an 1800s mansion, you do get a strong sense of the spaciousness and elaborate decor in South Carolina plantations. The grounds are beautiful, with live oak trees and the Cooper River in the background. As Doris Krasprak, the proprietor, says, "It is everything you think of when you picture a Southern plantation in your mind." What remains of the original plantation acreage today is the eleven acres of live oaks and gardens and the 371 acres of old rice fields bordering the Cooper River. Rice planting ceased to be profitable and was abandoned by about the mid-1800s. The acres that used to be rice fields are now tidal marsh, but you can still identify some of the embankments of the old fields. The formal gardens, with statuary, now cover about an acre of terraces. Brick paths lead through banks of camellias, which bloom October through April, on to drifts of azaleas, which bloom in spring. Live oaks draped with Spanish moss and low plantings of flowers complete the scene.

Visitors used to stay for long periods of time at plantations, so they would have found the pastimes at Rice Hope appropriate: tennis, bird watching, lawn games, bicycling, and boating. Breakfast is included in the rates. You can arrange for lunch and dinner, too. This is a popular place for weddings. If you think such a party would disturb your stay, make sure when you make your reservation that no weddings are scheduled. To get to Rice Hope Plantation, drive north on U.S. Highway 17, turn onto State Highway 41, and, finally, follow country roads. You will receive detailed instructions when you make reservations. Phone (803) 761–4832 or (800) 569–4038, or write 206 Rice Hope Drive, Moncks Corner, SC 29461. Rates are about $60 to $75 per room.

Driving north on U.S. 17 for about an hour brings you to the third oldest city in South Carolina, **Georgetown.** As in so much of the area, the history of the Old South and the Revolutionary War period run together. Georgetown's historic district, on the Sampit River, dates back to the 1700s. The city's income came first from producing indigo, then rice. By the mid-1800s Georgetown County alone accounted for about half the rice crop of all the United States. Georgetown's deep harbor still serves as an important shipping port. This area is now pretty well modernized, but you might stop in the **Rice Museum,** at the corner of Front and Screven Streets, to study the details and history of producing rice in the United States. The museum has information about the development of Georgetown as well as maps, dioramas, photographs, and a cross-section of a model of a rice mill. The museum is open Monday through Saturday 9:30 A.M. to 4:30 P.M. Admission is about $2.00. Phone (803) 546-7423.

You might also stop at the **Georgetown Chamber of Commerce,** 600 Front Street, for tapes and brochures to lead you through self-guided tours. Phone (803) 546-8436.

Without question, though, you will learn the most by taking a plantation tour with **Captain Sandy's Tours.** Sandy Vermont lives here, knows the area intimately, and has a thorough understanding of how the past evolved into the present with many of the old ways intact. "We're still close to our history here," he said. "Industrialization came but it didn't take away what we know." Sandy is a master storyteller. His boat tour of the plantations includes narration of what life was like through the Civil War and some explanation of how that experience created the community that exists today. He tells it like good biography—warts and all. Some of Sandy's storytelling takes place on the Sampit River, where he relies on natural effects to enhance the mood. Some stories go back to what the settlers faced: water, animals, other people. Other stories are about ghosts and legendary local people. Sandy made up "The Legend of Spanish Moss" himself. To get full details, costs, and make arrangements for a tour, call Sandy at (803) 527-4106. He answers in a rich, Southern baritone.

Farther north on U.S. 17, about 18 miles south of Myrtle Beach, at Murrells Inlet, **Brookgreen Gardens** brings yet another interpretation to the plantation concept. The place was originally a rice and indigo plantation. You can still see how it was laid out as you drive down a wide road with live oaks dripping Spanish moss along each side. In its early days the plantation had a formal garden; it has been incorporated into the design of

the plantation's many gardens today. You won't see rice and indigo growing anymore, but you will find more than 2,000 different plants, mostly
flowering, intermingled with more than 500 statues. Serious botanists come
here to study native flora and to see what exotic plants have been intro-
duced successfully. A wildlife park provides nooks and crannies for deer,
foxes, otter, and many kinds of birds. You can wander along a nature trail
through an aviary to study the birds and some very old trees. You can picnic on the grounds after you've walked around, making a nice outdoors
kind of day. Brookgreen Gardens is open every day but Christmas. Admission is about $5.00 for adults, half that for children; the price includes free
programs and tours. Phone (803) 237–4218.

While you are in this area, plan on having at least one meal in the little
town of Murrells Inlet. This fishing village doesn't flaunt antebellum
grandeur, but is an excellent place to taste seafood so fresh that it has only
just stopped squirming, the way it would have been served all along the
coast in the Old South, when seafood was a staple in the diet if only
because it was *available*. The Murrells Inlet restaurants are casual places
where you can indulge in an oyster roast (huge buckets full of steamed rock
oysters that you pry open with small knives) or order fresh broiled and fried
seafood. Fishermen selling shrimp with the heads still on, fresh from their
boats, add to the authentic feel of the community.

THE SOUTHERN COAST

If you drive south from Charleston on State Highway 17 for a little less than
an hour, you will come to the seaport town of **Beaufort** (pronounced
"BEW-fort"), close to the Georgia border. You might plan to stop here on
your way on into Georgia. Settled in 1711, Beaufort is the second-oldest
town in South Carolina. The town faces the Intracoastal Waterway and has
a natural harbor on the Atlantic Ocean. The waterfront and some fine old
homes are the main attractions. The place feels kind of sleepy, with a peace-
fulness that must have prevailed during the prewar years. One reason so
much of the town remains as it was probably is that at the beginning of the
Civil War, most of the population left and Union soldiers occupied it. Consequently, it is one place in South Carolina that Sherman's troops didn't
burn. The houses that remain today are modest homes from before the

Revolutionary War plus a few grand antebellum homes. Most of these are not open for tours, but if you stop at the **Visitor Information Center,** 1006 Bay Street, you can arrange for a carriage tour that includes a narrated history of the town. It takes an hour and costs about $9.50 for adults, half that for children. Phone (803) 524–3163.

You might prefer to pick up a free map for a walking tour of the town that tells you about twenty-six historical sites, including several old churches and the **George Elliot House Museum,** housed in a building from about 1849, that served as a Union hospital during the Civil War. The visitors' center is open Monday through Saturday 9:30 A.M. to 5:30 P.M.; Sunday 10:00 A.M. to 5:00 P.M.

A romantic place to stay in Beaufort is the **Rhett House Inn,** 1009 Craven Street. The inn is a block from the Intracoastal Waterway, at the corner of Craven and Newcastle Streets. The restored house has wrap-around verandas with classic columns and porticos. Entry stairs on two sides sweep upward in a most Scarlett-and-Rhett manner. Live oaks dripping with Spanish moss shade the glistening white building. Inside, the rooms are large and bright, furnished with English and American antiques. One of the lower-level rooms opens onto a courtyard with gardens and a trickling fountain. You can arrange ahead of time for dinner. Continental breakfast is included in the inn's rates, which begin at about $100 per room. Phone (803) 524–9030.

From Beaufort, you can also pick up the unique **Gullah-n-Geechie Mahn Tours** to St. Helena Island, one of the South Carolina sea islands. Many of the inhabitants of these islands are direct descendants of South Carolina slaves. Because they were isolated from the mainland, the people of the sea islands developed a distinct language and culture of their own, strongly reflecting their African origins. The roots of the Gullah-speaking people have been traced back to the west coast of Africa, and much of the African "rice coast" culture survives today in the crafts, including the sweetgrass baskets, and the Gullah language, which is still spoken by many island natives. You can experience their culinary traditions at the **Gullah House Restaurant,** 761 Sea Island Parkway, St. Helena Island, about 10 miles east of Beaufort off State Highway 21. Phone (833) 838–2402. The food includes such entrees as fish-'n'-grits, stewed shrimp with grits, crab cakes, hot wings, and fried low-country shrimp with slaw and okra rice perloe; this is classic low-country cooking. The restaurant is open for lunch

Talkin' de Talk

Hey! De Gullah-n-Geechie Mahn Tours wish fa vite ya to de Sea Islandts ob Bufat, Sous Carolina.

Translation: Greetings!—Gullah 'n' Geechie Mahn Tours invites you to visit the Sea Islands of Beaufort, South Carolina.

and dinner Tuesday through Thursday, for all three meals Friday and Saturday, and all day Sunday. Live jazz and blues are performed beginning about 8:00 P.M. on weekends.

Adding a tour to the day will tell you a great deal about the rich, varied Gullah history. Guides speaking in the dialects indigenous to the sea islands tell their stories and explain the history of the islands. In the spring the Gullah Festival focuses on language, arts, music, dance, and food. For greater detail about the tour possibilities, call Kitty Green at (803) 838–3758, (803) 838–7516, or (803) 838–7560.

THE MIDLANDS

Columbia, the capital city of South Carolina since 1786, retains the feel of the gracious Old South to a remarkable degree, in spite of its growing numbers of new industries and people who have moved here from other areas. Early in the Civil War, South Carolinians considered Columbia a safe haven. Sherman's march threatened the coastal areas, but the Rebels did not expect him to come into the center of the state. They figured wrong. Sherman burned most of the city, sparing only a few public buildings and the **University of South Carolina** (then South Carolina College) because it was being used as a hospital for Union troops.

The burning of Columbia means that you will not find many antebellum tour homes and certainly none that offers lodging. What remains of the era, in structural terms, is the State House (over which the Confederate Stars-and-Bars flag still flies—controversially) and a few homes, in addition to the university.

A Passion for a Party

Mary Chesnut's Civil War Diary offers some fascinating glimpses into the determination of people in Columbia to maintain the niceties of polite social life even in the face of disaster. From the safety of Lincolnton, North Carolina, where she had retreated from Columbia, Mary Chesnut wrote about meeting her husband—and weeping on the day they learned that Columbia had been burned. Nine days later, she wrote, "Appliances for social enjoyment are not wanting. Miss Middleton and Isabella often drink a cup of tea with me. One might search the whole world and not find two cleverer or more agreeable women."

The university is a good place to start your explorations. Founded in 1805, its "horseshoe" was created like the quadrangles on the campuses of universities in England, with symmetrically arranged brick walks and buildings set off by flowers and stretches of grass. Young women in hoop skirts would look appropriate here even today. The buildings are open to all during normal school days and hours. The **McKissick Museum** is on the horseshoe. Exhibits reflect the area's development, emphasizing regional history, folk art, textiles, Southeastern art, and African-American culture. The museum is open Monday through Friday 9:00 A.M. to 5:00 P.M.; Saturday 10:00 A.M. to 5:00 P.M.; Sunday 1:00 to 5:00 P.M. Admission is free. Exhibits change often. Phone (803) 777–7251 for information about current exhibits.

If you walk from McKissick west across the square on campus, you will come to the **South Carolina Confederate Relic Room and Museum,** 920 Sumter Street. This tiny museum provides a poignant glimpse of what it meant to be a South Carolinian before, during, and after the Civil War. Small signs explain what you are seeing. One exhibit, reminiscent of Scarlett O'Hara's ball gown made from draperies in the movie *Gone With the Wind,* shows a dress that was made during Reconstruction from drapery fabric. A shabby beaded purse lies beside it. A dramatic exhibit shows two Confederate war uniforms, one glorious and bright, from the beginning of the Civil War, and another, sad and rough, made near the end of the war, of homespun dyed with extracts from roots. The museum is open Monday through Friday 8:30 A.M. to 5:00 P.M. Admission is free.

A quick walk northwest of only a couple blocks will take you to the **State House,** at Gervais and Main Streets, between Assembly and Sumter Streets. This building was under construction when Union troops fired on it in 1865. They didn't do much damage, because they were across the river, but each of the spots where a cannonball hit is marked today with a bronze star. This is where the South Carolina General Assembly first met, in 1869. If you go inside this Italian Renaissance building, you will see some interesting mahogany woodwork topped by balconies with brass railings. The building is open for tours Monday through Friday, 9:00 A.M. to 4:00 P.M., closed at noon for lunch. Tours are offered every half hour. Admission is free. Sometimes the building is closed because of special events. Phone (803) 734–2430.

Because they have so few significant old buildings left, Columbians take good care of the ones that remain. The Richland County Historic Preservation Commission manages four important old homes: Robert Mills Historic House and Park, Hampton-Preston Mansion and Garden, Woodrow Wilson Boyhood Home, and Manns-Simons Cottage.

Which of these you choose to tour depends on your interests. The **Robert Mills House** is an elegant, formal house, important because of its designer, Robert Mills, who also designed the Washington Monument and the original Mills House Hotel in Charleston. The house has two matching drawing rooms, marble mantels, and silver doorknobs, but these things have not been intact since the building's early days. Preservationists rescued the building from being torn down in 1961 and restored it using information from old manuscripts of Robert Mills.

Next door, the **Hampton-Preston Mansion,** 1615 Blanding Street, belonged first to the Confederate general Wade Hampton, and, later, to the Preston family. This is a good house to tour to understand how important entertaining was in Old Columbia. One exhibit shows a tablecloth with "The Legend of the Tablecloth," a little story about how the Hampton sisters, who took entertaining very seriously, had the cloth made from a bolt of linen that Wade Hampton II had ordered from Ireland for his Millwood Plantation. After the Civil War they presented the cloth to their minister so he wouldn't have to dine on a bare table. The guides here do a wonderful job of telling you about Columbia's polite society of the time.

Much less grand, the **Woodrow Wilson Boyhood Home,** 1705 Hampton Street, built in about 1872, is a cottage that belonged to President Wilson's father, a Presbyterian minister.

In yet another contrast, **Manns-Simons Cottage,** 1403 Richland Street, belonged to an antebellum black family. Celia Mann, a slave in Charleston, bought her freedom. Then she walked to Columbia, bought this small frame house, built in about 1850, and created a family home. Today the building is used to show the black history of the region. It has a gallery showing work by black artists.

These four homes are open Tuesday through Saturday 10:15 A.M. to 3:15 P.M.; Sunday 1:15 to 4:15 P.M. Closed major holidays. Admission is about $3.00 for adults, half that for children. Phone (803) 252–1770.

During and after the war, food was scarce in Columbia, but these days you will find plenty of places to eat. Until recently, eating at almost any restaurant in Columbia meant that you automatically got Southern cooking. As the city has become more multicultural, a variety of cuisines, ranging from Indian to Japanese to Mexican, have found their way into local restaurants.

One place, at 919 Sumter Street, just across from the horseshoe on campus, **Lizard's Thicket,** phone (803) 765–1373, specializes in regional, Southern-style country cooking for three meals every day. For lunch and dinner, this means a meat, perhaps fried chicken or ham, and several vegetables chosen from a list including pinto beans, greens, green beans, rice, okra, black-eyed peas, and so on, served with corn bread or biscuits and copious amounts of iced tea (sweetened unless you request otherwise). The breakfast menu includes country ham, sausage, grits, and biscuits. Lizard's Thicket has several other locations in the area, including one at 402 Beltline Boulevard, phone (803) 782–0618.

Another way to find old-fashioned Southern cooking is to look for the small lunch places scattered around the city. They serve Columbia's traditional country cooking, using the ingredients that have typically been produced in the area: ham, chicken, okra, corn and cornmeal, black-eyed peas, field peas, greens, cabbage prepared as cole slaw, rice, and sweet fruit-based pies and cobblers. Barbecue appears on many of their menus, too.

Maurice's Piggie Park, 1600 Charleston Highway in West Columbia, (803) 796–0220, is the area's most famous barbecue restaurant. The sauce, which is mustard based, as is most South Carolina barbecue, mixes with the juices of roasted pork, which you can order either chopped or sliced, to create a concoction that inevitably tempts you to eat too much. Barbecue is traditionally served on soft, white round buns with slaw and hush puppies. The sauce at Maurice's has become so popular that many Southern grocery stores sell it, but somehow the barbecue you make at home just isn't as good.

You might also try the **Dixie Seafood Company, Inc.,** 902 B Gervais Street, which specializes in fried fish and oysters. Phone (803) 771–6753.

It's a drive of less than an hour on U.S. 76/378 from Columbia to **Sumter,** where you can ignore Shaw Air Force Base as being too contemporary and concentrate on the excellent self-guided tours offered by the **Sumter Convention and Visitors Bureau,** 21 North Main Street. Although the town was named for a Revolutionary War hero, Thomas Sumter, there is Civil War history here, too, in a distant sort of way. The first shot of the Civil War was fired in Charleston by a Sumter native, who happened to be a cadet at the Citadel when he fired at a Union boat. But here you will be looking at gracious plantation life, not battlefields. The area was developed by well-to-do planters who appreciated culture enough to have had an opera house.

The Visitors Bureau publishes brochures for three different tours: the plantation tour, the tour of governors, and the lakes tour. Of the three, the governors tour evokes the Old South most strongly. It begins in the Rembert/Spring Hill area, where planters spent their summers, needing a respite from summer heat and disease on their plantations. The plantation tour takes you past several actual plantations. The lakes tour includes a country store and restaurant, the Wedgefield Presbyterian Church, and an excellent 1881 Gothic frame building. You can request brochures ahead of time to plan your tours by calling (803) 773–3371 or (800) 688–4748 or by writing the bureau at P.O. Box 1149, Sumter, SC 29151.

These tours, combined with a visit to **Sumter County Museum,** 122 North Washington Street, give you a good idea of life in Sumter's antebellum years. The museum is located in what used to be the home of Andrew Jackson Moses and his wife, Octavia Harby Moses. They raised fourteen children here, so the doll and toy collection will be of interest; it is the kind of exhibit that you do not often have the chance to see. Other rooms have exhibits of war artifacts and a textile gallery, where some vintage clothing and old quilts are on display. The museum is open Tuesday through Saturday 10:00 A.M. to 5:00 P.M.; Sunday 2:00 to 5:00 P.M. No admission is charged, but the museum welcomes donations. Phone (803) 775–0908.

One more look back in Sumter should please you if you like antiques. In the 200 block of Broad Street, **Antique Row** has a number of shops in old houses where you can sometimes find some excellent Southern pieces. Antique Row is not a mall or formal arrangement, but the shops are concentrated in this area, making it easy to walk from one to another. The shops are closed Sunday.

UPSTATE

To appreciate the importance of the mountainous upstate area to antebellum South Carolinians, all you need to do is drive around Charleston and Columbia in August without air-conditioning. Planters fled the heat for the relative coolness of the higher elevations—just over 1,000 feet for **Greenville,** a little more than 800 feet for Spartanburg. The Blue Ridge Mountains, which dominate this area visually, are as inviting today as they must have been then. Today the area is devoted to manufacturing and industry, not to providing resorts for rich planters, but some important overtones of the Old South still exist here to be explored.

Greenville was originally Cherokee country; white men took it over by treaty toward the end of the 1700s. The community flourished as a mountain resort area until the Civil War, when it served as a hospital center for Confederate soldiers. Textiles—specifically, cotton—became the main industry during Reconstruction. Since then the area has attracted other industries as well. But by visiting the state parks of this region, you can get a true feeling of the relief and comfort that must have come in the years before the Civil War to those Southerners who made the long, slow journey from the coast and midlands into the mountains each summer. These places were not state parks then, of course, but they make a good place to approximate the summer mountain escape of earlier times. The four parks in the immediate area are Caesars Head State Park, Jones Gap State Park, Keowee-Toxaway State Park, and Table Rock State Park.

Caesars Head State Park is on U.S. 276, northwest of Greenville at the South Carolina/North Carolina border. In a classic piece of Southern storytelling, the most popular tale about the park is that it was named for Caesar, a hunting dog that got carried away in the chase and ran right off the mountain. A more likely explanation for the name, however, is that a granite outcropping resembles Julius Caesar's profile, in much the way that Grandfather Mountain in North Carolina got its name because people could "see" an old man's profile in the outcropping there. The park is more than 3,000 feet above sea level and is rich in all kinds of wildlife. The vistas are wonderful, and the park is good for fishing and hiking. Open daily. Phone (803) 836–6115.

Jones Gap State Park, off U.S. Highway 276, some 3 miles northwest of Marietta, is another wilderness park with a diversity of plant and animal life. The middle branch of the Saluda River has cut a rocky gorge that is stunning to look down into. This is a good hiking park. Open daily. Phone (803) 868–2605.

If somebody tries to tell you how the old Confederates loved the lake here, run fast the other way, because you're being had. The 18,500-acre Lake Keowee was built by the Duke Power Company. But it is worth a stop anyway. It has tent camping sites with water, and RV sites with water and electricity. (It is true that absolute power corrupts, but we do need electricity.) You can learn about the Cherokee Indians in the area at an interpretive center in the park. Native Americans were a part of the Old South that has not had much attention until recent years, but now their story is increasingly coming to light. You can fish here and hike some challenging trails. Open daily. Phone (803) 868–2605.

Finally, **Table Rock State Park,** on S.C. 11, about 16 miles north of Pickens, offers great mountain vistas with a few more amenities, including some cabins, one hundred tent sites, and a restaurant. You can fish and swim in the lake, and boats are available for rental. This park has some of the most challenging hiking trails in South Carolina.

Don't get the idea as you roam the upstate that only tourists came here in the early days. Some of the plantations belonging to permanent settlers go back to Revolutionary War times. A short drive from the Greenville-Spartanburg area, for instance, takes you to **Walnut Grove Plantation,** in the little town of **Roebuck.** Walnut Grove will give you an especially good sense of the self-sufficient nature of those plantations that were fairly isolated. In addition to the main house, detached kitchen, and separate school building at the center of the plantation, a re-created doctor's office about a mile down the road duplicates the one run by the county's first physician. A nature trail about ¾ mile long wanders past the family cemetery—not necessarily the doctor's fault—through a wooded area to the kitchen.

The plantation remained in the same family from the time King George III granted the land to Charles Moore until Moore's descendants donated it to the Spartanburg County Historical Society in 1961. The family kept detailed records of everything from furniture to wills, which has made the restoration and re-creation process more accurate than it otherwise could have been.

You will learn something about early education here, too, because the plantation owner was also the plantation teacher. He had been a teacher in his native Ireland; soon after settling on the plantation, he began gathering the children of the area into his school. The plantation is open April through October, Tuesday through Saturday 11:00 A.M. to 5:00 P.M.; Sunday 2:00 to 5:00 P.M. The rest of the year, it is open Sunday 2:00 to 5:00 P.M. Closed holidays. Tickets are about $3.50 for adults, $2.00 for children. Phone (803) 576–6546. To get to the plantation, take exit 28 from I–26 onto U.S. 221. Turn left to go east toward Columbia on 221. At the first street past the intersection, you will see a sign directing you about 1 mile farther to the entrance.

While you are in this upstate area, try to see **Price House,** at 1200 Oak View Farms Road, in Woodruff. It sits on what was once a 2,000-acre plantation built in the 1700s to show off Thomas Price's wealth. According to records of the property, Price kept the post office, a general store, and a bed-and-board lodging. What you see when you visit is largely restoration, because over the years transients burned up all the wood in the house. Even the walls had to be rebuilt. The bricks had been made on the property, but they were held together with too much wet sand and too little mortar to survive the wear of time. Fortunately, the Spartanburg Historical Preservation Commission has been able to restore the building with accuracy, because Price kept good records.

One interesting aspect of the house is the eclectic mix of its architectural features. It has walls one board wide, like those in Charleston, along with steep Dutch gambrel roofs and inside end chimneys typical of buildings in Virginia and Maryland. Researchers speculate that Price may have been a military deserter who learned about architecture in different parts of the country while he was running and hiding. To get to the Price House, take exit 35 near Spartanburg off I–26, and turn right onto Price House Road. Continue to a sign identifying a driveway to the house. The property is set off with a chain-link fence, so you will need to ring the big bell at the entrance to summon a guide. Open April through October, Tuesday through Saturday late morning to 5:00 P.M. Open Sunday afternoon year-round. Admission is about $2.50 for adults, $1.50 for children.

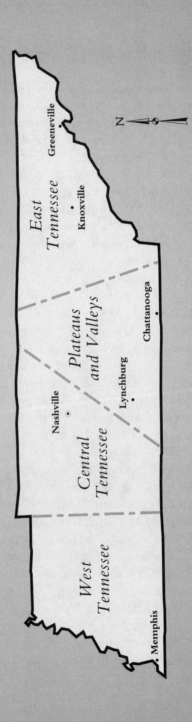

Tennessee

A TRAVELER CALLED TENNESSEE "THAT STRANGE and wonderful state where nothing is what you expect." To wit: It *is*
part of the South, and it *did* figure prominently in the Civil
War. But what you will find in Tennessee differs from any
stereotypical notions of hoop skirts and magnolias that you might associate with the antebellum South. Moreover, the western, middle, and eastern regions of the state differ from one another enough to make them
seem like three independent countries.

You can attribute the differences partly to geography. Western Tennessee, with both the Mississippi and Tennessee Rivers, reflects the influence of the early riverboat culture, when many people passed through on
their way to someplace else. The middle of Tennessee spreads over rolling
terrain from the Tennessee River to the foothills. Fertile soil and relatively
open spaces have invited farming and husbandry, especially horses. Eastern
Tennessee lies on and between ridge after ridge of mountains. Pockets of
civilization in the Smokies and the Appalachians developed, until recently
isolated from one another by the rugged mountains. Even today, getting
from one small mountain community to another can be a heart-stopping
challenge along steep, narrow roads with hairpin turns and switchbacks.
The rule—sometimes posted on crude signs nailed to trees for the enlight-
enment of "flatlanders"—is "uphill traffic has the right of way."

What remains of the Old South in these three regions for visitors to experience is often unexpected, and always fascinating. Much of it reflects Tennessee's position as a border state when the Civil War divided the nation. The state was by no means united in its wish to secede from the Union. Tennessee was the last state to leave the Union. According to the book *The Border States* (Time-Life Library of America series), although more than 100,000 people voted to join the Confederacy, more than 47,000 others voted to stay in the Union. This led to instances of neighbor against neighbor, family against family, and even brother against brother. These differences show up in the attractions available to travelers looking to understand the Old South.

WEST TENNESSEE

Spending time in **Memphis** will quickly demonstrate that not all the Old South was glamorous. One local resident says, "Memphis is not lovely, never was. She just squats there by the river. But she sure is interesting."

Not that the city didn't have some good years. This land originally belonged to the Chickasaw Indians, who didn't turn it over to the United States (and Andrew Jackson) until 1818. To see the role of the early Indians, visit the **Chucalissa Archaeological Museum,** 1987 Indian Village Drive, next to Fuller State Park. This museum is part of the anthropology department of Memphis State University, at the site of an Indian settlement that remained active until sometime in the 1500s. A slide show and exhibits explain the history and findings on the site. There are nine reconstructed thatched huts, including a chief's house in the little village, and an exhibit of a sample archaeological excavation. To get to the site, drive south 5 miles on U.S. 61, then turn to go west on Mitchell Road for 4.5 miles more. The museum is open Tuesday through Saturday 9:00 A.M. to 5:00 P.M.; Sunday 1:00 to 5:00 P.M.; last admission at 4:30 P.M. Admission is about $3.00 for adults, $2.00 for children. Phone (901) 785–3160.

After Jackson and his partners laid out the town that would become Memphis on the bluffs over the Mississippi River, the settlement boomed. Steamboats navigated the Mississippi from Memphis to New Orleans. Within just a couple of decades, railroads connected Memphis to the Atlantic seaboard. Trade, travel, and population grew. Business associated with river trade, including the largest slave-trade market in the South, thrived. To see this once-wealthy aspect of old Memphis, you'll want to check some of the restored homes and churches in the **Victorian Village District,** on Adams, Jefferson, and Poplar Avenues.

The district has a number of preserved homes and churches built in the late 1800s. Some of these are open to the public. **Historic Fontaine House,** 680 Adams Avenue, is a restored 1870 French Victorian house furnished with antiques and including exhibitions of vintage clothing. You'll see real opulence here—Chippendale, Sheraton, and Queen Anne antiques, crystal chandeliers, and marble mantels. The house is open Monday through Saturday 10:00 A.M. to 4:00 P.M.; Sunday 1:00 to 4:00 P.M. Closed Fourth of July, Thanksgiving, and Christmas Eve and Christmas Day. Admission about $4.00 for adults, $2.00 for children. Phone (901) 526–1469.

Another home of the wealthy, the **Mallory-Neely House,** 652 Adams Avenue, is an 1852 brick-and-stucco home in the Italian villa style. The three-story building has twenty-five rooms with original furnishings, demonstrating how the James Neelys, a prosperous cotton family, lived in Memphis in the late nineteenth century. The house is open Tuesday through Saturday 10:00 A.M. to 4:00 P.M.; Sunday 1:00 to 4:00 P.M. Admission is about $4.00 for adults, $3.00 for children. Phone (901) 523–1484.

To see life at a more middle-class level in the district, visit **Magevney House,** 198 Adams Avenue. This small clapboard cottage was built in the 1830s, then sold a few years later to Eugene Magevney, an Irish immigrant who founded the Roman Catholic community in Memphis. It is the oldest remaining residence in Memphis, and in some ways is the most interesting of the tour homes. Some of the family's furniture is still in place, along with some family portraits. Open Tuesday through Saturday 10:00 A.M. to 4:00 P.M. Admission is free. Phone (901) 526–4464.

In contrast to this genteel preservation, you'll find the **Beale Street Historic District** full of people and parties and activity. Beale Street, famous as the birthplace of the blues, runs east–west from Main Street to Fourth Street. In its heyday, it teemed with the kind of nightlife that you might think of as lowlife—people hanging around the nightclubs, bars, gambling establishments, and, inevitably, pawn shops. The sounds of the blues, simultaneously somehow cookin' and cryin', filled the Orpheum and the Palace and rocked the saloons along the street. Beale Street's fame grew from music there about the turn of the century, when William Christopher Handy published such songs as "Memphis Blues," "Beale

Street Blues," and "St. Louis Blues." He is honored by a statue in the W. C. Handy Park where Beale and Third Streets meet. But the roots of the blues go back to the fields and the songs of the slaves. To understand why their music and the culture from which it grew marked Memphis so indelibly, you need to know a little more about the city's early history.

Runaway slaves on the Underground Railroad passed through Memphis on their way north. Ironically, Memphis was also one of the largest markets for slave trade in the South. During the Civil War the city was an important port for supplying provisions to the Confederacy until Union troops sank a Confederate fleet, took over the city, and cut off its vital river trade. That was the first economic disaster. After the war Reconstruction ruined the plantation economy of the area, as it did elsewhere in the South.

Then "The Yellowjack" struck. Memphis historian Phyllis Tickle says that yellow fever hit the city so violently and so fast that between Sunday, August 19, 1878, when it began, until the following Friday, more than half the Memphis population of 40,000 had been buried. Everyone who could, especially the well-to-do, such as those living in what is now known as Victorian Village, fled north. Those who remained were mostly slaves, with no way to escape nor anyplace else to go. By an unpredictable quirk of biology, it turned out that while yellow fever made black people very sick, it did not kill them, as it did white people. When it was all over, only 6,000 people, most of them former slaves, remained to rebuild the city. In fact, in 1879 the city lost its charter, becoming a ward of the State of Tennessee for the next thirteen years because its population had dwindled so drastically.

When you walk Beale Street, you will still hear the rhythms and see the influence of people who, as Billie Holliday put it much later, had "a right to sing the Blues."

These days Beale Street thrives as a tourist attraction. In addition to the specialty shops that are found in tourist areas everywhere, you will find many nightclubs, with food, drink, and live music. The best way to get the sense of Beale Street is to walk the street and follow your ear.

If you don't want to get into the nightlife scene, learn about the area and the times by stopping at the **Center for Southern Folklore,** 130 Beale Street. (This address is in the old Lansky building, where Elvis used to buy his clothes. Hey, he's not the *old* South, but you can't go to Memphis and ignore *The King!*) This is a center that the Chamber of Commerce people like to call "intimate." It is, in that the staff are all personally fascinated with Memphis's past and tell you about it with authority and enthu-

Singing the Blues

The blues follows a twelve-bar pattern. In three-line stanzas, the lyrics talk about life's troubles. The second line of each stanza repeats the first. In Memphis they say, "It's wrote in no books. You inherit the Blues; it's born in you." The music was performed first in tiny local night spots in the country, where the audience comprised mostly local friends and neighbors. Later the musicians came to Beale Street to play for larger audiences.

siasm. Generally, the exhibits in the center explain Beale Street and the folk arts of the region. The film, "All Day and All Night: Memories of Beale Street" is screened several times a day. Don't miss it. You'll see and hear musicians of the 1930s and 1940s hanging out, eating chili, and playing music, exuding the history from which their music and lives grew. The film is narrated by B. B. King. Other films give you insights into the origins of the Delta blues and different aspects of Memphis life.

An especially striking series of photographs taken by an African-American minister shows images of the daily lives of people in the local black community—people going to school, watching parades, working in and patronizing businesses, attending churches. The center has a gift shop selling recordings of Southern music and books about the South and folk art. Outside, up and down Beale Street, you will find outdoor interpretive exhibits that one employee at the center says are "like historic markers but more interesting because they tell you more."

The Center for Southern Folklore is open Monday through Thursday 10:00 A.M. to 8:00 P.M.; Friday and Saturday 10:00 A.M. to 10:00 P.M.; Sunday 11:00 A.M. to 8:00 P.M. Admission is free, though donations are encouraged. Phone (901) 525–3655.

And then there are the ducks at **The Peabody Hotel.**

Nothing reflects the quirky Southern sense of humor or the Southern reverence for ritual better than the ducks at the Peabody Hotel, 149 Union Avenue, just a block from Beale Street. After hours the ducks live out in a rooftop pen; but during the day they swim happily in the marble, cherub-adorned fountain in the lobby of the hotel. Twice a day—11:00 A.M. and

5:00 P.M.—uniformed, gloved porters roll out the red carpet and, with great ceremony, the ducks parade to and from the fountain to the measured four-beat of the "King Cotton March." People gather at the lobby bar and along the rails of the second-story balconies overlooking the lobby to watch the parade. Even if you don't hang around for the show, you can't really escape those ducks. Their motif is everywhere: on matchbooks and billheads, on napkins, stamped onto butter pats, and even impressed into the sand of ashtrays. The hotel has four restaurants, more than 400 rooms, and such amenities as a swimming pool, exercise room, and lounge. Phone (901) 529–4175 or (800) 732–2639.

CENTRAL TENNESSEE

Driving on I–40 takes you from the western to the eastern border of Tennessee. When you reach **Nashville,** you are in central Tennessee, often called "the heartland." These days the city is associated primarily with country music, recording studios, and the Grand Ole Opry. But things were happening here long before Minnie Pearl ever pinned a rose on her bonnet.

The Native American tribes were here first, of course. By the mid-1700s Cherokee, Choctaw, Chickasaw, and Creek tribes were hunting the hills.

North Carolina migrants moved into the area in 1779, founding the city as Fort Nashborough, and creating what was then a new western frontier. By the 1800s, with steamboats navigating the Cumberland River, which skirts the city, and the St. Louis Railroad linking Nashville to Atlanta and Louisiana, the city had become a thriving center of commerce. It was named Tennessee's state capital in 1843.

When Union forces seized Nashville in 1862, they were taking over such an important Confederate supply center that the Rebels tried to take it back, in the Battle of Nashville. The battle lasted two days, but Union troops won by sheer force of numbers. This defeat of the Confederates was the last battle of the Civil War.

When you walk what is now Second Avenue, you are on **Historic Market Street,** where huge brick warehouses once held cotton, tobacco, and grain. These Victorian buildings now house an assortment of specialty shops, restaurants, and, poignantly, stores selling shiny new guitars and Western boots next to pawn shops selling slightly used versions of the same items.

The best place to begin orienting yourself to Nashville's history is the **Tennessee State Museum.** It is in the lower level of the James K. Polk Cultural Center, in the block bounded on the west and east by Sixth and Fifth Avenues north, and on the north and south by Deadrick Street and Union Street. Enter at 505 Deadrick Street. This museum charms even those people who usually don't care for museums, with exhibits going all the way back to prehistoric Indians. That puts a wild spin on the notion of the "Old South." One visitor to the museum kept wandering off in different directions, then running back to the people he came with, saying, "Come here, you gotta see this!" Some of what he saw included tools used by the first inhabitants of the area, perhaps some 17,000 years ago; a 200-year-old dugout canoe; a waterwheel that works; the hat that Andrew Jackson wore to his presidential inauguration in 1829; Davy Crockett's rifle; and a middle-class farmer's cabin. Representing the antebellum period, silver made in Tennessee, a Tennessee painting gallery, and a fully furnished middle-class parlor, all are from the prosperous years in the 1840s and 1850s, attesting to the good life.

The museum's collection of Civil War uniforms, battle flags, and weapons is considered one of the best in the country. Throughout the museum, documents, old books, and interpretive markers bring Tennessee's history to life. The museum is open Tuesday through Saturday 10:00 A.M. to 5:00 P.M.; Sunday 1:00 to 5:00 P.M. The museum is closed Easter, Thanksgiving, Christmas, and New Year's Day. Admission is free. Phone (615) 741–2692.

About a block from the museum, at the corner of Charlotte and Fifth Avenues, St. Mary's Church, built in 1847 in Greek Revival style, is the oldest church standing in Nashville. It was used as a military hospital during the Civil War Battle of Nashville.

At the corner of Fifth Avenue north and Church Street, the **Downtown Presbyterian Church,** built in 1851, is considered one of the best-preserved examples of Egyptian Revival architecture in the United States. It is listed as a National Historic Landmark.

While you're in this part of town, you could walk to the **Satsuma Tea Room,** 417 Union Street, for a lunch of some genuine Southern food. The food is home-style, with an emphasis on fresh vegetables, hot breads, and homemade desserts. Well established in Nashville, the restaurant has been serving Southern food since 1918. Open for lunch Monday through Friday 10:45 A.M. to 2:00 P.M. Closed weekends and major holidays.

After you have stoked up your furnace, look into another longtime Southern tradition—tobacco. This crop has been almost as important as religion in the South. You can study the history and uses of the now-controversial stuff going all the way back to A.D. 700 in the **Museum of Tobacco Art and History,** at 800 Harrison Street. In earlier times pipes for smoking tobacco and containers for storing it in were often genuine works of art. The museum displays photographs and folk art, old advertising, antique pipe collections, Indian pipes, and all the items you would expect to find in an old tobacconer's shop. Several especially interesting exhibits stem from the early association of tobacco with Native Americans: A collection of peace pipes, an advertising poster from the 1890s promoting "Tomahawk Scrap" as "an excellent chew," a 6-foot cast zinc Indian warrior standing in the lobby, and a carving of Tecumseh, the chief of the Shawnee tribe. Pipe collections include glass pipes from Nalisea, England, made early in the 1800s, and an elaborate meerschaum pipe carved to show Diana, Goddess of the Hunt, astride her horse. The museum has a gift shop and is open Monday through Saturday 9:00 A.M. to 4:00 P.M. Closed major holidays. Admission is free. Phone (615) 271–2349. The museum is in the U.S. Tobacco manufacturing facility at the corner of 8th Avenue North and Harrison Street, north of the James Robertson Parkway and the state capitol.

A different sort of museum, the **Nashville Toy Museum,** shows you what children used to play with—toy soldiers, antique dolls, European bears before Teddy, and, most popular of all, trains. The train room's operating layout demonstrates how the old steam engines would have chugged through western and central Tennessee. The museum is open seven days a week 9:00 A.M. to 5:00 P.M.; to 9:00 P.M. in summer. Closed Thanksgiving and Christmas. Admission is about $3.00 for adults, $1.50 for children. Phone (615) 883–8870.

When you have finished exploring the downtown area, a short drive will take you to **Belle Meade Plantation,** 5025 Harding Road, the embodiment of the romantic South. In the nineteenth century Belle Meade was famous as a thoroughbred stud farm. It produced outstanding horses and dispensed hospitality on a grand scale to those who came to the plantation. The people at Belle Meade are proud of maintaining that hospitable tradition now that the plantation operates as a tour facility. The house is an 1853 Greek Revival mansion with 14-foot ceilings and a massive curving stairway. The first thing you see when you come through the main entrance is the huge hallway, its walls lined with pictures of the plantation's thoroughbred racehorses. Many of the pictures have been in place since the early days of the plantation. The hall is really like another big room. Standing here, it is easy to imagine groups of people standing around chatting, the men sipping bourbon, studying the pictures and discussing the horses.

The tour includes a video entitled "A Lady As Game As That . . ." (based on an episode in the Civil War), giving you an overview of the one hundred years of the plantation's life. After you view the video, costumed guides take you through the house. You then are given a map of the property and are on your own to explore the grounds and outbuildings, including the carriage house and stable filled with a collection of carriages and sleighs.

Exactly what you will find in the house depends on when you visit. Special exhibits change regularly, and the entire house is decorated thematically and seasonally—for Christmas, for instance—as it would have been when it was a home. The guides' custom-made costumes also change to suit the themes. This means that you can come to Belle Meade more than once and count on seeing something different each time. A particularly effective theme is the wedding: Life-size mannequins are dressed in antique clothes, including a wedding dress, and the entire house is decorated with flowers and candles as it would have been for a wedding. Staff members base their presentations on information gathered from old newspaper stories, family records, diaries, journals, and literary accounts of the times.

A gift shop in the house's attached kitchen sells Victorian ornaments, books and pictures, and souvenirs of Belle Meade. The plantation is open year-round, Monday through Saturday 9:00 A.M. to 5:00 P.M.; Sunday 1:00 to 5:00 P.M. The last tour begins each day at 4:00 P.M. Admission is about $6.00 for adults, with reduced rates for senior citizens, and children ages five and under are free. Phone (615) 356–0501. To get to Belle Meade Plantation, drive 7 miles southwest of Nashville on U.S. Highway 70S.

Another mansion that more than meets one's expectations for opulence and romance is **Belmont Mansion,** on the campus of Belmont College. Built in 1850, it was the summer home of Adelicia Acklen, one of the country's wealthiest women. The mansion, built like an Italian villa, is the only one of its kind in Tennessee. It has iron balconies, an octagonal cupola, and fifteen rooms, one of them a ballroom with an arched ceiling. The rooms are fully furnished with period furniture, marble statues, gilded mirrors, and art collected by the Acklens.

You can learn about the history and restoration of the mansion in guided tours, which begin on the hour. The mansion is open Monday through Saturday 10:00 A.M. to 4:00 P.M.; Sunday 2:00 to 5:00 P.M.; hours end each day at 4:00 P.M. in fall and winter. Admission is about $5.00 for adults, $1.00 for children. Phone (615) 386–4459. To get to the mansion, take the Wedgewood exit from I–65, drive on Wedgewood 2½ miles west to Magnolia Avenue, and then go ⅛ mile on Eighteenth Street to the Belmont campus. Signs will direct you.

Finally, stop at **The Hermitage,** 4580 Rachel's Lane, to see the mansion and grounds that were the home of President Andrew Jackson and his wife, Rachel. Now a National Historic Landmark, the Hermitage operates frankly commercially, but it is done so well that you end up being glad that more people will have an opportunity to enjoy the place. The story of the mansion is complicated. It was built in 1821 as a Federal-style building, but in 1834 part of it burned. In the rebuilding, the style was changed to Classical. But since the old house did not burn completely, many of the earlier features remain intact. Inside, the mansion is still furnished with a lot of the Jacksons' original pieces and personal items.

Outside is Mrs. Jackson's formal nineteenth-century garden, still maintained and growing much as it was when she enjoyed it. Depending on the season, the borders bloom with crocus and tulips, peonies, hollyhocks, periwinkle, spice bush, winter honeysuckle, and so on. It is the kind of garden that you might have if you could have all the free labor you needed. If you are seriously interested in old gardens, consult with the people in the visitors' center, who can provide a list of the perennials and shrubs and trees that are growing. The Jacksons are buried in a tomb in a corner of the garden. One employee at the Hermitage said that visitors usually find the tomb "awesome."

Elsewhere on the property, you will find the original log homes, with dependencies (outhouses to most of us) and slave quarters. There are a smokehouse, a church, and Tulip Grove, the mansion in which Jackson's nephew and his wife lived. Audiocassette tours explain all that you are seeing.

In the visitors' center, you can grab a bite in the restaurant, browse through the museum, and watch the orientation film "Andrew Jackson: His Story, His History." A museum shop sells gift items. The Hermitage is open seven days a week 9:00 A.M. to 5:00 P.M. Closed Thanksgiving, Christmas, and the third week in January. Admission is about $7.50 for people age thirteen and up, $4.00 for children, and a maximum of $23.00 for families of four or more. Senior citizens receive discounts. To get to the Hermitage, drive 12 miles east of Nashville on I–40 or I–65/24N. Take the Old Hickory Boulevard/Hermitage exit. Signs will direct you.

Nashville makes a good base from which to take side trips in all directions—to Dover, Franklin, Gallatin, Columbia, and Murfreesboro. Of these, **Dover** is the farthest—about 80 miles from Nashville, going north on I–24 and then west on U.S. 79. Whether you stop here or not depends on how interested you are in the Civil War. Near Dover, the **Fort Donelson National Battlefield** is a park of more than 500 acres where you can study the fort, perimeter defenses, and battle sites where General Ulysses S. Grant won the first major Union victory of the Civil War in 1862. You can visit the hotel where Confederate general Simon Buckner surrendered to Grant, turning over 13,000 of his men as prisoners of war. The earthen fort, river batteries, outer earthworks, Dover Hotel, and National Cemetery are all preserved. To take in these landmarks, you can take a 6-mile, self-guided auto tour, beginning at the visitors' center. The visitors' center also has a museum and a slide presentation describing the battle, which are a good way to get a sense of what happened before you begin the actual tour. In the summer park staff, dressed in appropriate costumes, sometimes present programs about the Civil War era. The park is open every day 8:00 A.M. to 4:30 P.M. Closed Christmas. Admission is free, but it costs about $3.00 to rent the cassette for the driving tour. Phone (615) 232–5706.

Franklin, just about 18 miles from Nashville via U.S. 31 or I–65 (take exit 65 off I–65), is the site of another Civil War battle, the 1864 Battle of Franklin, on the banks of the Harpeth River, also won by the Union. Eight thousand soldiers, about two thirds of them Rebels, died in the fighting. Important spots are noted with markers.

The **Carnton Plantation and Confederate Cemetery,** 1345 Carnton Road (on State Highway 431), was a Civil War field hospital during the Battle of Franklin. Next to the main property is the two-acre McGavock Confederate Cemetery, where about 1,500 Confederate soldiers who were killed in that battle lie. The plantation is open Monday through Saturday 9:00 A.M. to 5:00 P.M.; Sunday 1:00 to 5:00 P.M.; it closes at 4:00 P.M. during fall and winter months. Closed Thanksgiving, Christmas, and New Year's Day. Admission is about $5.00 adults, half that for children, and there are discounts for senior citizens. Phone (615) 794–0903.

Still another Civil War site in Franklin, **The Carter House,** 1140

Columbia Avenue (on U.S. 31), was caught in the middle of the fighting during the Battle of Franklin. The house has both original and period furnishings. Civil War artifacts are displayed in a museum. Admission includes the museum, a guided tour of the house and grounds, and a video presentation about the Battle of Franklin. Admission is about $3.00 for adults, half that for children. Open Monday through Saturday 9:00 A.M. to 4:00 P.M.; Sunday 1:00 to 4:00 P.M. Closed major holidays. Phone (615) 791–1861.

Franklin has a lively, 15-block downtown historic district, with specialty shops, restaurants, antiques shops, and historic houses. The entire 15-block original downtown area is listed in the National Register of Historic Places, as are many old homes in the county. You can pick up a brochure to guide you at the Williamson County Courthouse or at almost any of the businesses there. During the first week in May, the Franklin and Williamson County Heritage Foundation offers special tours featuring at least ten historic homes, some of which would not ordinarily be open to the public. For more information about these tours, call Williamson County Tourism at City Hall, (615) 794–1225 or (800) 356–3445, or write P.O. Box 156, Franklin, TN 37065–0156.

About 30 miles north of Nashville, on U.S. 31 east, the little town of **Gallatin** offers a tour home from the early 1800s and what may be the largest log building in Tennessee. The historic downtown area is unusually intact. Most of the homes and businesses were not destroyed during the Civil War, probably because Union forces were occupying the town. About twenty-five of the buildings have been restored and are now occupied by antiques stores, a book shop, restaurants, and specialty shops.

About 2 blocks from the town square, **Trousdale Place,** 183 West Main Street, is a two-story brick house where one-time Tennessee governor William Trousdale lived in the mid-1800s. Civil War items and the Trousdale furniture remain in the house. Open Tuesday through Saturday 9:00 A.M. to 4:30 P.M.; Sunday 1:00 to 5:00 P.M. Closed Thanksgiving, Christmas, and New Year's Day. Admission is about $3.00 for adults, with discounts for children and senior citizens. Phone (615) 452–5648.

You may find **Wynnewood** a blessed change from all the grim Civil War battle sites. This place represents yet another facet of the Old South. To get to this long, long log cabin, drive on U.S. 25 8 miles east of Gallatin to Castalian Springs. But if you need to stop for directions (the area has always been rural and still is), don't ask the way to Castalian Springs or Wynnewood, ask how to get to "The Lick." That is what local folks call it, a name going back to when the area was known for the mineral springs at Bledsoe's Lick. The log building was built in 1862 as a stagecoach stop. At one time, when the post office was in this log building, Castalian Springs became the post-office address. In ensuing years the building was variously called Castalian Springs Inn or Mineral Springs Resort, or something similar, depending on the era. People who came Castalian Springs to "take the waters" used it as a resort; they took the baths or water treatments in little cabins at the springs and stayed at the inn. None of the cabins remain, but you can still sample the salty, sulphurous water at one of the artesian springs.

The restored building stands two stories tall and is 142 feet long. The building is furnished in period furniture. In some places, the chinked log interior walls show; elsewhere, later residents added plaster and wallpaper. One of the most interesting items is the old post-office desk, dating from the 1830s. The people here are pleasant and knowledgeable. They can tell you lots about the history of the old desk, the building, and the area. Wynnewood is open Monday through Saturday 10:00 A.M. to 4:00 P.M.; Sunday 1:00 to 4:00 P.M. Closed Sunday and open shorter hours in late fall and winter months. Closed major holidays. Admission is $3.00 for adults, with substantial discounts for children and senior citizens. Phone (615) 452–5464.

After exploring the battlefields and rural oddities of this region, you might like to get back to the more traditional South. Try a bit of Maury County. It advertises itself as the "Antebellum Home Capital of Tennessee." The headquarters is in **Columbia,** about 65 miles south of Nashville on I-65, where **The Athenaeum** and the **James K. Polk Ancestral Home** deserve your attention.

The Polk Ancestral Home, 301 West Seventh Street, was built in 1816 by the parents of James Polk, the eleventh president of the United States, and is furnished with items from the Polk White House as well as many portraits belonging to the older Polks. Next door, in the Polk sisters' house, Mrs. Polk's inaugural ball gown and her jewelry are on display. The Polk Ancestral Home is open Monday through Saturday 9:00 A.M. to 5:00 P.M.; Sunday 1:00 to 5:00 P.M. The hours are shorter in winter. Closed Thanksgiving, Christmas Eve, and New Year's Day. Admission is about $2.50 for adults, with reduced rates for children and senior citizens. Phone (615) 388–2354.

President Polk's nephew, Samuel Polk Walker, had a fine Gothic home, **The Athenaeum,** 808 Athenaeum Street, built in the late 1830s. To give you an idea of the size of this place, in 1837 it became the Columbia Female Institute, a progressive school for its day. The building has been restored to show how the well-known and well-to-do of the region lived. The Athenaeum is open June 1 through August 31, Monday through Friday, with tours available at other times by appointment. Hours and rates may change, so call ahead. Phone (615) 381–4822.

With more than 300 listings on the National Historic Register, Maury County specializes in antebellum home tours. They can provide you with a self-driving antebellum trail tour. Stop during normal business hours at the **Convention and Visitors' Bureau** at 1116 West Seventh Street, Columbia, or phone (615) 381–7176 for full details about the homes and tours.

Finally, about 32 miles south of Nashville via I–24, **Murfreesboro** has a plantation-house museum, a living-history village, and a national Civil War battlefield. Visiting these sites could easily fill a day or more. From 1819 to 1825 Murfreesboro was the capital of Tennessee, then lost that honor to Nashville. It is the geographic center of the state and, for a time, was also the center of some Civil War fighting.

The **Oaklands Historic House Museum,** 900 North Maney Avenue, is an Italianate-style antebellum plantation house built in four phases from about 1815 to 1860, and restored now to the style of the early 1860s. Both Union and Confederate forces had a turn occupying the house. It is the site of the surrender of Murfreesboro to the Union in the summer of 1862 and of a visit by Confederacy president Jefferson Davis in December of that year. The museum is open Tuesday through Saturday 10:00 A.M. to 4:00 P.M.; Sunday 1:00 to 4:00 P.M. Closed major holidays. Admission is about $3.00 for adults, with discounts for senior citizens and children. Phone (615) 892–0022.

To see what middle Tennessee life was like before the Civil War, stop at **Cannonsburgh Pioneer Village,** South Front Street. This living-history museum of restored buildings includes a log house, blacksmith shop, general store, grist mill, one-room schoolhouse, church, and museum. The village is open May through October, Tuesday through Saturday 10:00 A.M. to 5:00 P.M.; Sunday 1:00 to 5:00 P.M. Admission is free. Call the Chamber of Commerce at (615) 893–6565.

And there is yet another battlefield that may lure you. **Stones River National Battlefield,** 3501 Old Nashville Highway, is a National Park Service area commemorating the Civil War Battle of Stones River. More than 83,000 soldiers fought here; 23,000 of them died. A national cemetery and the oldest intact Civil War memorial are on the grounds. Admission is free. Phone (615) 893–9501.

From this part of the state, you might head toward Chattanooga, via I–24, stopping to check out Lynchburg, famous for Jack Daniel's sourmash, and the Monteagle Assembly Grounds, sometimes called "the Chautauqua of the South," on your way. You are almost into eastern Tennessee at this point.

PLATEAUS AND VALLEYS

Tennessee tourism people like to call this part of the state "the land of plateaus and valleys," with Chattanooga its main city and astonishing vistas its outstanding natural characteristic. They distinguish it from "the mountainous east," where Knoxville and the Great Smoky Mountains are the most notable features. In fact, it is a useful, if slightly artificial, division. Chattanooga and Knoxville differ in character; and the peaks, valleys, and plateaus are surprisingly different visually from the views in the mountains of eastern Tennessee.

If you are traveling toward Chattanooga from Memphis on the interstates, you will come to a couple of interesting stops on your way. If you are approaching the area from the east, you will make these stops after you have been to Chattanooga.

From I–24 near Manchester, State Highway 55 west takes you to **Lynchburg** (population 361 or 700, depending on your source). You can also get there from I–65 by way of U.S. 64 and State Highway 50. By far the most famous thing in Lynchburg is **Jack Daniel's Distillery,** established in 1866, famous over generations for its Tennessee sippin' whiskey. The entrance to the distillery is off State Highway 55, next to Mulberry Creek Bridge. A hostess at the distillery's visitors' center will set you up for a tour. The free tours of the distillery take you through all the steps of whiskey making, beginning with the limestone water that comes out of Cave Spring at 56° F no matter the time of year through the processes of filtering, aging, and so on. The distillery has a gift shop selling all sorts of Jack Daniel's gift items, including everything from a wooden whiskey chest and replicas of the original Jack Daniel's stoneware jugs to decks of gentleman's playing cards with the Jack Daniel's insignia. Open every day 8:00 A.M. to 4:00 P.M. Closed Thanksgiving, Christmas, and New Year's Days. Phone (615) 759–4221.

Lynchburg has developed its historic district well enough to have a visitors' center on the edge of the town square where you can pick up brochures, local maps, and suggestions for sightseeing. If you like to plan ahead, write P.O. Box 421, Lynchburg, TN 37352; phone (615) 759–4111. The community has three places where you can sample down-home Southern cooking. The most famous is in the first house built in the town, the Bobo House (1812), on Main Street. Now known as **Miss Mary Bobo's Boarding House,** it was famous for feeding everyone who mattered in town, including Jack Daniel himself. Dinner (at midday) is still an event. It is served family style and includes two meats, six garden vegetables, homemade bread, dessert, and beverage. You will need a reservation here. Phone (615) 759–7394.

Also on Main Street, at the other end of the town square, **Iron Kettle Restaurant** features basic Southern plate lunches. Open Monday through Saturday 6:00 A.M. to 6:00 P.M. Phone (615) 759–4274. Just a little west of the town square on Lynchburg Highway, **The Countryside Restaurant** serves three meals a day—all Southern country food, including a variety of vegetables, breads, and homemade desserts. Buffet lunch. Open Monday through Thursday 6:30 A.M. to 8:00 P.M.; Friday and Saturday 6:30 A.M. to 11:00 P.M.; Sunday 11:00 A.M. to 8:00 P.M. Phone (615) 759–4430.

In addition to shopping in the gift and specialty shops on the town square, you might enjoy the **Moore County Courthouse,** which is still functioning as a courthouse. It was built in 1855 of bricks made in Lynchburg. A monument on the courthouse lawn honors the Confederate soldiers of Moore County.

Now, anyone who knows Tennessee knows that while Jack Daniel's is the most famous distillery, it is not the *only* one in the state. **George Dickel Distillery,** established in 1870 in the scenic countryside of Cascade Hollow, not far from I–24, welcomes visitors for tours, too. In addition to touring the distillery, you can watch a video presentation about the distillery and shop in the old-fashioned general store. Tours are available Monday through Friday 9:00 A.M. to 3:00 P.M. Closed holidays. For more information, write the distillery at P.O. Box 490, Tullahoma, TN 37388; phone (615) 857–3124. The distillery is near Normandy Dam. Get off I–24 at Junction 105 and head south on State Highway 41. Turn right onto Road 4291 toward Blanton Chapel Road, and follow the signs to Normandy Dam. Pass the dam and go through the town of Normandy. Signs will direct you to the distillery, about a mile outside Normandy.

Normandy is only a few miles, via U.S. 41A, from **Shelbyville,** Tennessee's "Walking Horse capital."

Shelbyville has a town square laid out in 1810 as a prototype for town squares in the South. The square and its stores are listed on the National Register of Historic Places. The annual national Tennessee Walking Horse Celebration is held nearby. And the **Tennessee Walking Horse Museum,** on Whitthorne Street, shows you a history of the Tennessee Walking Horse. These horses are really the "Southern gentlemen" of the equestrian world. They are known for their good dispositions and stylish, refined movement. The museum has interactive displays and artifacts related to the Walking Horse. It is open Monday through Saturday 9:00 A.M. to 5:00 P.M. Closed holidays. Many farms near Shelby breed and raise Tennessee Walking Horses. If you would like to learn more about them, contact the Chamber of Commerce (615–684–3482).

Eventually, wend your way back onto I–24, from which you can exit again, about an hour north of Chattanooga, to explore **Monteagle.** The main points of interest are Adams Edgeworth Inn, a fine Victorian inn on the Monteagle Assembly Grounds, and **Jim Oliver's Smoke House,** on U.S. 64 and 41A, exit 34 off I–24. Jim Oliver's Smoke House is a huge, resortlike place with a rustic appearance. Here you can find accommodation in everything from motel rooms to camp sites. If you are looking for old-fashioned Southern cooking, your main interest will be the restaurant, which serves, among other things, country ham and sweet ham cured on the property in huge slabs. Although the operation is big and commercial, the service is down-home friendly, and the country cooking is as Southern as you can get. Open every day 6:00 A.M. to 10:00 P.M.; Saturday 6:00 A.M. to 11:00 P.M., Jim Oliver's can be reached by phone at (615) 924–2091 or (800) 489–2091.

Adams Edgeworth Inn, on the Monteagle Assembly grounds, has thirteen rooms. This three-story Victorian house was built as an inn, not as a private home. Consequently, the rooms are spacious, and the traffic patterns are efficient. The innkeepers, Wendy and David Adams, have refurbished the old building to brighten the interior and have furnished it with an eclectic collection of museum-quality art and antiques gathered in their world travels. In most of the rooms, shelves bulge with books, and classical music fills the air. Perennial gardens and a heavily wooded lot make the setting feel more rural than it really is. The overall effect is serene and peaceful. Dinner is available by reservation. The rates, which begin at about $75 per room, include continental breakfast. Phone (615) 924–4000.

A short drive west from Monteagle on U.S. 41A/64 is **Sewanee,** the University of the South, a lovely old Southern campus with some of the most magnificent views anywhere. The school was established in 1857 by twenty-eight Episcopal dioceses. Most of the buildings on campus were destroyed during the Civil War; in the next decade the campus was essentially rebuilt to resemble a British campus. As a result, Breslin Tower and All Saints Chapel are designed like structures at Oxford University. The sandstone buildings on the central campus are Gothic in style, surrounded by great stretches of lawn so green that you'll think you're in Ireland. Beyond the lawns stretch about 10,000 acres of woodlands, hidden lakes, and bluffs overlooking unexpected plateaus of farmland. About 4 miles south of the school, on U.S. 56, is the **natural stone bridge,** a 25-foot-high wonder that you can walk across if you have the nerve. Otherwise, it is a nice area for just walking around and enjoying the woods.

The entire area around Monteagle and Sewanee has hiking trails of every degree of difficulty, as well as so many remote lakes that innkeeper David Adams says you can skinny-dip without getting caught. The National Park Service publishes excellent trail maps. If you enjoy outdoor activity, hiking some of these trails would be a perfect way to understand another aspect of Dixie—those wilderness areas once known only to some Indian tribes and some intrepid outdoorsmen.

For balance after this stint of rusticating, head on down I–24—a beautiful drive—to **Chattanooga,** to learn about some important Civil War battles. If you have become interested in Native American history, you will want to know that this was also a point where Cherokees were moved onto the Trail of Tears. And if you are interested in African-American sites, you will want to know that Chattanooga is the location of the **Mary Walker Historical and Educational Foundation,** named in honor of the ex-slave who learned at the age of 117 to read, write, and do arithmetic. A museum commemorates her accomplishments as part of the foundation's programs for promoting education, helping inner-city children, and spreading information about black history. The foundation is located at 3031 Mary Walker Place. For more information on exhibits, call (615) 622–3217.

Chattanooga is one of the most important Civil War sites in the South. This is where General William Tecumseh Sherman began his march to the sea. Chattanooga's railroads went to Nashville, Memphis, Knoxville, Atlanta, and Charleston, and gaining control of this transportation center was a major part of Sherman's strategy. Union forces failed to take the city immediately, but they occupied it in 1863. The battles during October and November of 1863 were the deadliest of the war. It is hard to grasp the big picture by just touring the battlefields. A better place to start is at **The Battles for Chattanooga Museum,** 3742 Tennessee Avenue, at the foot of **Lookout Mountain.** An electronic, three-dimensional topographical battle map, with 5,000 miniature soldiers, narrative, and sound effects, gives you the details of the five major battles fought in October and November 1863, in Chattanooga. These include Missionary Ridge, Orchard Knob, Browns Ferry, Wauhatchie, and Lookout Mountain. During the fighting on Lookout Mountain, on November 24, 1863, heavy fog moved in; the fighting here thus became famous as the "Battle Above the Clouds."

The figurines used in the exhibit are themselves collectors' items, made in Africa by the Swedish African Engineers, which is no longer in business. When the company closed, the museum's owners bought up all the remaining stock to keep in reserve for when pieces are broken or disappear.

It is a plus if you can get to the museum when Sergeant Fox Jim McKinney is there. He is a passionate Civil War reenactor who wears his uniform, sets up his Civil War tent, demonstrates his musket, shows you

Four Decades of Passion and Play

The Battles for Chattanooga Museum has been operating for nearly forty years. It was the brainchild of Lee Anderson, now editor and publisher of *The Chattanooga Free Press.* Anderson designed the battle map, wrote the script, and helped build the display. Much of the topography was done by Anderson's friend Pendell Meyers, who loved modeling and gave special attention to representing the rivers and Lookout Mountain accurately. The men's wives, Betsy Anderson and Barbara Meyers, painted and helped get the building ready for the exhibit. Betsy named it "Confederama," which is how the museum was known until the name was changed recently. Barbara has worked at the museum since it opened, but her interest has not waned: "Right this minute I'm reading another new book about the Civil War," she said.

the soldiers' equipment, explains how the Confederate troops were trained, and philosophizes. He is knowledgeable, erudite, and dramatic. In the summer Fox Jim is around most of the time to talk to all who are interested. After Labor Day he is available only for special group presentations. The museum is open June 1 through Labor Day, every day 8:30 A.M. to 8:30 P.M. During the fall and winter months, it is open daily 9:00 A.M. to 5:00 P.M. Closed Christmas Day. Admission is about $4.00 for adults, $2.00 for children. Inquire about discounts. To get to the museum from Nashville, take I–24; take exit 174 and turn right on State Highway 41 to Tennessee Avenue. From Knoxville, take I–24 to Lookout Mountain, exit 178; bear left at the bottom of the down ramp, drive 2 blocks to Broad Street, and turn left on Tennessee Avenue.

While you are close to Lookout Mountain, it would be a mistake not to go up to the top to enjoy the spectacular view. It is a lot of fun to take the **Lookout Mountain Incline,** billed as the world's steepest passenger railway. As you reach the top, the grade is more than 72 percent. When the railway was built in 1895, it was powered by steam; now it is electrically powered. The railway is listed on the National Register of Historic Places, and Lookout Mountain is a National Historic Site, so a visit here does not mean that you're abandoning history for a quick thrill.

When you get to the top of the mountain, you will be a short walk away from Point Park, a military park and museum. From this place, you can see the Tennessee River, the Chattanooga, and the east Tennessee foothills. In the park, you'll find cannons, monuments, and the museum commemorating the Battle Above the Clouds. If you board the incline railway at the Battles for Chattanooga Museum, you will be about halfway up the mountain. You can also begin the ride at the foot of the mountain at St. Elmo Avenue, near State Route 58 South. Since the higher points are the most exciting part of the ride, though, you may decide to get on when you come out of the Battles for Chattanooga Museum, in the interests of convenience.

Either way, the people who operate the incline assure you that even though it is steep, it is not really scary. "It goes six miles an hour. That's a nice slow ride," noted one employee. The incline runs in June, July, and August, daily 8:30 A.M. to 9:20 P.M.; the rest of the year, it runs daily 9:00 A.M. to 5:40 P.M. Tickets are about $6.00 for adults, half that for children. Phone (615) 821–4224.

Having studied the miniaturized battle scene in the Battles for Chattanooga Museum and climbed the mountain to look over the terrain of Chattanooga, you are now ready to stop at the **Chickamauga and Chattanooga National Military Park.** The park comprises more than 8,000 acres; some of them are in Georgia, but many of the markers and monuments commemorate the battles for Chattanooga. Stop in the visitors' center at the north end of the park to pick up a self-guided tour map for visiting the sites of the Battles of Chickamauga, Lookout Mountain, and Missionary Ridge. The visitors' center also has a museum with Civil War and weapons exhibits. For a modest fee, you can watch a multimedia presentation about the Battle of Chickamauga or rent a taped tour telling the park's history. The visitors' center and park are open in the summer, daily 8:00 A.M. to 5:45 P.M.; in other months, 8:00 A.M. to 4:45 P.M. Closed Christmas. Phone (706) 866–9241.

EAST TENNESSEE

Driving north on I–75 from Chattanooga, you will come to the little town of **Athens,** where you should plan to stop at the **McMinn County Living Heritage Museum,** 522 West Madison Avenue. The building does not look at first like a place for experiencing the Old South, because the museum is in three floors of a remodeled portion of a high school building. But, in the words of the museum folks, the exhibits in this 21,000-square-feet-museum "follow the early McMinn County settler and their descendants through Tennessee's early pioneer years, the Cherokee heritage, Tennessee's secession from the Union, the impending Civil War and its dramatic economic transformation." In other words, this is one of those rare places where you can concentrate on the flow of history in a small locality and can see how one era relates to the next. Twenty-eight exhibit areas show clothing, transportation, a pioneer log cabin, Native-American artifacts, a general store, a Victorian parlor and dining room, and Civil War uniforms. An area devoted to religious items includes pulpits, organs, christening gowns, chalices, books, and other items from local churches.

If you visit from February through April, you can see the annual quilt show, in which 300 antique and contemporary quilts are displayed The museum features antique and contemporary dolls in November and December. The museum is open Monday through Friday 10:00 A.M. to 5:00 P.M.; Saturday and Sunday 2:00 to 5:00 P.M. Admission is about $3.00

for adults, $2.00 for senior citizens and children. To get to the museum, take the Decatur Pike, Exit 49 from I–75 to West Madison Avenue.

Your next major stop is **Knoxville,** a sophisticated little city at the intersection of three heavily traveled interstates—I–74, I–40, and I–81. The skyline, a thoroughly modern collection of high glass and steel buildings, gives the city so contemporary a look that one does not drive into it expecting to find history. But Knoxville was settled near the end of the eighteenth century and was the state capital for a time; its history is lively. Don't come looking for plantations, though. Knoxville's economy was based on shipping trade from the Tennessee River. Historians say that having trade rather than plantations as an economic base helped the city rally from the Civil War faster than the devastated planting regions of the South. Both Union and Confederate forces occupied the city (not at the same time, though) during the Civil War.

Civil War issues are addressed at **Confederate Memorial Hall,** 3148 Kingston Pike. This Victorian mansion was used by Confederate general James Longstreet as his headquarters in 1863. It is furnished as it would have been during that period. In addition to Civil War memorabilia, the museum has a good library of Southern literature. The museum is open February until Christmas, Tuesday through Friday 1:00 to 4:00 P.M. Admission is about $2.00, less for children and senior citizens. Phone (615) 522–2371.

To see what was going on before the Civil War, visit **Blount Mansion,** 200 West Hill Avenue. It was one of the first frame houses built west of the Alleghenies. This 1792 house is where the governor of the Southwest Territory, William Blount, lived and kept his office. In this office, Blount signed the constitution for the State of Tennessee. Originally from North Carolina, Blount was a delegate to the Constitutional Convention of 1787 and a signer of the U.S. Constitution. Several things here reflect the Old South: an assortment of antique furnishings (some original to the house), displays of eighteenth-century American glass, and a detached kitchen. The Colonial-style gardens typify the popular gardens of the 1800s. The house is open March through October, Tuesday through Saturday 9:30 A.M. to 4:30 P.M.; Sunday 2:00 to 4:30 P.M. Closed weekends the rest of the time as well as Christmas week and New Year's Day. Admission is about $3.00 for adults, less for children and senior citizens. Phone (615) 525–2375.

Another attraction in Knoxville deserves note. The **Beck Cultural Exchange Center,** 1927 Dandridge Avenue, has served since 1975 as a place to learn about African-American history in Knoxville. The center is in the former home of Mrs. Ethel Beck. Four large rooms downstairs and six upstairs form a museum, library, art and photography exhibit area, meeting place, and gift shop. The center has African-American newspapers from the 1840s to the present. Of the books sold here, two were written by Robert J. Booker, executive director of the Beck Cultural Center. *Two Hundred Years of Black Culture in Knoxville, Tennessee* covers the story of life and how it has changed in the years from 1791 to 1991. *And There Was Light* tells the story of **Knoxville College,** 901 College Street Northwest. The college, founded in 1875, is one of Tennessee's oldest black colleges. Some campus sites are on the National Register of Historic Places. The Beck Center is open Tuesday through Saturday 10:00 A.M. to 6:00 P.M. Admission is free, though donations are accepted. Phone (615) 524–6461.

If you are in a more playful mood, hang around the fishin' hole of **The Crosseyed Cricket** for an experience that is somewhat ersatz Southern, but still fun. This is a fifty-six-acre recreation area centered around a restored working grist mill that is 140 years old. The two lakes are stocked, one with catfish, the other with trout, for visitors to set 'n' fish a spell. People at the restaurant in the mill will dress your catch and cook it to order. If you don't catch anything (unlikely), or if you prefer just floating around in the canoes, rowboats, and paddleboats, you can go to the restaurant and order catfish and trout. The fish is served with hush puppies, slaw, and fries. For folks who don't eat anything with fins, the menu includes hamburger steak and grilled chicken. After dinner take a short walk to the Dessert

African Americans in Knoxville

Tennessee Tourist Development has published a special booklet about the history of Knoxville's African Americans. It gives a brief history of blacks in Tennessee and describes sites and landmarks related to black history and accomplishments. It also includes a schedule of special events and celebrations relating to African American history. To get a copy of the booklet, write the Tennessee Department of Tourist Development, P.O. Box 23170, Nashville, TN 37202; phone (615) 741–2158.

Barn, a gazebo with little round tables, to eat homemade desserts such as hot French coconut pie and Hummingbird Cake. The cake contains bananas, pineapple, and pecans, a mixture that seems to be the quintessential Southern dessert. The restaurant is open March 1 through October 31, Monday through Friday 5:00 to 9:00 P.M.; Saturday 4:30 to 9:00 P.M.; November 1 through February, Thursday, Friday, and Saturday 5:00 to 9:00 P.M. Closed major holidays.

In addition to the restaurant and lakes, The Crosseyed Cricket has a full-service campground with two bathhouses, a swimming pool, spa, and playground. During the last two weeks of November and the first three weeks in December, The Crosseyed Cricket invites you to visit the Christmas-tree plantation, ride past a Nativity scene, and then progress to the main buildings for cocoa or wassail in front of an open fire. In the fall you can take a hayride up to the pumpkin patch, pick your own pumpkin, and climb into the hay again to ride back. Phone (615) 986–5435. To get to The Crosseyed Cricket, take exit 364 off I–40 at Lenoir City and go 2 miles.

A 16-mile drive to the north of Knoxville on I–75 takes you to **Norris,** where you'll find the truly remarkable **Museum of Appalachia,** called the most "authentic and complete replica of pioneer Appalachian life in the world" by the "Official State of Tennessee Blue Book." Visiting here, you gain a sense of life and immediacy that is rare even among "living" museums. Much of what you see comes from the southern Appalachians of the 1700s. You will learn about the diversity of the early mountain cultures and how they evolved in the Southern states.

John Rice Irwin, whose ancestors—mountain people—lived in the Appalachians, started the museum, almost casually, to preserve the "old-timey" primitive items that his grandfather had collected. The museum opened in 1960 in a single log building on a two-acre piece of ground. Now the museum covers sixty-five acres and has an ever-growing number of authentic old log buildings, donated by area owners and moved onto the museum property. Live animals inhabit the barns, henhouses, sheep pens, and so on.

To give you an idea of the human connection, visit the Arnwine Cabin one of the cabins in the museum complex. The notation on the tour map explains that old Wes Arnwine reared a large family in the 1830s and 1840s. Many of his descendants still live in the east Tennessee region. The last occupants of the cabin were "old Aunt Julie and Polly Ann" Arnwine. This cabin was built in about 1800 on Clinch River, about 40 miles away.

Later, like the other buildings in the museum, it was moved to its current location. The cabin, fully furnished in Frontier style, is included in the book *Tiny House*, a volume dedicated to special and unusual small houses.

Another cabin, the McClung House, built near Knoxville, was used as a hospital for wounded soldiers during the Civil War.

As you tour the grounds of the museum, inspecting the vegetable gardens and checking out the underground dairy, the smokehouse, and maybe even the privy, you'll hear fiddlers on the porches of the cabins, playing and singing old mountain songs. Cassettes of their music are sold in the huge gift shop, along with books about Appalachia, local crafts, and such foods as cornmeal, bean-soup mix, and preserves.

Speaking of food, you should eat in the lunchroom beside the gift shop. It's plain and unpretentious, with long tables covered by oilcloth, and the food is served on paper plates. But it's the real McCoy. The corn bread, for instance, is crisp and brown on the outside, moist inside. The women who work here say that they accomplish this by pouring the corn bread batter into a preheated iron skillet. Try the corn bread with pinto beans and a slice of raw onion for an authentic Southern meal.

The museum is open during daylight hours year-round, except Christmas. Admission is about $6.00 for adults and $4.00 for children, with a maximum family rate of about $16.00. For a schedule of special events, phone (615) 494–7680 or (615) 494–0514.

East Tennessee has another living museum in Rugby, 50 miles or so west of Norris. This site is entirely different from the Museum of Appalachia but is equally fascinating. **Historic Rugby** was founded in 1880 by Thomas Hughes.

Hughes established a "colony" in the Tennessee mountains where England's second sons could come to farm and practice the trades without losing face. He named it "Rugby" after the school in his novel *Tom Brown's School Days*. What Hughes had in mind was a cooperative, classless community where the second sons could join tradespeople and farmers to create a new agricultural community, based on Christian principles.

By the summer of 1881, the community had 300 members, a dozen or so buildings, a newspaper, a cafe, and a boardinghouse. By the turn of the century, however, the experiment had obviously failed. The main reason probably was that the second sons didn't know anything about farming or physical labor and didn't like it when they tried it. The local

Down with the Establishment!

Thomas Hughes was a writer and social reformer in England who once berated "the establishment press and establishment politicians" in both England and America for causing bad relations between England and the Union during the Civil War. England had declared itself neutral and had refused to recognize the Confederacy, but British newspapers and politicians objected to America's holding the American Union together "by force of arms." Union supporters were annoyed. Hughes spent a lot of time trying to improve feelings between the two countries. Although he was widely admired as a writer and author of the novel *Tom Brown's School Days,* he did not make much headway as a negotiator.

In the late 1870s Hughes found a new cause—the sorry plight of the second sons of the English upper class. In England at the time, the eldest sons in upper-class families got not only the family money but also the best jobs. That didn't leave much for second sons. They weren't supposed to work at trade jobs, which were beneath their status, and they had trouble getting jobs in law or medicine, because their older brothers were taking them—along with the family inheritance. Rugby, a utopian community, was his solution to this problem.

mountain people in the community, though used to such work, could not take up all the slack.

The community is much more successful today as Historic Rugby Inc., called by the National Trust "one of the most authentically preserved historic villages in America."

If you visit, plan to stay a while—there is a lot to see. You can spend the night in the restored **Newbury House** and eat in the cafe on the grounds. When you stay at Newbury House, the entire staff of Historic Rugby is, in a sense, your innkeeper. You will find a letter on your bed telling you about the activities and features of the village and about any special events that may be going on during your visit. Everyone on the staff is able to answer your questions about the village and its history. The cafe

Historic Rugby was established by the British crusader Thomas Hughes to provide a colony where England's second sons, who weren't allowed to do much in their own country, could farm and practice the trades. Although this building looks like a church, it has always housed the community's Thomas Hughes Free Public Library.

Maybe It's the Mountains

Tennessee was the site of no fewer than twelve different attempts to establish utopian communities. In addition to Rugby, there was one especially interesting community: Nashoba, an interracial experiment. All these communities failed, as utopian experiments seem to do. For a full and interesting account of the utopian experiments in Tennessee and what happened to them, see John Edgerton's excellent book *Visions of Utopia* (University of Tennessee Press, Knoxville, 1977).

serves your choice of a full Southern breakfast or a continental breakfast. Both are described on a Victorian menu.

The Victorian theme carries over in a book shop jammed with books about the Victorian era. The craft commissary sells excellent work by about one hundred crafters in the area. Some of them learned their crafts during workshops in quilting, weaving, making regional white-oak baskets, cornhusk crafts, and so on, sponsored by Historic Rugby. To get a complete, current list of workshops and special events, write P.O. Box 8, Rugby, TN 37733; phone (615) 628–2430. To get to Historic Rugby from I–75, take State Highway 63 east, then go south on State Highway 27 to State Highway 52. Go west on 52 for about 6 miles. From I–40, go north on Highway 27 or Highway 127 to Highway 52.

As you move on toward Tennessee's eastern border and the Appalachian Mountain Range, you will come to an area sometimes referred to as "The First Frontier." Three places in this region deserve special attention, each for different reasons.

Rogersville is about 65 miles east of Knoxville. Its downtown has enough old buildings to warrant a walking tour, but the most interesting place is **Hale Springs Inn,** half a block from the courthouse. The people at the inn will treat you with the kind of small-town friendliness that made one style of Southern hospitality famous. The inn was built in 1824. If you stay here, you're sleeping where Presidents Andrew Jackson, James K. Polk, and Andrew Johnson stayed. The nine-room inn has been beautifully restored; it looks as it would have in earlier times without a sacrifice of comfort. All the rooms are big and bright, with high ceilings. All but one have a working fireplace. When the rooms are not occupied, the doors are open so that you can walk in and look around. A self-guided tour brochure points out the special features in each room, including an authentic east Tennessee bed, wardrobe, and chest of drawers in the John McKinney Room. In the inn's restaurant, you will dine by candlelight, served by attendants in Colonial costume. The menu always includes many versions of the old Southern standby, chicken. The inn is at 110 West Main Street. Phone (615) 272–5171 or (800) 272–5171. To get to the inn, take State Highway 11 west and follow the main street to the town square and the inn.

On the east side of I–81, you will come to **Greeneville.** During the Civil War this little town had both Union and Confederate supporters in nearly equal numbers. It is the only county seat to have monuments to soldiers of both sides. A statue of a Union soldier stands at one end of Courthouse Square and a statue of a Confederate soldier at the other end, commemorating the service of soldiers from Greene County.

Greeneville was the home of Andrew Johnson, the president who took office after Abraham Lincoln's assassination. Two of Johnson's homes have been preserved, along with a tailor shop where he once worked and the cemetery in which he is buried, as **The Andrew Johnson National Historic Site,** at College and Depot Streets. You can tour the site at your leisure for free, or you can take the homestead tour, guided by a National Park Service ranger. Admission is $2.00 for anyone 18 to 61 years of age, free for those younger or older than that. Open daily 9:00 A.M. to 5:00 P.M., except Thanksgiving, Christmas, and New Year's Day.

While you are touring the old buildings in the town, stop at the **Dickson-Williams Mansion,** at the corner of Irish and Church Streets. This is another of those places where famous people (Andrew Jackson and Henry Clay, for instance) stayed. The house was built in 1821 for the first postmaster of Greeneville and was one of the most elegant homes in the region. A Civil War general who stayed here was killed one morning when he woke to find himself surrounded by Union men and couldn't escape. As of this writing, the mansion is in the final stages of a massive restoration project, but it should be open for visitors by the time you read this. The historic downtown district of Greeneville also has major restoration projects in process. To learn what will be going on when you plan to visit, contact the Greeneville/Greene County Area Chamber of Commerce, 115 Academy Street, Suite 1, Greeneville, TN 37743; phone (615) 638–4111.

Johnson's Better Half

Andrew Johnson worked as an indentured servant in his early years. It wasn't until he met his wife, Eliza, that he became literate; she taught him to read and write. Once he had mastered reading and writing, Johnson became an advocate for public education in Tennessee. He spent much of the rest of his life studying the Constitution of the United States and working for its literal interpretation—a stand that almost got him impeached.

This historic photo of the taylor shop where Andrew Johnson once worked is preserved at the Andrew Johnson National Historic Site.

When you are in Greeneville, you might stay at **Big Spring Inn,** 315 North Main Street. This huge Greek Revival building has operated as an inn for about a decade. It has six rooms, two of them with a fireplace. The current owners are building a good library of Civil War material, to fit the character of the town. You may request a candlelight dinner during your stay; if your preference is for Southern cuisine, you can ask for that, too. Phone (615) 638–2917.

About 30 miles east of Greeneville, **Jonesborough,** Tennessee's oldest town (1779), offers you everything from a living restored community, where people actually live and work in the old buildings, to storytelling festivals. Not only have the people of this town done a notably good job of historic preservation, they have also done a good job in making it accessible to visitors. Andrew Jackson spent a lot of time here—in fact, he once was nearly tarred and feathered at the Chester Inn, which still stands.

Stop first at the **Historic Jonesborough Visitor Center,** 117 Boone Street, to browse through the **Jonesborough-Washington County History Museum,** see the slide show about the town, and pick up brochures for tours. The people who work here are friendly, helpful, and knowledgeable. Exhibits in the museum include such mementos as small cannon balls from a Civil War battle, a Victorian parlor, and part of an old log courthouse, all arranged to tell the story of the town. Exhibits also explain the "Lost State of Franklin" and its brief life, with Jonesborough as its capital, before the state of Tennessee was established. The museum is open Monday through Friday 8:00 A.M. to 5:00 P.M.; Saturday 10:00 A.M. to 5:00 P.M.; Sunday 1:00 to 5:00 P.M. Closed weekends in January and February. Admission is about $1.50. Phone (615) 753–5961.

The restored downtown area has a variety of specialty stores and restaurants, and many of the buildings have historic markers detailing their significance. You can shop for quilts, antiques, Indian crafts, and gift items.

And then there are the stories. Everyone who's ever known Southerners knows they love to tell stories. And they do it amazingly well. Exploding in popularity, Jonesborough's annual storytelling festival, held over the first full weekend in October, attracts storytellers, writers, and story lovers from all over the country. The gift shop in the **Jonesborough Visitors Center** sells books and cassettes of the stories told at the festivals. For full details on the festival, phone (615) 753–2171.

For a meal that reflects the more sophisticated possibilities of Southern cuisine, try the **Parson's Table,** a restaurant in an old Gothic-style church

Geography Is Destiny

The great diversity in Tennessee's culture and among its people does not seem so surprising when you consider the geography of the state. The topography ranges from the Mississippi River Delta on the west to the Great Smoky Mountains on the east, from an elevation of 188 feet to 6,000. The state covers two time zones, and it is bordered by eight different states: Virginia, Kentucky, Missouri, Mississippi, Arkansas, Alabama, Georgia, and North Carolina.

at 102 Woodrow Avenue. The owners, Jeff and Debra Myron, call their food "refined Southern, with a little bit of French—and a whole lot of love." This is *not* down-home fare. The food, like much of the South itself, reflects the influence of many countries without directly copying any of them. The most popular entree, for instance—shellfish medley in a pastry with a cream reduction sauce—whispers its French origins. The interior of the restaurant is fine Victorian, with plum-colored tablecloths, dusty-rose napkins, and fresh flowers. Open for lunch and dinner Tuesday through Sunday. For reservations, phone (615) 753–8002.

Come day's end, you might choose to stay at **Hawley House Bed and Breakfast,** a three-guest room (all with private bath) inn housed in a 1793 log-and-frame building at 114 East Woodrow Avenue. The place is furnished with antiques and folk art. In good weather, sit and rock in true Southern fashion on the wraparound porches overlooking the town. In cooler weather, guests gather around the fireplace in the old kitchen. The innkeepers serve a full Southern breakfast. Rates begin at about $65 per room. For reservations, phone (615) 753–8869.

The Ubiquitous Hush Puppy

You get hush puppies with your order almost anywhere in the South that serves down-home cooking. The most basic hush-puppy recipe is nothing more than cornmeal, flour, eggs, and baking powder, but every restaurant has its own special recipe. Hush puppies may contain sugar and taste almost like dessert, or onion and be more savory. Their texture may be soft and cakelike or dense and gritty inside, depending on the recipe, but they are always deep-fried and should be crisp and brown on the outside.

The classic story about the origins of hush puppies is that they were made of the batter left from frying fish over a campfire. When the dogs got rowdy, the cook fried up lumps of the batter and threw them to the dogs, calling, "Hush, puppy."

Virginia

THE HISTORY OF VIRGINIA IS DENSE. Consider, for example, that the British formed their first permanent New World colony at Jamestown; Virginia was the home of Thomas Jefferson, who wrote the Declaration of Independence; the city of Richmond was the capital of the Confederacy; and eight American presidents came from Virginia. And although Virginia was reluctant to leave the Union, refusing until there was no other way to avoid having to fight with Union troops against fellow Southerners, this state bore the brunt of Civil War battles.

Because Virginia was so central in both colonial and Confederate history, it is one of those places where you truly can see the continuity with which one era runs into the next. People in Virginia don't just "know" their history. They revel in it. They celebrate their historic sites and preservation with the kind of enthusiasm that some states reserve for championship football teams or award-winning city skylines.

What this means for you, in search of Old Dixie, is that sometimes you may have to decide whether or not to stop at an interesting colonial site on your way to a Civil War battlefield, whether to focus exclusively on the antebellum years, or whether to slide into the flow from colonial to later times and visit sites from both eras. You can be sure, however, that no matter where you stop, you'll find something of historic interest.

Virginia

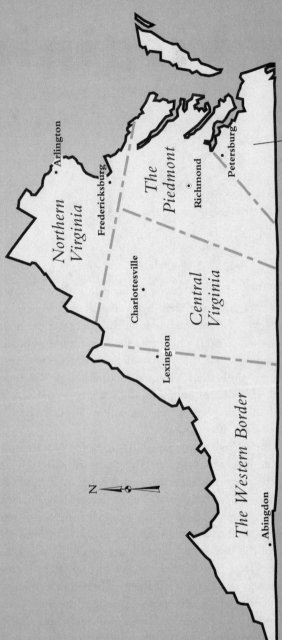

Northern Virginia

Arlington

Fredericksburg

The Piedmont

Richmond

Petersburg

Southeast Virginia

Charlottesville

Central Virginia

Lexington

N

The Western Border

Abingdon

Since this is a guide to Old Dixie, here you'll find only the briefest mention of those sites that are mainly colonial in their significance. But keep in mind that many attractions that are not included because they do not closely fit the Dixie theme are nonetheless important to Virginia's history.

NORTHERN VIRGINIA

Arlington is probably better known for being a suburb of Washington, D.C., than for its antebellum ambience. But **Arlington National Cemetery** includes **Arlington House, the Robert E. Lee Memorial.**

The famous cemetery was originally part of General Lee's estate. The Union took control of the estate and in 1864 began burying Union casualties virtually in what had been the Confederate general's backyard, as an act of sheer nastiness, to ensure that the place would never feel like home to Lee again. Today Arlington House is maintained and managed by the National Park Service.

Lee and his wife, Mary Anna Randolph Custis, were married here and lived in the house from 1831 to 1861, when the Civil War disrupted the good life. The restored house contains some of the original Lee family furnishings and portraits, which have been tracked down and returned. The "Official National Park Handbook" contains photographs and details of nineteenth-century daily life to lead you on a self-guided tour of the house. Some of the details in the handbook are taken from family documents. Thus you learn that the Lees were married in the parlor in 1831 and that while they lived there, Lee placed a rosebud he'd picked outside on the plate of each lady when the dining room table was set for breakfast. Other family records have made it possible to set the table and arrange furniture as the Lee family would have done. Gardens to the south and north of Arlington House are also kept as the Lees would have done, with vegetables and flowers. Another document shows that Lee freed the family's slaves in 1862, in accordance with his father-in-law's will. Learning about Arlington House gives you an understanding of Lee that goes well beyond a limited image of him as merely a military strategist and determined fighter.

The house is directly across the Potomac River from Washington, D.C., and affords a splendid view of the capital. Arlington House is open April through September, daily 9:30 A.M. to 6:00 P.M.; October through March daily 9:30 A.M. to 4:30 P.M. Hours may vary seasonally. Admission is free.

Phone (703) 557–0613. To get to Arlington House, park at the Arlington Cemetery Visitor Center and walk or take the bus to the house.

The restoration of Arlington House gives you a wonderful sense of the good years in the Old South, while the cemetery in which it's located reminds you how forcibly the Civil War disrupted that life. Head south to **Manassas** to see the place where, in a sense, the good antebellum years ended. In the mid-1800s this was just a little town where two railroads came together. Nothing else much went on in Manassas and, were it not for the Civil War, you might not ever hear of it. But this was the spot where the Union commanders, soldiers, and citizenry realized that a war to preserve the Union was going to be more than a sporting skirmish.

The first and second battle of Bull Run were fought here. At the first battle, on July 21, 1861, the people of Washington, D.C., had so little concept of what the fighting would be like that they packed picnic hampers and went with their families to watch the show. They thought that Union victory would be assured within half a day or less, and they must have had some sort of pre-television storybook concept of a bloodless battle.

At this point, however, some 35,000 Union soldiers and 38,000 Confederates had moved into the area. Neither army had any experience at soldiering, but the Confederates had the advantage of some good information from spies in Washington. The Union troops, thinking that they had already won the battle, and presumably the war, regrouped to charge up a hill—where they were surprised by Southern reinforcements. The upshot was that after a day of fighting, 2,700 Union soldiers had died, as had 2,000 Rebels. Spectators, dazed and shocked, made their way back to Washington, D.C., in subdued confusion. This came to be called First Battle of Manassas or the Battle of Bull Run, for the creek near where it was fought. A second battle, which the Confederates also won, was fought here in August 1862.

The visitor center at the park has interpretive displays about both battles. In the museum they are illustrated on a three-dimensional map. The park is open daily 8:30 A.M. to dusk. The visitor center is open June through September 1, daily 8:30 A.M. to 6:00 P.M. Admission to the park is about $2.00 for adults, free for those over 61 and under 17. Phone (704) 361–1339 or (704) 754–1861.

South of Manassas on I–95 is **Fredericksburg,** at the falls of the Rappahannock River. This spot encompasses a great sweep of Virginia history. It was the boyhood home of George Washington and the site of four major

Civil War battles. Today the city's National Historic District contains 40 blocks of buildings old enough to have been familiar to Washington himself; the triumph of the district is that these buildings survived Yankee bombardment and occupation during the Civil War.

At the **Fredericksburg Visitor Center,** 706 Caroline Street, you'll find brochures for a walking tour of the district as well as a two-part, self-guided walking tour of the Battle of Fredericksburg. The building housing the Visitor Center was built in 1824 as the shop and home of a confectioner. Now it stands as the starting point for self-guided historic tours. If you are interested in Civil War battles, be sure to ask for the two-part walking tour, "Fire in the Streets" and "The Assault on Mayre's Heights." The brochures give maps and walking directions to track the two encounters of the Fredericksburg Campaign of November–December 1862, along with detailed accounts of the fighting. Excerpts from the letters and journals of Confederate and Union soldiers bring the action to life with stunning reality—no romance here. While you're in the center, see the twelve-minute audiovisual presentation that orients you to the city. You can gather information about food and lodging and also pick up parking passes here. The center is open mid-June through Labor Day, daily 9:00 A.M. to 7:00 P.M., it closes at 5:00 P.M. the rest of the year. Phone (703) 373–1776 or (800) 678–4748.

Some of the interesting stops in the historic district also dim the romantic notions we entertain in thinking about the past. The **Hugh Mercer Apothecary Shop,** Caroline Street at Amelia, shows you more about eighteenth- and nineteenth-century medical practices than you may have wanted to know (though leeches and bleeding probably aren't any more gruesome than periodonture or chemotherapy). Living-history presentations explain the old ills cures and their "cures." The shop is open March through November, daily 9:00 A.M. to 5:00 P.M.; December through February, daily 10:00 A.M. to 4:00 P.M.; closed Thanksgiving, Christmas, and New Year's Day. Admission is about $3.00 for adults, with discounts for children. Phone (703) 373–3362.

There is nothing romantic about the **Rising Sun Tavern,** 1306 Caroline Street, either. The tidy building of brick and frame was built by Charles Washington, George Washington's youngest brother, who lived in it from 1760 until 1790. After that it was opened as the Golden Eagle Tavern; a new owner renamed it Rising Sun in 1821. Now it is a museum. The restored building contains sections of the original bar. What the tour guides (costumed as serving wenches) have to tell you about guests being served on wooden plates that weren't washed between seatings leaves you hoping that the tavern beer was good at killing germs. The tavern is open March through November daily 9:00 A.M. to 5:00 P.M.; December through January, 10:00 A.M. to 4:00 P.M. Closed Thanksgiving, Christmas Eve, Christmas Day, and New Year's Day. Admission is about $3.00 for adults. Discounts are given for children. Phone (703) 371–1494.

Even if sanitation left something to be desired, life in the antebellum years must have been good here, where so many affluent and astute people lived. The attractions that remain, however, speak less about the good life than about how the Civil War disrupted that life. Soldiers' accounts describe not only combat but also looting and deliberate destruction, streets pummeled to mud by combat boots, furniture and household utensils broken and strewn along the streets, and—inevitably—soldiers wounded, sick, and dying. These things have all left their mark in Fredericksburg's historic district and the nearby area.

The **Town Hall,** 907 Princess Anne Street, where people had once gathered for everything from concerts and balls to meetings of the Masons, was used as a hospital during the Revolutionary War. The original building was demolished and replaced with a new town hall in 1814, and during the Civil War, this, too, was used as a hospital. Now it is the home of the **Fredericksburg Area Museum and Cultural Center,** with six permanent exhibit galleries detailing area history from prehistoric times through Indian and colonial settlement, the Revolutionary War and Federal eras, the Civil War, Reconstruction, and the early twentieth century. The displays include old photographs, tools, toys, clothing, and other artifacts of day-to-day life. The museum is open March through November, Monday through Saturday 9:00 A.M. to 5:00 P.M. and Sunday 1:00 to 5:00 P.M.; and December through February, Monday through Saturday 9:00 A.M. to 4:00 P.M. and Sunday 1:00 to 4:00 P.M. Admission is about $3.00 for adults, with discounts for children. Phone (703) 371–3037.

At Princess Anne and George Streets, **St. George's Church and Graveyard** date back to 1849. General Lee's troops held religious revivals in this Episcopal church, and, like so many other buildings in the area, it was used as a military hospital for a time. Parishioners paid for the church by renting box pews. The pews survived both the Civil War and a major fire, so you can still sit in them today. The church is open every day 8:00 A.M. to 5:00 P.M. Admission is free. Phone (703) 373–4133.

Just across George Street, still on Princess Anne, walk by **The Court House,** a Gothic Revival–style building that also played a central role in several Civil War activities. Union hospitals and signal stations operated from the site, and escaped slaves hid here. During Reconstruction, a freedman's court in the building was the site of civil cases between white people and former slaves.

Cross the street again to visit **The Presbyterian Church,** George Street at Princess Anne, built in 1833. The Greek Revival–style building served as a hospital during the Civil War; Clara Barton, founder of the American Red Cross, nursed Union soldiers in this church. Being a military site was hard on the building. Pews were broken up for use as stretchers and coffins, and the church gave its bell to the Confederacy to melt down for ordnance. After the war the bell was replaced and the congregation rebuilt the pew boxes, which are still in place.

At 900 Princess Anne Street, the **National Bank of Fredericksburg,** was opened in 1820 as part of the Farmers' Bank of Virginia. President Abraham Lincoln addressed the troops and citizens from the steps of the building on May 22, 1862; and during the war Union commanders headquartered in the bank. Restoration has brought the building back to the way it looked before the Civil War. It is open during usual business hours and still functions as a bank.

Today the National Park Service maintains almost 6,000 acres preserving Civil War sites.

Four battlefields and a Union headquarters site, in the **Fredericksburg and Spotsylvania National Military Park,** round out the area's Civil War story with museum exhibits, tours, and the stories of the park historians. The Union headquarters is outside of town, 1 mile east on State Road 218, at 120 Chatham Lane, at **Chatham,** a 1700s Georgian-style mansion, where Clara Barton and Walt Whitman stopped to treat wounded soldiers. The mansion contains exhibits relating to its history and is owned and operated by the National Park Service. Open daily 9:00 A.M. to 5:00 P.M., except Christmas and New Year's Day. Admission is free.

The four battlefields are famous, and the park service has detailed information about the battles and their significance. In a conflict from December 11 through December 15, 1862, at Fredericksburg Battlefield, Robert E. Lee and his troops triumphed, making it obvious that Union troops were going to have much more to do than whup a few rural Rebs. Thanks to some brilliant strategy by Lee and Stonewall Jackson, the Confederates were doing well until the day Jackson was mistakenly shot by his own troops. (This is detailed at Chancellorsville Battlefield, in recounting the fighting taking place from April 27 to May 6, 1863.) After his arm was amputated, however, Jackson actually died because he caught pneumonia. At the **"Stonewall" Jackson Shrine,** the room in a plantation office where he died on May 10 is kept as it was then. It is open mid-June through Labor Day, daily 9:00 A.M. to 5:00 P.M., with shorter hours the rest of the year. Meanwhile, at Wilderness Battlefield, on May 5 and 6, 1864, Union general Ulysses S. Grant encountered Lee in battle and was brought to a stalemate. At Spotsylvania Courthouse Battlefield, which lay on the crossroads of the most direct route to Richmond, troops fought for two weeks, including twenty hours of bloody hand-to-hand combat, from May 8 to May 21, 1864.

A self-guided tour of the battlefield begins at the Fredericksburg Battlefield Visitor Center. Park historians are on duty here and at the Chancellorsville Visitor Center. From June until Labor Day interpretive programs re-create Civil War scenes. The Visitor Center, at Lafayette Boulevard and

Kindness Remembered and Honored

The following words are inscribed on the base of the Richard Kirkland Monument:

IN MEMORIAM

RICHARD ROWLAND KIRKLAND

CO. G. 2ND SOUTH CAROLINA VOLUNTEERS

C.S.A.

AT THE RISK OF HIS LIFE THIS AMERICAN

SOLDIER OF SUBLIME COMPASSION BROUGHT

WATER TO HIS WOUNDED FOES AT

FREDERICKSBURG. THE FIGHTING MEN ON

BOTH SIDES OF THE LINE CALLED HIM

"THE ANGEL OF MARYES HEIGHTS"

Sunken Road, is open mid-June through Labor Day, daily 8:30 A.M. to 6:30 P.M. Near the Visitor Center be sure to see the widely known statue of the Confederate soldier who left his lines to give water to wounded Yankee soldiers.

Stratford Hall Plantation, on the Potomac River about 20 miles east of Fredericksburg, off State Highway 214, is the birthplace of General Robert E. Lee. The impressive H-shaped mansion was built in the late 1730s of brick made on the property and timber cut from the virgin forest on the site. In the center of the house, a 29-square-foot tray ceiling soars 17 feet high. Some of the furnishings are original pieces of the Lee family, dating from 1730 to 1810. The house has Revolutionary War and Colonial as well as antebellum significance, because two members of the Lee family signed the Declaration of Independence. Before the Civil War was even a thought, a young Robert E. Lee rode horses with his brothers in the meadows of the property. You can walk the same paths where Lee rode and also see a formal boxwood garden and orderly kitchen gardens. A waterwheel at the reconstructed mill turns wooden gears to power millstones that grind grains as they have for more than 200 years; you can buy the flour at the Stratford store, which is open every day. And every day from April 1 to November 1, you can have a plantation lunch in a log-cabin dining room, open 11:30 A.M. to 3:00 P.M. The plantation is open daily 9:00 A.M. to 4:30 P.M., except Christmas. Admission is about $5.00 for adults, with discounts for children and senior citizens. Military personnel are admitted free. Phone (804) 493–8038 Monday through Friday, 9:00 A.M. to 5:00 P.M.; phone (804) 493–8371 weekends and holidays, 9:00 A.M. to 5:00 P.M.

THE PIEDMONT

The South doesn't get more Southern than this! The Piedmont is characterized by rolling farmland, old plantation homes, and the formal, gracious manners of an earlier time. **Richmond,** south of Fredericksburg on I–95 where it intersects with I–64, was the center of antebellum Virginia. It continues to reflect that history in its historic attractions. More Civil War battles were fought in Virginia than in any other state, and Richmond, once the capital of the Confederacy, has several important sites related to those struggles.

One of the most fascinating is **Valentine Museum,** 1015 East Clay Street, a museum that deliberately portrays a deromanticized version of Richmond's history. It gives special attention to what life was like in the homes of slave-owning families, not only for the owners but also for the slaves. About a decade ago the people at the museum committed themselves to treating the social, as opposed to, say, the architectural, history of Richmond as their primary perspective. Several of the buildings that compose the museum today thus include changing exhibits, ranging from photographs to costumes, documenting the city's history.

The museum includes the **Wickham-Valentine House,** an 1812 Federal-style structure with a freestanding spiral stairway, elaborate woodwork, and splendid wall murals. This house, furnished with antiques and

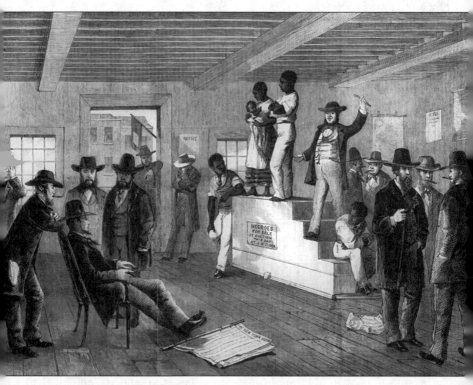

"A Slave Auction in Virginia by Our Special Artist" was published in the Illustrated London News *in 1861 and is part of the exhibit at Valentine Museum.*

Part of Valentine Museum, the interior of the Wickham-Valentine house, furnished with fine antiques, shows how typical wealthy Richmond citizens lived in the early 1800s. In some rooms you hear recordings of dramatized conversations that might have taken place among the family members and the family slaves.

collections of crystal, china, and silver, typifies the life of well-to-do Richmond citizenry of the time. In some rooms, you will hear recorded dramatizations of conversations that might have taken place among the slaves both in private and in the presence of the Wickham family; the private conversations are about rumors of slave beatings on nearby plantations and about the hardships of servitude. In contrast, you will also hear dramatizations of conversations among the Wickham family members and guests about fashion, travel, fine wine, and how it is unnecessary for young women to be highly educated since they will soon be married, bearing children, and reading novels. These audio conversations are not documented word-for-word, but they are based on extensive research and are true to the character of the Wickham family.

The innovative programs at the Valentine are in continuous development and will provide in-depth understanding of the history of Richmond. A visit here is highly recommended. Also available through the museum is a self-guiding walking tour and map of the Court End historic district that leads you past sixteen sites that were important from the American Revolution, through the formative years of the nation, through the Civil War. Court End stretches from Thomas Jefferson's Capitol to include nine National Historic Landmarks and twelve buildings on the National Register of Historic Places. Some of the buildings are open to the public. Special block tickets offer savings over rates for touring individual sites. The museum is open Monday through Saturday 9:00 A.M. to 5:00 P.M.; Sunday noon to 5:00 P.M. Admission is about $5.00 for adults, with discounts for children, students with ID, and senior citizens. Children under seven are admitted free. Phone (804) 649–0711.

The White House of the Confederacy and the **Museum of the Confederacy** are side-by-side at 1201 Clay Street, in downtown Richmond. Jefferson Davis and his family lived in the stuccoed home while he was president of the Confederacy. Although everything was taken out of the house after the war and the building deteriorated, it has since been restored and many of the original furnishings returned, so now the house looks about the same as it did when Davis lived in it. You'll find that this White House contrasts startlingly with the quiet elegance of the White House in Washington, D.C. The decor in the Confederate White House is Victorian at its gaudiest (though tourist literature often prefers to call it "opulent"). Call it what you will, the elaborate brocade-and-velvet furnishings represent a triumph of restoration. Guided tours are offered. The house is open Monday through Saturday noon to 5:00 P.M.; Sunday 1:00 to 5:00 P.M.; closed Thanksgiving, Christmas, and New Year's Day. Admission is about $4.00 for adults, with discounts for senior citizens, college students with ID, and children. Phone (804) 649–1861.

The Museum of the Confederacy, located next door, contains art, artifacts, and exhibits about the history of the Civil War, including weaponry belonging to Robert E. Lee and Thomas J. "Stonewall" Jackson, as well as items related to the lives of African Americans at the time. The museum is open Monday through Saturday 10:00 A.M. to 5:00 P.M.; Sunday noon to 5:00 P.M. Closed Thanksgiving, Christmas, and New Year's Day. Admission is about $4.00 for adults, with discounts for senior citizens, college students with ID, and children. Phone (804) 649–1861.

Now leave Clay Street for a couple of interesting stops. **John Marshall House,** nearby at 818 Marshall Street, was the home of Supreme Court Chief Justice John Marshall from 1790 to 1835. The original paneling and woodwork, many of the original furnishings, and even some of Marshall's horseshoes remain. The house is open Tuesday through Saturday 10:00 A.M. to 5:00 P.M.; Sunday noon to 5:00 P.M. Admission is about $5.00 for adults, with discounts for children and senior citizens. Phone (804) 648–7998.

St. John's Episcopal Church, 24th and Broad Streets, dates back to 1741. This is where Patrick Henry made his famous "Give me liberty or give me death" speech. It's a good example of a historic site that predated the antebellum years but continued to be significant during them. Combination tickets for the Museum of the Confederacy, the White House of the Confederacy, St. John's Episcopal Church, the Valentine Museum, and the John Marshall House are available at the Museum of the Confederacy.

The antebellum connection is more direct at **St. Paul's Church,** Grace and Ninth Streets, where Robert E. Lee and Jefferson Davis both worshiped. Everything in the church is a memorial to them. Open Monday through Saturday 10:00 A.M. to 4:00 P.M.; Sunday 8:00 A.M. to 3:00 P.M. Sunday services are held at 7:45 A.M., 9:00 A.M., and 11:00 A.M. Closed holidays. Admission is free. Phone (804) 643–3589.

Next, moving out of downtown Richmond, not far from St. John's Church, you come to **Chimborazo,** the site of a Confederate hospital where more than 76,000 wounded soldiers were treated. The hospital no longer stands, but in **Chimborazo Park,** a visitor center at 3215 East

Broad Street serves as headquarters for the **Richmond National Battle-field Park.** A slide show and movie shown at the center orient you to events surrounding the battles for the Confederate capital and leading up to the burning of Richmond in 1865. You can pick up brochures at the center for several self-guided tours of the battlefields.

Touring the entire park takes several hours. It is made up of nine units that encompass the sites of two campaigns: the General George McClellan Campaign of 1862 and the campaign of General Ulysses S. Grant of 1864. Probably the best known of the battles fought here is the one at Cold Harbor on June 3, 1864, during which 7,000 soldiers died in half an hour. An electronic map and exhibits in the interpretive shelter at the Cold Harbor Battlefield amplify details on that battle.

More information is available at the Fort Harrison Visitor Center in the Fort Harrison unit of the park. This is also where you can pick up the route to trace the various Confederate forts in the park. The park is open daily during daytime hours. Admission is free. The **Chimborazo Visitor Center** is open daily 9:00 A.M. to 5:00 P.M. Closed Christmas and New Year's Day. The **Fort Harrison Visitor Center** is open during the same days and hours in June, July, and August. Admission is free. Phone (804) 226–1981.

While you are in Richmond, you might stay at **The William Catlin House Bed and Breakfast,** 2304 East Broad Street. The owners, Josephine and Robert Martin, are concentrating on re-creating antebellum ambience in this three-story 1845 home. Their furnishings are mostly Empire antiques, with which many of the better homes in Richmond would have been furnished during the antebellum years. The house is in the Historic Church Hill District, just a block from St. John's Episcopal Church and also close to the Richmond National Battlefield Park. As Josephine explains, you will find old homes standing in this district, despite the burning of Richmond at the end of the Civil War, because burning was concentrated mostly on the businesses and warehouses around Main Street and the fire did not come up the hill. Of the five guest rooms at The William Catlin House, three have private baths, and two, in a suite, share a bath. Rates, including breakfast, begin at about $75 per room, shared bath; $95 per room, private bath. Phone (804) 780–3746.

SOUTHEAST VIRGINIA

From Richmond, a drive of about 18 miles south on I–295 and 10 miles more on Route 5 along the James River brings you to the oldest plantation in Virginia: **Shirley Plantation,** at **Charles City.** The plantation is an ideal attraction to include in this guide because, as the people who promote the plantation point out, it is a fine example of historical continuity.

Shirley was founded in 1613, just six years after settlers came to establish the first permanent English colony in Jamestown. (Shirley is west of Jamestown.) The plantation was a social center in Colonial times, then a supply center during the Revolution. Anne Hill Carter, the mother of Confederate General Robert E. Lee, was born at Shirley. Some of Lee's schooling took place in a converted laundry house on the plantation. The current mansion was built from 1732 to 1738 and survives relatively unchanged. The carved walnut staircase, which seems to float between floors with no visible support, is famous among people interested in interior architecture. It is the only staircase of its kind in America. Members of the Carter family, now into the eleventh generation, still live in the mansion and manage the plantation. The mansion houses original family silver, furnishings, and portraits. The tour of the property also encompasses a number of brick outbuildings, including a large, two-story kitchen and two barns. The property is a National Historic Landmark.

The plantation is open daily 9:00 A.M. to 5:00 P.M. Closed Christmas. The last tour begins at 4:30 P.M. Admission is about $7.00 for adults, with discounts for children, military personnel, and senior citizens. Phone (804) 829–5121 or (800) 232–1613. To get to the plantation, take exit 22–A from I–295 onto Route 5. Drive 10 miles to Shirley Plantation Road. Follow signs on Shirley Plantation Road 1.5 miles to the plantation.

After you view Shirley Plantation, continue along the James River on State Highway 5, known as the Plantation Route, to see several more fine old plantation homes that are open for tours. And you can at least drive by to see the exteriors of several more that are open only on special occasions.

Berkeley Plantation, 12602 Harrison Landing Road, is where thirty-eight settlers from England came ashore on December 4, 1619, and observed the first official Thanksgiving in America, more than a year before the Pilgrims arrived in New England. The date of the three-story brick plantation mansion, 1726, and the initials of the owners, Benjamin Harrison IV and his wife, Anne, appear on a datestone over a door.

Berkeley claims a remarkable number of "firsts." An Episcopal missionary made a home brew from corn that the colonists found much better than British ale. This corn liquor was the first bourbon whiskey distilled in America—a first without which that revered antebellum libation, the mint julep, would not have been possible. This accomplishment is honored on the plantation by the presence of a gazebo-like structure known as the **Tea and Mint Julep House.** As colorful as the plantation's beginnings were, the antebellum and Civil War years here were equally dramatic. Benjamin Harrison, a signer of the Declaration of Independence, was born here. So was his son, William Henry Harrison, who was elected president of the United States in 1840. He returned to the plantation to write his inaugural address in the room where he was born. (*His* grandson, Benjamin Harrison, was the twenty-third president of the United States.) This is one of the rooms open for public tours. In 1862 President Abraham Lincoln visited Berkeley to review the 140,000 Union troops encamped there; that same year a Union officer at Berkeley composed the mournful melody "Taps," which was quickly adopted by troops on both sides. The mansion has been restored and furnished with fine eighteenth-century antiques; ten acres of formal terraced boxwood gardens extend to the James River. The house and grounds are open for tours daily 8:00 A.M. to 5:00 P.M. Closed Christmas. Admission is about $8.00 for adults, with discounts for children and senior citizens; half price for a tour of grounds only. Phone (804) 829–6018.

If you'd like to dine on a plantation, **Coach House Tavern,** on the Berkeley grounds, serves lunches and dinners that include but aren't limited to Southern favorites such as crab cakes. The chef calls other offerings "innovative American cuisine." The restaurant is on the site of the original coach house, which burned, but its foundation and part of its walls were incorporated into the newer building. Closed Monday, Tuesday, and Christmas. Phone (804) 829–6003. To get to the plantation, follow signs from State Highway 5 onto Harrison Landing Road and drive 1 mile.

Also on the Plantation Route, **Edgewood,** a restored 7,000-foot Gothic mansion built in 1849, offers an opportunity not only to tour the plantation but also to spend the night. Edgewood includes eight guest rooms furnished in antebellum opulence, two of them in the former slaves' quarters and six more in the main house. "Jeb Stuart's Room" is furnished to convey the illusion of that flamboyant Confederate general awaiting the arrival of his special love.

Confederate generals really did spend time in this mansion. During the Civil War the third floor of the main house was used as a lookout from which Confederate generals could spy on Union troops camped at nearby Berkeley Plantation. And on June 15, 1862, Confederate general Stuart stopped at Edgewood for coffee (not to await his love) on his way to Richmond to warn General Robert E. Lee that the Union Army was stronger than had been supposed.

The owners of Edgewood are natives of Virginia who can tell you in great detail about the history of the plantation. They are also collectors, so you can expect to see an astonishing number and variety of old items on display. The guided tours of the mansion include eleven rooms filled with antique furnishings, vintage clothing, and interesting antebellum artifacts. The plantation is open Tuesday through Sunday 11:00 A.M. to 5:00 P.M. Admission is about $5.00 for adults, with discounts for children. Rates for the bed-and-breakfast guest rooms begin at $148 per room. Phone (804) 829–2962.

Evelynton, the next plantation along this route, also has interesting Civil War connections. Edmund Ruffin, the soldier who fired the first shot of the Civil War at Fort Sumter, in Charleston, South Carolina, bought the plantation in 1847. It was originally part of William Byrd's larger Westover Plantation and was named for Byrd's daughter, Evelyn. Three Civil War battles were fought at Evelynton in 1862, during which the original house and outbuildings burned. The house there today was designed and built by Edmund Ruffin's great-grandson and his wife to combine features typical of several plantation homes in the area. Family members still own and operate the 2,500-acre plantation. Historical markers on the grounds detail the Civil War fighting that took place there. The plantation house, grounds, and gardens are open for guided tours daily 9:00 A.M. to 5:00 P.M. Closed Thanksgiving, Christmas, and New Year's Day. Admission is about $6.00 for adults, with discounts for children, senior citizens, and grounds-only tours. Phone (804) 829–5075 or (800) 473–5075.

Continuing a few miles more on State Highway 5 will bring you to **Colonial Williamsburg,** which, of course, is beyond the scope of this guide. However, if you decide to see it while you are in the area, you can request further information from the visitor center in Williamsburg by calling (800) 447–8679.

When you've seen enough plantations, return to I–295 and continue south for about 10 miles to **Petersburg,** where touring the **Old Towne** historic district points up again the rigors of the Civil War. A couple of miles east, the **Petersburg National Battlefield** preserves the battlefields on which the Confederate Army suffered nearly a year of debilitating trench fighting. You can best orient yourself by starting at the **Visitor Center** at Old **Market Square.** The staff can supply you with a map of Petersburg and tour guides for the Old Towne and can suggest sites appropriate to your specific interests. In addition to the historic attractions of the historic district, you'll find restaurants and lots of antiques and specialty shops in the Market Square. The Visitor Center is open daily 9:00 A.M. to 5:00 P.M. Phone (804) 733–2400 or (800) 368–3595. (These phone numbers pertain also for the following three attractions.)

For those in pursuit of the antebellum experience, **Siege Museum,** 15 West Bank Street, is an important stop. Exhibits and a film show what it was like for ordinary people living in Petersburg during the ten months that Petersburg was at the center of attacks from the troops of General Grant beginning in the summer of 1864. Petersburg had been an important center of commerce before the Civil War, but the fighting devastated the town's homes, businesses, and services. The museum is open daily 10:00 A.M. to 5:00 P.M. Closed Thanksgiving, Christmas Eve, Christmas, and New Year's Day. Admission is about $2.00 for adults, with discounts for senior citizens, children, and military personnel with ID.

A tour leaving from the Siege Museum will take you to **Trapezium House,** North Market Street. The home was built in the shape of a trapezium to keep out ghosts. The man who built it in the early 1800s believed that evil spirits lived in right angles; the result was that the house has no right angles, and hence no parallel walls. A tour costs about $1 for adults, with discounts for senior citizens, children, and military personnel with ID.

Old Blandford Church and Reception Center offers perhaps another approach to warding off evil spirits. Located at 319 South Crater Street, the church dates to 1734. Its cemetery is the resting place of 30,000 Confederate soldiers. Records and pertinent artifacts are displayed in the Reception Center. The church and Reception Center are open daily 10:00 A.M. to 5:00 P.M. Closed Thanksgiving, Christmas Eve, Christmas, and New Year's Day. Admission is about $2.00 for adults, with discounts for children, senior citizens, and military personnel with ID.

Petersburg National Battlefield covers more than 1,500 acres, with interpretive trails and historical markers to explain the Civil War battles that led to the defeat of the Confederacy. Five miles of original earthworks are in the park. At the entrance, a visitor center has an electronic map, artifacts, and exhibits pertaining to the Petersburg campaign. A 4-mile self-guided tour begins from the center, and a 16-mile tour of the siege line begins where the battlefield tour stops. The park is open daily 8:00 A.M. to 7:00 P.M. Admission is about $1.00 per person, or $3.00 per private vehicle. Phone (804) 732–3531.

CENTRAL VIRGINIA

Charlottesville, located midway between Richmond and Staunton on I–64, in the foothills of the Blue Ridge Mountains, is notable as the location of Monticello, the home of Thomas Jefferson, and Ash Lawn-Highland, the home of James Monroe. The ways of life practiced by these two early presidents effectively shaped the antebellum concepts of "the good life." Indeed, Jefferson's concepts regarding architecture, gardening, cooking, and wines still pertain in many ways.

Monticello is considered one of the country's architectural masterpieces. Jefferson lived in it from 1770 until he died in 1826. He repeatedly remodeled the house for at least the first forty years, indulging his pleasure in architecture and "putting up and pulling down," as he put it. The gardens also reflect Jefferson's love of experimenting. He tested more than 250 varieties of vegetables and herbs, keeping such detailed records that gardeners have since been able to re-create his gardens accurately. Jefferson's interest in growing vegetables led naturally enough to an interest in cooking, and it is possible today to cook from recipes that he devised at Monticello.

Monticello is located on a mountaintop overlooking Charlottesville and the countryside of Albemarle County. The preservation of the property is an ongoing project, as is the effort to bring the home's original furnishings back to re-create the interior as it was during Jefferson's lifetime. Tours include the main rooms of the house, where many of Jefferson's furnishings are in place, while tours of the grounds cover vegetable and flower gardens like the ones Jefferson kept. Monticello is also home to the Thomas Jefferson Center for Historic Plants, an interesting stop for learning about what grew in antebellum gardens before hybridization became commonplace; you can even buy some of the plants. Monticello is open for guided tours March through October, daily 8:00 A.M. to 5:00 P.M.; November through February, daily 9:00 A.M. to 4:30 P.M. Closed Christmas. Admission is about $8.00 for adults, with discounts for children and senior citizens. Phone (804) 295–8181 or (804) 295–2657. Monticello is located 3 miles southeast of Charlottesville on State Highway 53. From I–64 exit onto State Highway 20, drive south 0.5 mile, and turn east onto State Route 53. Continue 1.5 miles.

After you exit I–64 onto State Highway 20, you may want to stop at the **Thomas Jefferson Visitors Center** before continuing to State Highway 53. Archaeological excavations and research at Monticello have produced so much information about Jefferson's domestic life that the exhibit "Thomas Jefferson at Monticello" was set up to display some of the pertinent items to supplement what you learn at Monticello. You can procure a special "President's Pass" here—a discounted combined admission pass to Monticello, Ash Lawn-Highland, and Historic Michie Tavern. The center is open daily 9:00 A.M. to 5:30 P.M.; it closes at 5:00 P.M. from November through February. It is closed Thanksgiving, Christmas, and New Year's Day. Phone (804) 293–6789.

On the side of a mountain about 2.5 miles from Monticello, **Ash Lawn-Highland,** the home of Jefferson's friend James Monroe, gives you a chance to learn more about a working farm of the nineteenth century. Monroe moved here partly because of his friendship with Jefferson, and the property reflects their similar tastes and interests. In fact, it was Jefferson who chose the site, and Jefferson's gardeners put in the orchards. The Monroes moved into the house on the 535-acre tobacco plantation in 1799. When you tour the main house, you'll find many of the family's furnishings still in place. Cooking and crafts demonstrations are held from time to time. The site is open March through October, daily 9:00 A.M. to 6:00 P.M.; November through February, daily 10:00 A.M. to 5:00 P.M. Closed Thanksgiving, Christmas, and New Year's Day. Admission is about $6.00 for adults, with discounts for children and senior citizens. Phone (804) 293–9539.

The logical place to eat while you're visiting Monticello and Ash Lawn-Highland is **Historic Michie Tavern,** which is both a restaurant serving traditional Southern cooking and a museum of eighteenth-century travel and hospitality. This is one of the oldest homesteads in Virginia; it was moved from what had been a stagecoach route, where it once operated as a tavern, to its current location in the early 1900s. Major attractions today are the furnished ladies' and gentlemen's parlors, outbuildings, and Virginia Wine Museum. A buffet is served in the Ordinary, a 200-year-old log outbuilding, daily 11:30 A.M. to 3:00 P.M. The museum is open daily 9:00 A.M. to 5:00 P.M. Closed Christmas and New Year's Day. Admission to the museum is about $5.00 for adults, with discounts for children and senior citizens. Phone (804) 977–1234. To get to the tavern, go 0.5 mile south of I–64 on State Highway 20, then drive 1 mile east on State Highway 53.

Clifton, a country inn about 5 miles east of downtown Charlottesville, offers luxurious bed-and-breakfast accommodations with antebellum ambience. The manor house, circa 1799, sits atop a wooded cliff. Listed on the National Register of Historic Places, Clifton was the home of Thomas Mann Randolph (1768–1828), who served as governor of Virginia and member of the U.S. Congress. He married Thomas Jefferson's daughter Martha. The mansion still has its original wide-plank pine floors, paneled walls, and fireplaces. In the Martha Jefferson guest room, the walls, bed hangings, and rug are a rich cream color. The inn has fourteen rooms, all with private bath and fireplace. Some are in the main house, while others are in the Carriage House, the Livery, and what was once Randolph's law office. Dinner is served at the inn in an elegantly appointed dining room. Rates begin at about $165 a night per room. Phone (804) 971–1800.

Another choice for lodging is **Prospect Hill Plantation Inn,** about 15 miles east of Charlottesville on State Highway 613. This is a twelve-room inn on a 1732 plantation with beautiful grounds and gardens. Some of the guest rooms are in the main house, others in cottages that used to be out-buildings and slave quarters. Some of the rooms have a working fireplace. Rates, which include afternoon tea, a full breakfast, and dinner, begin at about $200 a night per room, double occupancy. Phone (703) 967–0844.

THE WESTERN BORDER

Running along the western border of Virginia, I–81 more or less parallels the Blue Ridge Parkway, taking you to a series of sites in the mountainous area of the state that are rich in antebellum history and are also situated along some of the state's most scenic routes. Along much of the stretch, you can drive on the Blue Ridge Parkway for a while, then easily get back to the interstate when the parkway's 45-mile-per hour speed limit gets tiresome. Beginning on the southern end of I–82, almost at the Tennessee border, **Abingdon,** founded in 1778, is the oldest town west of the Blue Ridge Mountains. The town is situated where Daniel Boone once camped at the junction of two Indian trails. Today the town is known mostly for fine arts and crafts and for tobacco auctions as well as for some interesting old buildings.

The Martha Washington Inn, 150 West Main Street, built in 1832, is a good place to stay for a taste of antebellum luxury. The building has been a private home, a Civil War hospital, and a women's college. Now it's a four-diamond, four-star hotel. The 150-year-old Federalist mansion has sixty-one luxuriously restored guest rooms, some with fireplaces. Many of the furnishings are fine antiques. The inn is also reputed to house some fine old antebellum ghosts. The inn's restaurant, **The First Lady's Table,** has the same elegant ambience, though the cuisine is—South American! Rates at The Martha Washington Inn begin at about $89 a room. Phone (703) 628–3161.

Continuing north on I–81, **Lexington** was the home of Confederate Generals Thomas J. "Stonewall" Jackson and Robert E. Lee. It is also the home of the Virginia Military Institute, whose young cadets fought in the Civil War on May 15, 1864, against seasoned Union forces, in the Battle of New Market, managing to hold their position long enough to force the more experienced Union troops to retreat north. The event is held in such reverence that every May 15, the military school holds ceremonies honoring the ten cadets who died during the battle. Moreover, both Lee and Jackson are buried in Lexington.

But quite apart from its military significance, Lexington is a pretty little town, almost the prototype of what one imagines an old Southern town should look like, with a shop-lined main street presided over by two important schools atop a hill, and great expanses of green lawn and deciduous trees offering generous shade. Stop first at the **Lexington Visitor Center,** 106 East Washington Street, to view a slide show and exhibits about the history of the area. The center is open during June, July, and August, daily 8:30 A.M. to 6:00 P.M.; the rest of the year, hours are 9:00 A.M. to 5:00 P.M. Closed Thanksgiving, Christmas, and New Year's Day. Phone (703) 463–3777.

Downtown, you can visit **The Washington & Lee University,** and **Lee Chapel,** on the campus of the university. General Lee was president of the college after the Civil War. The president's house and the chapel were built under his direction. The Victorian brick chapel, still containing his office as he left it in 1870, with chairs set around a conference table, is maintained as a museum and a shrine to Lee; the scene is old-style academic, decidedly not military. Part of its significance is that when Lee came here at the end of the Civil War, having lost practically everything, he did not engage in bitter rhetoric but urged Southerners to put the past behind them. He, his family, and various relatives are buried underneath the chapel. His war horse, Traveller, is buried outside. There is a famous statue of Lee in the chapel showing him lying as if on a battlefield, with a hand on his chest, looking like the worn old soldier he was. The chapel is open Monday through Saturday 9:00 A.M. to 5:00 P.M.; Sunday 2:00 to 5:00 P.M. Admission is free. Phone (703) 463–8768.

Another, quite different, school, **Virginia Military Institute,** mentioned earlier, is right beside the campus of Washington and Lee. Hank Burchard, writing in *The Washington Post,* once called the school's buildings "so ugly they achieve a sort of eclectic elegance." Stonewall Jackson taught here for a decade before the Civil War. Founded in 1839, the school remains predominantly military in its orientation. Cadets give guided tours Monday through Friday at 11:00 A.M. and 3:00 P.M.; Saturday at 10:00 A.M. and 11:00 A.M. Admission is free. Phone (703) 463–7103.

An oil painting showing the Battle of New Market is in the **Jackson Memorial Hall** on the VMI campus, while in the **VMI Museum,** downstairs in the memorial hall, exhibits show Jackson's old school uniform and his stuffed and mounted horse, Little Sorrel. A replica of a cadet room in the barracks gives you an idea of cadet life. The museum is open Monday through Saturday 9:00 A.M. to 5:00 P.M.; Sunday 2:00 to 5:00 P.M. Closed Thanksgiving and December 24 through January 1. Admission is free. Phone (703) 463–7103.

Probably the most popular attraction in this area is **Cyrus McCormick's Farm and Workshop,** also known as **Walnut Grove,** on State Highway 606. This is where Cyrus McCormick and his father made the first successful mechanical (horse-drawn) grain reaper in 1831. The success of the device helped turn the Shenandoah Valley into an agricultural center. The original reaper is in what used to be the blacksmith shop. The McCormick home, shop, and grist mill are all National Historic Landmarks and part of Virginia Technical Institutes' Shenandoah Valley Agricultural Research Station. Open daily 8:00 A.M. to 5:00 P.M. Admission is free. Phone (703) 377–2255. To get to the farm, take exit 205, the Steeles Tavern exit, from I–81, and drive 1 mile east on State Highway 606.

Continuing north on I–81, your next stop is **Staunton.** The town boomed in the 1800s, with its railroad and mining nearby, but it was untouched during the Civil War. Now it's pretty much a farm town, notable for being the home of the country-music performers the Statler Brothers. The two attractions in Staunton that pertain to Old Dixie are **The Woodrow Wilson Birthplace and Museum** and **The Museum of American Frontier Culture.**

Woodrow Wilson, the twenty-eighth president of the United States, was born in the Greek Revival home at the corner of Coalter and Frederick Streets in 1856, a decade after the structure was built. Woodrow's father was a Presbyterian minister, and the home was a manse for the First Presbyterian Church. The manse has been restored and furnished to look as it did when the Wilson family lived in it. Family memorabilia are displayed along with exhibits depicting Wilson's political and academic life. The museum is open March through December, daily 9:00 A.M. to 5:00 P.M.; January and February, Monday through Saturday 9:00 A.M. to 5:00 P.M. and Sunday 1:00 to 5:00 P.M. Admission is about $6.00 for adults, with discounts for college students, teenagers, and children ages 6 to 12. Phone (703) 885–0897.

At the edge of town, The Museum of American Frontier Culture is a remarkable, unromanticized, living-history village where you can learn about farmsteads from the seventeenth through the nineteenth centuries. Three of the farms are European and demonstrate how the early settlers who came to America had learned to farm in their native countries—England, Ireland, and Germany. The third farm is American, from the Valley of Virginia. It shows how the European influences came together in this part of the South. The buildings on the farms were brought to this site from their original locations in England, Ireland, Germany, and the Valley of Virginia and have been restored to usable condition. The Irish cottage, for instance, has been whitewashed, its thatched room made solid against the elements, and the interior arranged to show how the farmers and their livestock used the same shelter. The later American log house is sturdy but clearly would be cold in winter. Reconstruction of the English and German buildings is still in process. Appropriately costumed staff demonstrate farming activities, including planting, feeding the animals, and working in the kitchen.

The museum is on the Warrior's Path, an Indian trail through the Shenandoah Valley that later came to be known as the Great Wagon Road, which settlers followed from the north into Appalachia and, later, into North Carolina. Seeing these farms, where everyone obviously worked desperately hard, makes the opulent plantations seem even more remarkable. The museum is open daily 9:00 A.M. to 5:00 P.M., except December to mid-March, when hours are 10:00 A.M. to 4:00 P.M. Closed Thanksgiving, Christmas, and New Year's Day. Admission is about $7.00 for adults, with discounts for children and senior citizens. Phone (703) 332–7850. To get to the museum, take exit 222 off I–81 onto U.S. Highway 250, and drive 0.5 mile west.

From Staunton, if you continue driving north on the interstate for less than half an hour, you will come first to **Dayton** and then to **New Market,** where more Civil War lore awaits. In Dayton, **The Shenandoah Valley Heritage Museum,** 382 High Street, has exhibits relating to Stonewall Jackson's Valley Campaign of 1862. In addition to artifacts, photographs, and documents, you can study an electronic map that shows the progression of battles in his campaign. The museum is open Monday through Saturday 9:00 A.M. to 4:00 P.M., Sunday 1:00 to 4:00 P.M. Closed Thanksgiving, Christmas, and New Year's Day. Admission to the museum is free; it costs $1.00 to operate the map. Phone (703) 879–2616.

It was at New Market that the Virginia Military Institute cadets (see page 300) fought the battle that enabled the Confederates to hold the line and force the Yankees to retreat. **New Market Battlefield Historical Park** and **New Market Battlefield Military Museum** commemorate the event. New Market Battlefield Historical Park is maintained by VMI as the site of the battle where more than 250 VMI cadets, all about age 18, fought the much more experienced Union troops. **The Hall of Valor** in the park provides a movie and exhibits about the battle as well as a movie about Stonewall Jackson's Valley Campaign. The events are also depicted in dioramas. The park is open daily 9:00 A.M. to 5:00 P.M. Closed Thanksgiving, Christmas, and New Year's Day. Admission is about $5.00 for adults, half that for children. Phone (703) 740–3102.

The Newmarket Battlefield Military Museum, also on the battlefield, was built to replicate Robert E. Lee's home. It contains more than 2,500 military items from the Revolutionary War through the Persian Gulf War. Many of the artifacts are from the Civil War period. A film in the museum describes the Battle of New Market. The museum is open March 15 to December 1, daily 9:00 A.M. to 5:00 P.M. Admission is about $5.00 for adults, with discounts for senior citizens and children. Phone (703) 740–8065. To get to New Market Battlefield, take exit 264 off I–81 onto State Highway 305, and go north 1 mile.

Mint Juleps

Mint julep. The very name sounds romantic and somehow soft. Gentlemen in white suits should sit on the veranda, in the company of hoop-skirted ladies, chatting as they all sip mint juleps. Old-time recipes reinforce this notion, calling as they usually do for choice sprigs of mint plucked just as the evening dew settles, or pure, cold springwater, or fine sugar and shaved ice. Heady stuff.

But what a mint julep actually is—a drink consisting of bourbon, mint, and sugar with ice—can't be considered soft, though it may be heady. A standard recipe directs you to dissolve a teaspoon of sugar in a silver goblet with a little water, crush fresh mint leaves into the syrup, pour in a jigger and a half of bourbon, and fill the goblet with crushed ice. An alternate approach has you rub a glass with crushed mint, fill the glass with cracked ice, then pour in bourbon and sugary syrup and let them trickle through the ice before you begin to imbibe.

The Savannah Cookbook (published by Farrar & Rinehart), a collection of old recipes published in 1933 by Harriet Ross Colquitt, offers a mint julep recipe using rye whiskey rather than bourbon and directing that the glass be garnished with slices of apple, orange, pineapple, strawberries, and cherries as well as mint. This, of course, is heresy but perhaps forgivable coming as it does from Georgia. The *real* mint julep originated either in Virginia or Kentucky—great controversy over the true birthplace continues.

Index

Entries for Inns and Bed and Breakfasts appear on pages 311–312.
Entries for Historic Sites, Cemeteries, and Battlefields appear on page 312.

Index

Index

West Feliciana Historical Society, 121
Wetlands Acadian Culture Center, 146
Weymouth Hall, 167–68
White House of the Confederacy, The, 290
Whitecastle, La., 130–32
Wilmington, N.C., 197–99

Windrush Gardens, 128
Woodrow Wilson Birthplace and Museum, 302
Woodville, Miss., 172
Wynnewood, Tenn., 258
Zam's Bayou Swamp Tours and Restaurant, 145

Index of Inns, Historic Hotels, and Bed and Breakfasts

Adams Edgeworth Inn, 263
Arrowhead Inn, 204–5
Ashley Inn Bed and Breakfast, 225–26
Barrow House, 121
Bay Breeze Guest House, 26
Beaumont Inn, 114
Big Spring Inn, 276
Boone Tavern Hotel and Dining Room, 105
Cannonboro Inn, 225
Casa de la Paz, 54
Catherine's Inn, 198
Cedar Grove Mansion–Inn, 161
Church Street Inn, 26
Claddagh Inn, 212
Clarion Telfair Inn, 90
Clifton, 299
Corners, The, 162
Dunleith, 166
Edgewood 294–95
Edwardian Inn, 43
Fairbanks House, 52
Father Ryan House Bed and Breakfast, The, 176
Florida House Inn, 5
Gastonian, The, 88
Generals' Quarters, The, 153
Grace Hall, 14
Hale Springs Inn, 274
Harbour Oaks Inn, 179

Harmony House Inn, 195
Hawley House Bed and Breakfast, 278
Jailer's Inn, 111
LaFitte Guest House, 142
Lamothe House, 144
Langdon House, 193
Lion's Head Inn, 88
Lowndes Grove Inn, 229–30
Madewood Plantation, 146–47
Magnolia Hill Bed and Breakfast, 43
Magnolia Place, 88
Malaga Inn, 24
Margland Bed and Breakfast Inns, 39
Martha Washington Inn, The
Monmouth Plantation, 166
Newbury House, 272
New World Inn, 56
Nottoway, 132
Oak Shade Bed and Breakfast, 175
Oak Square Plantation, 172
Oakwood Inn, 203
Old Talbot Tavern, 110
Old Washington Jail Bed and Breakfast, 46
Oscar's House, 190
Peabody Hotel, The, 251–52
Prospect Hill Plantation Inn, 299
Red Bluff Cottage, 11
Rhett House Inn, 237
Rice Hope Plantation Inn, 234

National and State Historic Sites, Cemeteries, and Battlefields